CHURCH, COMMUNITY AND POWER

Roy Kearsley tackles a neglected but important problem – that of power dynamics in Christian communities. Drawing upon an impressive range of secular and theological resources, he offers an analysis of how relations of power should be understood and handled within the church. An honest and perceptive appraisal of the issues, this work will repay study by theologians and church leaders.

David Fergusson, University of Edinburgh, UK

Roy Kearsley's treatment of power and authority in the church is penetrating and incisive. He has a remarkable skill in correlating his knowledge of the New Testament and of post modern thinkers such as Foucault. This book challenges any easy assumptions about how churches handle their belief in servant ministry, and also explores whether the concept of divine omnipotence can withstand the hermeneutic of suspicion in contemporary society. It is a lively book which manages to be both readable and scholarly. I recommend it with enthusiasm.

Peter Sedgwick, Principal, St Michaels College Llandaff, Cardiff

In the era of 'post-Christendom', how can church as a sociological reality be switched on to the destructive dangers, yet constructive possibilities, of 'power' flowing in and around its community? Attuned to the current distrust of church power, this book creatively works out responses that could turn painful censure into a re-visioning of church power relations, helped by neglected critical studies. The approach exposes a complexity to power, and filters that insight into a theology of church. Much attention is paid in the book to the relevance to a religious community of post-modern philosopher Michel Foucault and of recent feminism.

The topic of power has universal importance in the study of religion, though the response to analysis and critique in this book is drawn specifically from Christian sources. Kearsley concludes with an exploration for a future renovated, self-critical, authentic and growing community, sensitive to power while remaining in line with classic Christianity.

'To Jan'

Church, Community and Power

ROY KEARSLEY
Cardiff University, Wales

ASHGATE

Published by
Ashgate Publishing Limited
Wey Court East
Union Road
Farnham
Surrey, GU9 7PT
England

Ashgate Publishing Company
Suite 420
101 Cherry Street
Burlington
VT 05401-4405
USA

www.ashgate.com

British Library Cataloguing in Publication Data
Kearsley, Roy
Church, community and power
1. Church polity 2. Christian sociology 3. Power (Social sciences) 4. Church polity and Christian union
I. Title
262

Library of Congress Cataloging-in-Publication Data
Kearsley, Roy.
Church, community, and power / Roy Kearsley.
p. cm.
Includes bibliographical references.
ISBN 978-0-7546-6345-4 (hardcover : alk. paper) 1. Church. 2. Power (Christian theology) 3. Communities—Religious aspects—Christianity. 4. Authority—Religious aspects—Christianity. I. Title.

BV600.3.K43 2008
262—dc22

2008023032

ISBN 978-0-7546-6345-4

Printed and bound in Great Britain by
MPG Books Ltd, Bodmin, Cornwall.

Contents

Acknowledgements

This book has been helped along by a number of generous readers and discussion partners. Outstanding in their assistance have been several colleagues in the School of Religious and Theological Studies at Cardiff University. Stephen Pattison afforded much needed encouragement in the early stages together with important suggestions for proceeding. David Fergusson at the University of Edinburgh provided similar help. In the later stages I was particularly grateful to Christopher Norris, distinguished specialist in French Philosophy at Cardiff for his friendly, critical scrutiny of my treatment of Michel Foucault's ideas. His assistance was generous and his comments incisive. Paul Ballard showed considerable patience and acumen in reviewing the work as a whole, a task undertaken with Stoic generosity. His considerateness and patience generated major revisions and much smoothing of text.

Additional engagement with later drafts came from busy colleagues and was probably undeserved but greatly valued. In particular Josef Lossl, Christine Trevett and Peter Sedgewick have provided valuable comment and encouragement. And mention must be made of Helen Reynolds who had to scrutinize every line for an abundant harvest of typos and other deficiencies to test her patience and ingenuity. The shortcomings that remain in the book to haunt me in the future despite patient guidance from others, are of course entirely down to my bad decisions and other failings. Most of all, I am grateful to my wife Jan who has shown great patience throughout the task, particularly during the finishing period when all domestic timetables in her busy life were treated by me with not much respect. Whatever her reward, it will not be that of having to read the book.

Chapter 1

Introduction: Church as Community in the Presence of Power

Focusing on Power and Community

Why do churches split, splinter or become scarred? Most obviously, because people fall out. Less obviously, because the members have made no allowance for the effects of power in their church community, a social body which is vulnerable like any other to the sociological hazards carried around by power. This troubling tendency for power dynamics to take church leaders by surprise suggests that there is a place for a new critical exploration of power's effects in Christian local 'congregations' or 'local churches'. Apart from the obvious value to theory about groups, it could help to clarify claims in a sceptical world that church is 'just interested in power'. But most of all it could lay a basis for reducing through vigilance some unnecessary pain and emotional upheaval entailed in power's laying waste of church communities. This book is offered as but one contribution to such a cause today. The book's aim is to lay critical foundations for an analysis of power in local churches, to address these theologically and to mark out practical challenges and opportunities implied as a result. The hope is that critical theorists, theologians and practical theologians alike will be encouraged to continue turning to this subject and addressing its many aspects. Hence the work undertaken here is no more than a contribution at a specific point, hopefully, to a much wider work in progress.

Accordingly, in uncovering the mystery of power's working in a church group, the following pages concentrate on power within the local church, though of course this will have implications for church's wider networks. Moreover, the book makes theologies of church as community a major resource for this task and newly applies some recent epoch-making, ecumenical agreements for the same end. As a result of all these factors, certain terminology will crop up frequently, such as 'church community', 'people on the way of Jesus', or 'those sharing in a common journey'. The preference for a community understanding of congregations is not designed to relativize all other depictions of church such as universal, national or ecumenical. Rather, a community portrayal proves particularly apt as a framework for a study of power dynamics.

It should be mentioned here that the decision to focus on local communities of the faith, as distinct from church as a universal or national body, is not a ploy to argue for a 'congregational' ecclesiology. There is no sectional, polemical aim in what follows. In fact the theological reflection throughout will throw up challenging questions for all traditions. Rather the purpose springs from a more catholic concern. It simply recognizes that all wider Christian streams are composed largely of such local churches and depend for their existence on the vitality and health of these grassroots communities. So here is the only place that a personal aside will be inflicted on the reader, and only so as to mention the biographical history behind the breadth of interest. That history includes regular attendance as a youngster in the Church of England, long and close contact with Methodism and branches of Presbyterianism, experience of independent churches and finally a long commitment to the Baptist tradition, including knowledge of at least three Baptist Unions. Teaching theology has meant involvement with students from most traditions, ranging from Salvation Army and Charismatic to Catholic and Coptic. I should also make mention of my three years in West Africa encountering Christian congregations at a time when new styles of church were burgeoning there and providing a challenge to established traditions. The aim therefore is to explore the handling of power in a way hopefully applicable to most types of local communities of the faith whatever their 'polity' or organizational preference. Of course someone from another tradition, might well have addressed the issues differently, but in general power is no respecter of differences. As a natural feature of a social unit it works similarly in all groups and therefore in all groups of a common faith.

Given such a focal point as that above it is obviously not possible to do justice at the same time to other related pressing concerns. So for instance we cannot in the same book also analyse in depth Christian thought on church responses to such critical topics as politics, social ethics, church and state, pastoral care or economics. Similarly we cannot give sustained attention to the fading glory known as Christendom and its meaning for today. Fortunately the literature is already abundant on such crucial concerns.[1] This book is focused differently from these endeavours, and yet it should still be seen as an overdue complement (and compliment also) to those big-canvas studies, for it is intimately connected with them. It works on their borders and even examines the anatomy of power in a way that is transferable to a larger scale. In any case, the way power works within any local church is obviously connected with that same church's attitude to its power relations among outside bodies such as ecumenical partners, political authorities and coalitions. For one thing, grassroots concerns, vitality and dynamics usually feed upwards into wider Christian thought on issues of 'big power'. Moreover,

---

[1] We note for instance, Paul Avis, *Authority, Leadership and Conflict in the Church* (London, 1992), Richard H. Roberts, *Religion, Theology and the Human Sciences* (Cambridge, 2002), S. W. Sykes, *Power and Christian Theology* (London, 2006), Walter Wink, *Engaging the Powers: Discernment and Resistance in a World of Domination* (Philadelphia, 1992), *Naming the Powers: The Language of Power in the New Testament* (Philadelphia, 1984), *Unmasking the Powers: The Invisible Forces that Determine Human Existence* (Philadelphia, 1986). Wink's attention, however, is trained on the broader, even global, 'domination system' in politics and society.

broader Christian pronouncements on major issues sometimes depend for their credibility on how well local church communities seem to handle their own internal power streams. Conversely, in this book broadly based political conceptions furnish a starting point for exploring more local forms of power such as those in a church. In summary then, the focal point from the outset is indeed going to be power in a local church, but a wider significance will be in evidence, and wider applications will be beckoning.

Clearing the Air on Terms

At this point a comment about terminology is needed with regard to all three terms of the book's title: 'power', 'church' and 'community'. For the sake of convenience we have already used 'power' somewhat carelessly as if it were a transparent word. But of course background will soon become necessary to address the problematic complexity in the word's varied uses. Though 'power' seems to have a vaguely common meaning to all speakers, in reality its varied deployment is far from simple or consistent. Muddling of categories easily occurs. Consequently the book endeavours to address the need for distinctions that assist conversation about power.

The word 'church' too is not straightforward. Here it will be used most frequently in the form: 'a church'. This convention is merely to remind constantly that power in local congregations is the main focus of discussion. But in addition the reader will encounter simply the single word 'church', as in 'church and power'. Then this single word on its own focuses sharply upon a quality, for example: 'to be church to the world' with all that means. It speaks of church-like traits usually valued in principle for all congregations, especially life as community or a 'life together', serving the world as Jesus did, not merely a meeting place or weekly event. In addition, it helps us not to speak of '*the* church'. Accordingly there will be less danger of unintentional sweeping assumptions about any particular wider tradition, association or coalition. That is, it does not raise contentious issues involved in talk of the 'true church' or 'the real church'. After all, the whole point of the discussion is to quarry some insights that might benefit all congregations of whatever stripe, with only occasional reference to any one body of the faithful.

One further clarification remains: the use of the word 'community'. The term nearly always denotes a local church considered as a community governed by the person, way and words of Jesus. Which means of course that here the word 'community' is not, as so often, a technical term referring to the various special orders, callings and vocations. Granted, the description 'community' here could actually be applicable to all kinds of Christian groups, including vocations, but more especially in what follows it emphasizes that congregations are communities. Their quality of community may not be as constraining as a specific vocational vow, but still a local church is community in biblical terms. It is an extended family with a calling for members to share in a life together on the way of Jesus, a 'household of the faith'. For reasons of comprehensiveness and simplicity, we leave open the vexed question of who exactly qualifies for inclusion in this family. These days even so-called 'gathered' congregations are much more accessible and hence broader in population than they used to be. They consciously make welcome a wide range of believers, searchers and doubters, including them in their activities, often under the heading 'friends'. This fact allows the term 'community' to be flexible, but usually implying that those calling themselves Christians are going to be in the majority and, at least by their own lights, receptive to their community being governed by Christian beliefs.

Why Power is Important

It is not difficult to identify the relevance of exploring power's presence in the community life of a local church. Disasters of dynamics in churches suggest that the time is ripe for bringing the subtle and complex questions of power into consideration of local church. It is here at street-level, in face to face church, that leaders and members often show troubling unpreparedness for power's sometimes destructive impact. Accordingly, the aim of what we are doing is to explore how power inhabits local communities of people of faith as they seek to build a life together on the Jesus way. This task naturally stirs up a variety of questions. What might 'power' mean specifically to church as a cluster of face-to-face relationships? Do the leaders themselves really enjoy as much power as they think? Or do they acquire more than they should? How should the people committed to a life together in the service of God and the world align and understand themselves in the presence of power? Can power be seen at all in a positive light? Is power a reality anyway or just a construct of human speech?

A response to such questions should be the concern not just of some unfortunate clergy but of every single leader of any kind in every church community, whatever stage it has reached in its life cycle. For meltdown can strike any company thinking itself to be on the way of Jesus, even one that seems buoyant. Such crises can occur whether the church concerned is healthy or in decline, traditional or contemporary, small or large, struggling or thriving. The sobering reality is that many a church bursting with vitality and on the brink of a seemingly great future has been cruelly blown away in a few hours by what is called in its midst, 'power dynamics' or 'power behaviours' (often to be termed in this book power patterns, power moves, or power streams). And it is likely that matters would indeed have been different if close attention had been paid to the sometimes half-hidden presence of these dynamics. Limited attention to power in ecclesiological literature also suggests there is a poorly developed awareness of power's role and an inadequate insight into its meaning and dynamics. Equally, it is possible sometimes to detect that little thought is given to the forms of natural defence available for church to combat power's more negative forms.

However, the study which follows does not simply concern the worst nightmare in a church. Consideration of power relates at every point to all the processes of church life including positive ones. This fact means that it is not enough to denounce all power, and hope for an upsurge of 'servanthood' in church leadership. To address social relations in the realm of church community, an inquiry like this must seek to throw light on the range of meanings for 'power' and unearth something of how it might work and might be conditioned by other influences. Therefore our task must not only explore measures against potentially harmful power in church community, but also recognize in what conditions it could be productive.

The uncomfortable truth is that power in churches often serves as the real cause of changes, whether positive or negative. Even in our highly democratized society, power rather than policy often still turns out to be the single most decisive factor in strategies developed by social groups. It can rise as the most immediate and pressing factor in every undertaking, despite accompanying solemn discussions about theology, finance and management. Power, this slippery element of human relations, frequently manages to mutate or reincarnate in some form – to live on in varying degrees and shapes. Probably there is no feast anywhere in the world of human relations without this spectre knocking on the door. And so it cannot be missing from church either. Power is possibly the element that is least understood, explored or explained in groups like churches, even though it is pervasive. Time and again it is the determining issue even around such core activities as mission, worship, pastoral care and sacrament.

Hence this is a journey which seeks to identify, dissect, and better understand forms of power faced in the social realities of a faith-community like church. The challenge is how a church seeks in the presence of power to be a company of authentic 'Jesus followers'.

The Critical Context for Church in the Presence of Power

Any critique of local church in connection with power at grassroots cannot ignore the wider sceptical environment for considering Christians and power. The following pages are therefore not produced without attention to wide-ranging, robust, critical examination today. Some of that criticism reaches right through history into the deep past and even to the fledgling Christian communities of the first and second centuries. Hence, for example, Henry Green claims that there has been from fairly early days, a clerical élite positioning itself nearest to the 'sacred-centre' and therefore to the divine power.[2] His suggestion implies at least that this, or some other kind of privileging, quickly sprang up in local churches and that it is likely to do so today as well. Gillian Evans reckons also that only the

2 Henry A. Green, 'Power and Knowledge: A Study in the Social Development of Early Christianity', in *Studies in Religion*, 20/2 (1991): 217–31, pp. 222–4, 229.

arrival of the sixteenth-century 'Protestant' reformation offered any challenge to now well-developed clerical privileges.[3] Yet another view insists that privileging only flourished in local churches due to a later and more encompassing factor: the peculiar culture called Christendom,[4] a centuries-long partnership between the political state and hierarchical Christian leadership. Opinions on that matter range from those less critical of Christendom[5] to serious criticism of the effects on churches in Western Christianity.[6]

Whichever view one takes, local churches in the West do in fact find themselves mainly stripped of the cosy security that surrounded and cushioned their predecessors in congregations through the centuries of Christendom. Churches could now, as some do, strive to hang on to the last crumbs of privilege, deep in denial. Or, as others urge, they could learn a new way to make bread enough for themselves and for others, as they seek to function in integrity as a healthy community for their own time. If they opt for the latter it would be essential to learn how to handle power within local church itself in a manner worthy of the Jesus way. This would set a gold standard for their wider relations and influence. Hence the contribution of word and action of churches in the world today will turn in great measure on their coming to terms with local power patterns, More than we may realize depends on how well churches understand the springs of power within their own local life and mission. Discernment here has implications for their relationship to the wider world. Struggling to gain clarity in such self-knowledge seems therefore to be inescapable.

Secular feminist writers have already provided one way into critical self-reflection for church, especially with their critiques of 'hierarchy' and 'patriarchy'. But more to the point for us now, is to ask if their claims could have further application and reach into the more general micro-world of each church community. The answer is probably positive. For these writers posed insistent questions on how power works, and so form primary resources for tackling the meaning, significance and dangers of power within local social groups. Moreover, in the writings of secular feminists the phrase 'power relations' came to be used frequently, in relation to group experience. Use of the term, of course, springs from the work of the French cultural critic, Michel Foucault. In the 1970s he turned from

---

3 Gillian R. Evans, *Problems of Authority in the Reformation Debates* (Cambridge, 1992), pp. 202–4.

4 Charles West, *Power, Truth and Community in Modern Culture* (Harrisburg, 1999), p. 66.

5 Oliver O'Donovan, noted by West: *Power, Truth and Community*, p. 66. See further the alternative offered by Sykes pp. 27–53 and Paul Avis, *Church Drawing Near: Spirituality and Mission In a Post-Christian Culture* (London, 2003).

6 E.g. Nigel G. Wright, *Disavowing Constantine: Mission, Church and the Social Order in the Theologies of John Howard Yoder and Jürgen Moltmann* (Carlisle, 2000), Linda Woodhead, *An Introduction to Christianity* (Cambridge, 2000), Stuart Murray, *Post-Christendom* (Carlisle, 2004), *Church After Christendom* (Carlisle, 2004).

his big canvas studies of power in society to analysing instead power's working in local groups or 'micro-settings' like school and family. The ideas explored here are significant for comparable groups such as churches.[7] In conclusion, the findings of feminists will in the light of these interests prove relevant and transferable to local church dynamics.

Foucault's work in due course reached feminist theologies too. It was welcomed, for instance, by Christian feminist Anna Hamar for the way it could move thought about power beyond the static '*status quo*'. Theological writings by women remain among the more challenging works on social power-hazards in church life. They have for instance provided a renewed impetus to probe power beyond simply historic Christendom's past effects on women.[8] Moreover, as a theologian, Hamar is typical in offering a challenge to established Western secular conceptualizing of power.[9] Like others, she wants to draw attention to the fact that power looks very different when seen from the standpoint of those who are at the wrong end of it. In addition she suggests that by entering into serious analysis it is possible to re-imagine the very form of power itself. Typically this process criticizes narrow attachment to the established political definitions of power relationships which are usually preoccupied with the necessity of stronger and weaker players. The aim of feminist writing instead is to promote a more creative and justice-shaping conception of power rooted in 'mutuality and reciprocity'.[10]

To take just one more example for the moment, Catherine Keller similarly critiques power relations in church. Apocalyptic in church preaching, she protests, is a force which can badly affect the way a church tries to energize its community life and to support its community relationships. Any failure of these overconfident visions leads to a reactive 'will to power' among Christians in this camp.[11] Fundamentalist preachers, over-focused on the last times, are the main offenders in Keller's mind of course but not perhaps the only possible targets. At any rate, we are assured by Keller that if churches want to seek an antidote for the will-to-power driven by apocalyptic vision, one is to hand. Churches need most of all to turn to 'relational power'.[12] Its more hopeful end result lies in a *vulnerable* relatedness and an unrestricted 'field of mutuality'.[13] The metaphor/image of a *king* for God has conversely been seen by many Christian feminist writers as an

---

7 Anna Karin Hamar, 'Some Understandings of Power in Feminist Liberation Theologies', *Feminist Theology*, 12/May (1996): 10–20, p. 20.

8 For those effects in a typical analysis see Margaret Miles, 'Patriarchy as Political Theology: The Establishment of North African Christianity', in L. Rouner (ed.), *Civil Religion and Political Theology* (Boston, 1986), 169–86, p. 184.

9 Hamar, p. 10.

10 Hamar, p. 17.

11 Catherine Keller, 'Power Lines', *Theology Today 55/2 (*1995): 188–203, p. 200.

12 Keller, 'Power Lines', pp. 201–2.

13 Keller, 'Power Lines', p. 202.

obstacle to a culture of mutuality in relationships.[14] Already, in this brief sample critical discussion raises real questions for handling the subject of power patterns in churches.

Various feminist views therefore seek to expose domination in churches, particularly in the marginalizing of women. A suitable metaphor for their main message could be that of a deep-sea predator lurking in the deeper fathoms that many have learnt to ignore by swimming in sunlit blue waves far above the dark waters. Up there among the power-holders domination cannot be seen – and so maybe does not exist. But it is there and will continue to have its victims. Accordingly feminism wants to stand out as an 'explanatory-diagnostic', breaking the spell of that denial by powerholders and addressing the *status quo* by giving 'the charm a name'.[15]

From this admittedly selective sample of skilled feminist challenges to church complacency about power's operations, we can at least detect the uneasiness with which many of their number, and other critics, view the track record of churches' understanding of power. The same critical contributions only underline the feeling that there is a crucial discussion to be had. The voices related above will be heard again at a later stage.

Ecclesiological and Social Realities

Already the term 'sociological reality' has cropped up in this chapter. It is necessary to consider more deeply the topic as an aspect of church. Pioneering applications of sociological theory to theologies of Christian church and community have indeed appeared from time to time.[16] But few writers have sharpened this up to a theological study of church able to resource a Christian handling of power in its communities. Modern theologies are of course not unaware of the tension between some traditional, reverential evaluations of church and other, sociological, perceptions. James F. Cobble's extended study twenty years ago drew out this tension.[17] On the one hand a church had to face the fact that it was a sociological

---

[14] The most famous version being: Sally McFague, *Models of God: Theology for an Ecological, Nuclear Age* (Philadelphia, 1987). But see further, Anna Case-Winters, 'The Question of God in an Age of Science: Constructions of Reality in Theology and Science', *Zygon,* 32/3 (1997): 351–75, p. 366.

[15] Marsha Hewitt, 'Woman, nature and power: Emancipatory Themes in Critical Theory and Feminist Theology', *Science Religieuses* 20/3 (1991): 267–79, p. 270.

[16] For example, James F. Cobble, *The Church and the Powers: A Theology of Church Structure* (Peabody, 1988), Gerald A. Arbuckle, *Refounding the Church: Dissent for Leadership* (London, 1993), Lewis S. Mudge, *Rethinking the Beloved Community: Ecclesiology, Hermeneutics, Social Theory* (Maryland, 2001). See also Duncan MacLaren, *Mission Implausible: Restoring Credibility to the Church* (Milton Keyes, 2004).

[17] James F. Cobble, *The Church and the Powers: A Theology of Church Structure.*

reality and so found itself inevitably hosting such features as political intrigue, bureaucracy, social layering and class conflicts.[18] At the same time church was still genuinely a tangible foretaste of something better, something still to come.[19]

Many cherished images cluster around that idea of 'foretaste of things to come': 'Body of Christ', 'People of God', 'Primal Sacrament', 'Fellowship of the Spirit' etc. Each of these can stand for some feature of church as transcending mundane social realities. And it must be admitted these *are* orthodox images, some very biblical in their origins. And just as truly, the biblical celebration can reach breathtaking heights (Gal 3.26–8, Eph 1.19, 22–3, 2.19–22; 3.10 etc). However, they do tend to make even more painful the classic tension between aspiring church and down-to-earth reality church. Certainly it is a help to realize that despite the ideal images, church actually turned up even in biblical writings as a fairly blemished article. For although this church in the Bible does indeed reflect the future and the transcendent, it is all the same still very flawed. It is only a reality on the way. And in the Christian Scriptures we find mainly pilgrim church. As such it is struggling, reforming, fragile and imperfect church (eg 1 Cor 1.11; 3.1–3; 13.5; 2 Cor 12.20; Eph 4.14–16 etc).

Hence recent ecumenical theology has come to accept and explore such an alternative 'sociological' standpoint.[20] Once inside this reality with eyes open we can of course look under rocks and discover very unappealing forms of life such as imbalances of influence, power-seeking, resistance, conflict, planned inertia and bureaucracy, just as is found in other forms of social organization. Yet the one constant ingredient of these, namely 'power', usually only merits a mention in textbooks of church when attention turns to a theology of Order and Ministry (if indeed even then). At any rate we frequently find ourselves with only half the story when some theologians get to work on a 'doctrine of the church'. That story sometimes unfolds in reverential tones, leaving hidden the unavoidable realities and sociological complexities of power as they really stand in a local church community as in any other form of small group dynamics. For this reason and many others, it will be necessary to examine power as a key term in the world of sociological reality. One major aim is to clarify as far as possible the patterns of power that play upon and within that sociological reality called church. Exploration of such matters will lead through a number of complexities towards serious conclusions for local church community life.

But sociological questions will not be left in complete charge. Few Christians could disagree with Paul Avis that sociological features are not the only ones affecting church. There are also socially relevant demands on church arising from

[18] Cobble, p. 93.

[19] Cobble, p. 94.

[20] Emmanuel Clapsis, 'Does the Church have a Sacramental Nature? An Orthodox Perspective', in Tamara Grdzelidze (ed.), *One, Holy, Catholic and Apostolic: Ecumenical Reflections on the Church. Faith and Order Paper No. 197* (Geneva, 2005), 18–26, pp. 23–4.

the Scriptures themselves. These directly focus upon the way of Jesus and have been attributed by churches in faith to God's own self-disclosure.[21] Therefore the story of how power became a major category in the modern mind is always balanced by another narrative, one which concerns Christian resources that are suited to checking dangerous power and deflecting power patterns towards positive results. Undoubtedly this is in part due to the contrasting life-settings that harbour power. For instance, Stephen Sykes comments that some people have power over others when conflict is in view but that a different approach is required where the power of whole community is in mind.[22] Contrasts between harmful and productive power sometimes come down to the relationship between 'power over' (power advantage obtained by one over another) and 'power to' (power as 'efficacy', or life-giving to the other). In fact this example just illustrates the varied play of prepositions attached to the word power, an ever-repeating and building theme from now on.

Power: A Word with a History

Those training for appointment to church leadership, nearly always want to dwell longer than time allows on discussion of the meanings and dangers of power. They are particularly keen on getting the words associated with power untangled, and on clearing their minds on definitions. However this is not just academic fascination with the conundrum of 'power' but also a sense of the subject's importance and for many crucial, practical reasons.

Writers on the subject of power are not always able for reason of space to interrupt their flow of argument to develop definitions of power. Stephen Sykes is blunt about the problems. The uses of the term power are so varied, he points out, that he has to settle for a 'thin' definition, though one shifting in its exact meaning according to setting.[23] It is indeed sometimes the only option for an author who therefore has to take a chance on 'power' being a transparent, commonsense word, hoping that everyone means roughly the same thing by it. However, as Sykes himself points out,[24] authors frequently do not mean anything like the same thing. For it is a word of many garbs and disguises. All the same, it can prove too great a diversion to grapple with distinctions, and hence avoidance takes its toll on many writings, even very useful ones.[25] However, this time, sorting through the varied usage is essential because a major part of this book aims to analyse power

21 Paul Avis, *Church Drawing Near: Spirituality and Mission in a Post-Christian Culture* (London: 2003), p. 165.

22 Sykes, pp. 6–7, 100–101, 113.

23 Sykes, p. 8.

24 Sykes, pp. 1–11.

25 For example Paul Beasley-Murray, *Power for God's Sake: Power and Abuse in the Local Church* (Carlisle, 1998).

patterns at grassroots. Whatever the difficulties, some clarification of thought on power is needed. To untangle the many lives of the word 'power' we resort to the 'play of the prepositions'. For example, power becomes a good deal more stark when presented as 'power *over*'. By this term we know for sure that we are in the domain of power sought and held by one party over another. But is this the only option for defining the notion of power and where might a wider use of the prepositions lead us? In answer to this question, we simply say for the moment that more prepositions will join this game of distinctions.

In picking its way through the varied faces of definition, therefore, this book aims to expose and inspect the subtlety and complexity of power as a concept turned this way and that for different ends. The effort must throw some light in due course on Christian community (life together in the way of Jesus), leadership and action in the world. So asking what power really is, promises solid fruit for healthy dynamics in church. In due course it will lead back to the idea of spiritual power which on the one hand has opened the door to forms of abuse.[26] Yet on the other hand spiritual power remains central to the Christian community's sense of calling and responsibility. 'The power of the Spirit' and 'authority in the church' become loaded and critical phrases requiring attention. Disentangling them theologically from negative association with power represents an important step.

In summary then the aim is to expose the anatomy of power patterns so that church need not be intimidated by power's possibilities and might fully appreciate the instability of power differentials in church life. This will enable alertness to power being, as Foucault once famously suggested, not exactly bad in itself but certainly dangerous. And yet there are constructive ends in view too, especially the use of distinctive Christian resources to build a community that can handle the unavoidable presence of negative power and channel or check power in a productive way. Hence, the theology of church can counterbalance the reality of power just as the sociology of church breathes sociological reality into theologies.

At the beginning of the discussion, analytical and sociological features will feature strongly, but gradually these will diminish in favour of ever fuller engagement with theological resources. 'Power over', as advantage by one player over another, will give way to further prepositions. But first we have to ask ourselves more about what is local church. Do we have a preferred key to its essence before we relate power to church?

---

26 Crucially raised by Stephen Sykes: S. W. Sykes, p. i.

Chapter 2

Church as a *Koinonia*. The Fellowship of the Way

The previous chapter indicated that the discussion ahead will primarily focus on the local congregation and its relationship to power. Hence, before turning to a clarification of power itself, we need to refine the intended working concept of church. As mentioned already, the chief factor at this point is the intention to emphasize specifically the local church's character as community. This move is rooted in recent ecumenical thinking about the biblical concept of church as a community of life together based on the *koinonia* or common sharing in the Spirit. The task of this chapter is in part to note the appropriateness of applying *koinonia* to the life of local church community. But it also has to pick up the wider associations of *koinonia* in connection with mission and justice as well as openness and transparency in churches. This helps to carry *koinonia* forward into domains of thought associated with power.

Koinonia **– The Fellowship of the Spirit**

In current ecumenical discussion the word *koinonia* ('common share or participation') often supports the development of a fellowship of church bodies sharing a common participation in the Spirit. Hence this theme of *koinonia* furnishes an underlying unity for broad frameworks such as catholicity, ecumenical endeavour or other global, regional or national dimensions to church. A similar note of deep unity appears even more strongly in Roman Catholic discussions of *koinonia*.[1] However, the attention for us is going to fall on translating such themes of *koinonia* from an ecumenical context into a congregational setting of face to face community. Hence, for instance, the theme of unity in the *koinonia* equally applies on the smaller scale, that is, in the concrete life of a local church community. Moreover, it supports other practical concerns especially those such as social relations in church and joint action in service to the world. *Koinonia* then connects with real and tangible traits at the grassroots, as distinct from universal or ideal concepts. It is here, on the ground, that one can most easily detect face to face sharing involved in a social reality, a real community rooted in ongoing church

---

[1] See, for instance, as a classic exponent of Vatican II, Walter Kasper, *Theology and the Church* (London, 1989), pp. 148–65.

life and witness.[2] In other words it is natural to attach *koinonia* as a concept to the local church as a living community. For local church is both the obvious place of concretely expressing *koinonia* and a natural way into exploring church power patterns and relations.

So it is clear that by 'community of the *koinonia*' we have in mind for this particular exploration simply church in its expression as a 'local', community of the *koinonia*. This, of course, is distinct from wider conceptions such as universal or worldwide church, or the purely representative, global or regional church,[3] and other ecumenical conceptions. But the idea is that the two angles of view are distinct, but not separate. Perhaps we may even say that the local is in the universal and the universal in the local. A perfect illustration of this paradox is found in Steven Croft's from an Anglican perspective. Under a section entitled 'Leadership within the Early Christian Communities', he immediately starts discussing not 'churches' but 'the Christian Church'. Plainly both perspectives are real and distinct for him, neither assimilated to the other yet closely related.[4] In addition, the term will also embrace not just traditional congregations, innovative and new forms of church. That immediately includes what are known as 'fresh expressions of church' or 'emerging church', or any other experimental forms such as niche networks. Perhaps it will even reach to 'virtual church' and the radically new forms of 'face to face' sharing found there. In fact the analysis ahead is meant to be applicable to any authentic, engaged community of like-minded fellow travellers whose people can describe themselves as being 'on the way of Jesus' together. We include here any such company that is truly interactive and bearing signs of being committed to each other in tangible ways. Their journey together ideally includes such elements as worship, sacrament, learning, friendship, caring and a mission to the world. That is, the journey is about being a healthily transformed and vitally transforming community of the faith. For David Clark, such a community ideally meets regularly and fosters such relational qualities as solidarity, friendship and

---

[2] Not including here the special sense of 'local' in some traditions to describe metropolitan, diocesan or regional administration.

[3] The main focus of the impressive and eirenic work of the Catholic writer Dennis Doyle: *Communion Ecclesiology: Visions and Versions* (New York, 2000). It is an impressive regional analysis of ecclesiology in North American Catholicism with many lessons for other contexts.

[4] Steven Croft, *Ministry in Three Dimension: Ordination and Leadership in the Local Church* (London, 1999), pp. 36–7. See also a similar crossing back and forth between ecumenical *koinonia* and local *koinonia* in the paper by Thorwald Lorenzen, 'The church as koinonia', *St Mark's Review*, 172 (1998): 7–13. Calls to take more interest in church as a local community intimately linked to a wider understanding of church is illustrated by the work of evangelical Anglicans. See the positive approaches to congregation as a *koinonia* community in an internet journal: David G. Peterson, 'The Locus of the Church: Heaven or Earth?' *The Theologian* July (2007): 1–11. www.theologian.org.uk/church/locus.html [accessed 28.06.07].

sympathy, while also being bedded down in society, whether on the margins or at the heart.[5]

In the light of the above clarifications, the form of 'church' lying behind the following discussion should be applicable to all congregations that acknowledge a community dimension and come from any of a varied range of Christian bodies. Moreover, all the reflection ahead has in any case been enriched by theological writing drawn from widely varied streams of church.[6]

Of course, therefore, the ecumenical, unifying and global expression of *koinonia* remains an indispensable backdrop for this focus. More important still, broad ecclesiological issues are, for sure, an ever-present partner in the exploration. All the same these broad brush tasks cannot divert us from the main quest, given the restrictions of space.

But how helpful is the choice of *koinonia* from among the rich variety of options available in ecclesiology? What is special about it? The attempt to answer these questions only leads us back for a few moments to broader discussions. For, ever since the publication of Avery Dulles's *Models of the Church*,[7] theological discussions of church have wrestled with the options for a possible, dominant root depiction of church. This is familiar ground and in any case there is no space to evaluate all the preferences here. Suffice it to say that a recent World Council of Churches guide,[8] *The Nature and Purpose of the Church*, still begins by conceding a plurality of approaches on offer.[9] It reminds us that while there are 'no systematic ecclesiologies' in the Christian Scriptures nevertheless a healthy range of images do appear, and are useful in their very diversity.[10] Between them they can look after a variety of portrayals of church: local or global, structural or organic, relational or active etc. However, this fact in no way detracts from themes receiving priority such as 'people of God', 'body of Christ' and living 'temple'.[11] These images, taken together, enjoy a crucial prominence, it is argued. For they point us beyond themselves in the direction of a deeper gift lying at the very heart of the idea of church and found already in the Hebrew Scriptures. This gift is *koinonia*, 'a dynamic impulse to communion', the possibility for communion between persons

[5] David B. Clark, *Breaking the Mould of Christendom: Kingdom, Community, Diaconal Church and the Liberation of the Laity* (Peterborough, 2005), pp. 28–9.

[6] We note especially, the key ecumenical contribution from Roman Catholic thought, the seminal article: L. F. Fuchs, 'Koinonia: Text and Context for the Church', *Ecumenical Trends*, 22/Fall (1993): 1–15.

[7] Avery Dulles, *Models of the Church* (Dublin, 1981). See Doyle, pp. 18–19 for an example of (acknowledged) indebtedeness to Dulles.

[8] World Council of Churches, *The Nature and Purpose of the Church: A Stage on the Way to a Common Statement: Faith and Order Paper No. 181* (Geneva, 1998).

[9] WCC, *Nature and Purpose*, pp. 12–15.

[10] WCC, *Nature and Purpose*, p. 12.

[11] WCC, *Nature and Purpose*, p. 12.

and, significantly, '*a gift for the whole world*'.[12] Its chief meanings are 'communion, participation, fellowship, sharing'.[13]

This more recent approach has come to command a wide degree of respect and interest because of its versatility but also perhaps because of its affinity with the Catholic *communio*.[14] As a respected Catholic ecclesiologist, Dulles did indeed connect *koinonia* to the community model of church, acknowledging in it a meaning of face to face community. But he also cautioned Protestants especially against too high expectations of deep social communion from congregational community in the real world. In addition he counselled against confusing community with the more mystical idea in *koinonia* of a communion of grace.[15] With such a caution *koinonia* as community helpfully emerges not as idealism and whimsy for the perfect community, but a vulnerable, flawed company of travellers together on the same journey. A willingness has also emerged in conversations between Catholic and Evangelical theologians to take *koinonia* to mean community, fellowship and shared aims in service.[16] This approach also squares perfectly with our perspective on *koinonia* as community and moreover only along with a sober sociological realism. Indeed this double sense of *koinonia*, mystical and concrete, ideal and realistic, only underlines further the duality of theological and sociological realities emerging in the previous chapter.

The extent of the consensus is illustrated in John Webster's uncompromisingly evangelical and reformed analysis of ecclesiology's shortcomings today, but which nevertheless approves *koinonia*'s pervasive use now whether speaking of the nature of church, or of its relation to God.[17] The article freely acknowledges the term's ecumenical and worldwide appeal though for ecumenism mainly in terms of family resemblances rather than identical doctrines.[18] Moreover, Webster recognizes *koinonia*'s positive possibilities. The term does after all lie at the heart of Ephesians[19] and is exemplified in the Lucan narrative and the Pauline ministry.

---

12 WCC, *Nature and Purpose*, p. 12.

13 World Council of Churches, *The Nature and Mission of the Church: A Stage on the Way to a Common Statement: Faith & Order Paper No. 198* (Geneva, 2005), p. 21.

14 Though it is important to note that the Catholic approach is more concerned with such topics under *koinonia* as sacraments and priesthood. See especially Kasper, pp. 148–65 and Doyle throughout.

15 Dulles, pp. 56–7. See a similar approach in Robert Gascoine, a Catholic writer sympathetic to Karl Rahner and Walter Kasper, *The Public Forum and Christian Ethics* (Cambridge, 2001), p. 94.

16 See *Church, Evangelization and the Bonds of Koinonia: A Report of the International Consultation between the Catholic Church and the World Evangelical Alliance (1993–2002)*, found online at www.efg–hohenstaufenstr.de ,(accessed 22.02.06.)

17 John Webster, 'On Evangelical Ecclesiology', *Ecclesiology* 1/1 (2004): 9–35, p. 14.

18 Webster, p. 13.

19 See Webster on this, p. 27.

Accordingly a *koinonia* centred on Christ and the Spirit seems to be, as Douglas Farrow suggests, the distinctive Pauline emphasis, remaining the lodestar of ecclesiology through the early crises and phases of church history.[20] If this is correct, an institution of power centuries ago must have overshadowed church's character as a grassroots community of the Spirit. This development is now being corrected and *koinonia* is returning to the agenda, for it really lies at the heart of any discussion of church and the problematic of power. We shall have good reason to return to this connection between *koinonia* and the Spirit at a later stage. Recalling this history also underlines once and for all the long pedigree of conceptualizing church primarily as *a common life* rather than a branch of an institution or organization. However, as we have seen a wide variety of emphases can in any case be embraced under *koinonia*.

The *Koinoinia* of the Local Church Community

So far it has become clear that the present state of discussion on *koinonia* underlines its importance, as long as the term is not overworked, or given jobs that it cannot do, or wielded as a weapon. At least we have settled on a loosely applied and widely received *lingua franca* these days for discussing church. Moreover it will not only contain something for everyone, from Catholic and Orthodox to traditional and Reformed, but it is likely to hold its charge for the immediate future. We are not saddled with a mere passing fad.

However, we have to return to the fact that many of the discussions of *koinonia* in our time are broad in scope even if they also underscore the validity of *koinonia* as a key to local church. It has become clear that questions are frequently trained on ecumenical links, and so function in a panoramic rather than microscopic way. That is, they display how various, multiple Christian communities in many cultures actually belong today to a vast, worldwide 'catholic' community. This is fair enough. The concern of such discussions is ecumenical – a communion ecclesiology of unity amid worldwide diversity. The word functions sometimes rather as the word 'family' does in talk of a worldwide human family – not exactly abstract but not local and familiar either. So how far can this upsurge of special usage validate what this book attempts to achieve?

The answer is surely that aspirations for *koinonia* life as being of ecumenical importance must spring from aspirations for church as it really is on the ground. It all comes down in the end to the action and resourcing that is located there. So for instance, the Catholic 'communion "ecclesiology"', must in the end surely define itself from what is hoped for in a multitude of specific communities in specific

[20] Douglas Farrow, *Ascension and Ecclesia*: *On the Significance of the Doctrine of the Ascension for Ecclesiology and Christian Cosmology* (Edinburgh, 1999), p. 42. Farrow asks whether the gradual fading away of this centrality was due to a loss of visions for the end-time resulting in a creeping institutionalism (Farrow pp. 42–3).

places. This is the case whether the focus is on action, worship, sacrament or common life etc. The *koinonia* life belongs first of all where the people are, where they have intentional, sustained face to face relationships – namely in the life of local church or social network. Hence *The Nature and Purpose of the Church* does not shrink from reaffirming that the one Church is made known in the life of the local church.[21]

Moreover *The Nature and Mission of the Church*, as a sister document appearing seven years later, speaks even more unambiguously. The notion of *koinonia* has now become central in the quest for a common understanding for church[22] and is in the course of being 'reclaimed' as a key to understanding not just the nature but also the mission of the church.[23] Dennis Doyle's writing,[24] incidentally, is just one more recent example of Roman Catholicism's parallel attention to this same central intent as the WCC discussion. But significantly Doyle freely notes 'fellowship' as a serious and historic alternative to 'juridical' understandings of church from the sixteenth-century reformations onwards right through to Schleiermacher, Vatican II and the present day. Doyle's preferred term 'communion' can be seen as a relational approach prior to all abstract theology of church.[25] Where then might communion, in any of its senses, apply most if not at the grassroots?

It does not seem so unreasonable, then, to make this simple, decisive move at the beginning of our own journey. In order to dissect local church in the presence of power we have elected to concur with the preferences currently sounding out in bringing Christians together, namely those of *koinonia* (sharing) and *communion* (fellowship, common life). To repeat therefore, 'church' in the discussion ahead points primarily to local and specific church seen as a community of shared life ordered by the way of Jesus and living in the constant presence and problematic of power. So the exploration aims to engage in the task of removing theological obstacles and opening up theological opportunities in respect of one question. That question is relatively simple: how might church as a located fellowship, a community inspired in *koinonia*, handle the challenge of *power* – in its midst and all around?

Koinonia and Church Community

Certainly, two important trails for the task ahead open up when we begin to consider *koinonia* as *the* characteristic feature of a particular Christian community. First a problem emerges with that familiar theme of unity. For whether within a family of churches or a local congregation, the most obvious danger of a sensed unity is that

21 WCC, *Nature and Purpose*, p. 50.

22 WCC, *Nature and Purpose*, p. 21.

23 WCC, *Nature and Purpose*, p. 22.

24 Doyle, pp. 1–8.

25 Doyle, pp. 7–8.

of introspection – a 'fellowship' existing primarily for itself and its own affairs, hermetically sealed in an introspective bubble. Hence *The Nature and Purpose of the Church* recognizes the danger when revisiting the four 'notes' of the church. Indeed it sometimes goes beyond a traditional structural concept of unity. Church is one, not primarily through organizational unity. Rather it is one through becoming a living foretaste of possible shared community. Church as *koinonia* is to be in action calling back all creation to its true being. Church is one through living this out in social reality.[26] This explanation is echoed in the note of church as catholic, that is, not united just in creedal orthodoxy but more importantly as it becomes 'saving, life-giving', and inclusive regarding 'race, class, sex and culture'.[27] Hence the unity is not merely a formal, Christian, mutual sharing in Christ and each other. It is also to be concrete, a form of testimony, a sign, to the world in general. But this occurs fully only when the community consists not just of words but of visible mutual love between members and service to those in need. This, incidentally, implies a place of 'fair distribution and exercise of power'.[28] We note in passing that most of these descriptions invite, even beg, the application of *koinonia* to the local congregation.

As just seen, the character of *koinonia* as community, in this ecumenical discussion, does not imply introspection but rather openness. The fact is underscored in *The Nature and Mission of the Church*. This companion document even more strongly describes *koinonia* as a form of open, serving community. To be 'sharing' in God's own passion concerns not just church but the whole of creation especially the common ties of human society. Creation has its integrity rooted precisely in this connection.[29] The full meaning of *koinonia* comes out in human qualities of relationship in community. But it does so, additionally, in the relationship of human beings to creation itself.[30] Moreover, the community's mutuality of service in a common life inevitably entails working together for justice and peace.[31] The community exists so that humanity and all creation may also be brought into communion.[32] The community participates in and anticipates the new community that is God's will.[33] Most of all, this *koinonia* is a calling to service together for the poor, needy and marginalized. That service plays its part in exposing and transforming unjust structures. It also cares for the integrity of creation and seeks to reverse abuses of nature, because *koinonia* is about participating in God's healing of broken relationships between creation and humanity.[34] David Clark's

26 WCC, *Nature and Purpose*, p. 10.
27 WCC, *Nature and Purpose*, p. 10.
28 WCC, *Nature and Purpose*, p. 42.
29 WCC, *Nature and Mission*, p. 22.
30 WCC, *Nature and Mission*, p. 22.
31 WCC, *Nature and Mission*, p. 24.
32 WCC, *Nature and Mission*, p. 24.
33 WCC, *Nature and Mission*, pp. 26–7.
34 WCC, *Nature and Mission*, p. 26.

view of church community converges with this approach and sets challenging targets. He has many valuable reflections on community from years of helping to build various forms of it. He makes clear he is concerned with many kinds of community in the world ranging from voluntary associations through to regional and institutional communities (church therefore being just one form with its own contribution to make).

What these, however, all have in common is the need to be sources of energy and transformation, as well as centres of life-giving and liberation.[35] They also must be learning communities. Moreover, to be solid, effective community a church's members must have a place to stand (a psychological security), a role to play (a feeling of its significance and relevance) and a world in which they feel they belong (a sense of solidarity).[36] For church, these all spring from that underlying reality of a share in the *koinonia*. What this portrayal says is that church community should not stand for anything superficial, ideal or sentimental.[37] It is a serious venture.

The second trail of importance is that of realism and candour in the community. The theme emerges more clearly in consequent discussion of the reports, some of it tackling painful differences and tensions with carefulness and honesty. The account of this process in 2005[38] came not only to re-emphasize the centrality of the *koinonia* but also to underscore the importance to it of honesty, mutual accountability and an environment of diversity.[39] This is illustrated from discussion of the sacraments. Even contributors from strongly sacramental traditions stress that in sacrament the church community becomes a channel of Christian confession[40] and is a token to the world insofar as it is a part of the world already transformed. The calling of the *koinonia* community is first authentically to be a place of the reconciled and reconciling and then to share with all people the grace by which its own life is created and sustained.[41] In local church such themes of candour and openness will be central to the discussion of power relations and patterns. They will be the key to lubricating relations of power and offsetting the tendency to power moves.

---

35 Clark, p. 13.

36 Clark, pp. 16–17.

37 See Clark's own comments pp. 19–20.

38 Tamara Grdzelidze (ed.), *One, Holy, Catholic and Apostolic: Ecumenical Reflections on the Church. Faith and Order Paper No. 197* (Geneva, 2005).

39 Grdzelidze, pp. 8–9.

40 Antii Saarelma, 'Church and "Sacrament" in Bilateral Dialogues', in Tamara Grdzelidze (ed.), *One, Holy, Catholic and Apostolic: Ecumenical Reflections on the Church. Faith and Order Paper No. 197* (Geneva, 2005), 51–61, p. 57.

41 Donna Geernaert, 'Church as Koinonia/Church as Sacrament', in Tamara Grdzelidze (ed.), *One, Holy, Catholic and Apostolic: Ecumenical Reflections on the Church. Faith and Order Paper No. 197* (Geneva, 2005), 62–77, pp. 72–3.

Koinonia and Society

Some approaches even go further than the WCC reports and debates on the relation of *koinonia* community to the world. They see Christian community as referring to human community in the world as a whole. Lewis Mudge is one of the better-known and skilled exponents of this view and represents it well. For him 'people of God' means not just the whole communal reality in the churches but also that which is *beyond them*.[42] Not only this but the Christian community is not actually itself exclusively 'the people of God' but mainly articulates the Spirit's people-forming activity in the wider world. Christian congregations simply pick up on these wider 'Spirit-formed' realities, setting them within a Christological context and so making them more explicit and visible.[43] This means of course that Christian congregations are not to be identified exclusively as *the* people of God. They merely signify a greater social reality of community.[44] Thus Christian congregations are a sign simply to keep the hope of a general civic human community open and alive.[45] Mudge, therefore, rejects a purely mystical and classic sense of Christian community such as explained, for example, in Dulles's account of the community model.[46] For Mudge, the Christian Scriptures present the people of God as moving towards a universal community of nations.[47] Hence, the term 'people of God' denotes all people living out what it means for Messiah to be incarnate and the church is simply that part which conveys to the whole human world its destiny as the space of God's reign.[48]

Mudge's startling reinterpretation of this biblical phrase has not met with an overwhelmingly positive reception. Indeed, official ecumenical discussion has virtually passed it by. It is easy to see why. For one thing the notion is quite difficult to support either from Christian Scripture or tradition. John Webster argues that in Christian thought, the common life of the Christian community is not in fact an adaptation 'of sociality in general'.[49] Clearly Webster will not be drawn into confounding sociological phenomena with confessional aspirations.[50] But for him, neither need the alternative choice be a dualism, opposing supernatural and natural, time and history or material form and inner substance. These oppositions would have a corrosive effect on ecclesiology by sharply dividing Christ (supernature) from church (nature). Rather church comes from the grace of God alone as bearing

42 Lewis S. Mudge, *The Sense of a People: Toward a Church for the Human Future* (Philadelphia, 1992), p. 30.

43 Mudge, *The Sense of a People*, p. 90.

44 Mudge, *The Sense of a People*, p. 90.

45 Mudge, *The Sense of a People*, p. 29.

46 Dulles, pp. 43–57.

47 Mudge, *The Sense of a People*, pp. 24–38.

48 Mudge, *The Sense of a People*, pp. 30, 51–3.

49 Webster, pp. 19–20.

50 Webster, pp. 10–11.

marks gifted by God. There is a closeness to God but there is also a dissimilarity and asymmetry.[51] This leaves church as still being part of a flawed creation but also willed and gifted by grace. As such it is 'visible' church with a form and human history. It genuinely belongs to our social history as 'a social project'. But it is church only through the work of the Holy Spirit.[52] What emerges for our interest here is that for Webster just as church cannot be confused and compounded with deity or with Christ, neither can it be confused and compounded with mere sociological phenomena. Accordingly, views of Christian community faithful to a grace-covenant conception of church cannot in the end settle for a sociological reductionism. It cannot view church as mainly a spiritualized or self-conscious phase of immanent community processes.

Does this conclusion despatch Mudge and similar approaches, removing them from our consideration? For some purposes it might indeed, but not for that which occupies us here. For we now return to our main point about *koinonia* and the danger of introspection. Mudge's work should not altogether be overlooked. For its intent in part overlaps that of consensus ecumenics in one important regard, and that is agreement that Christian community is inauthentic if obsessed with itself rather than opened outwards. Some agreed statements draw quite close to Mudge's ideas. Take for instance the claim that all creation has integrity only in '*koinonia* with God', and that communion has its roots right in the order of creation and in such things as family and kinship.[53] Salvation history concerns the divine restoration and advancement of *koinonia* in the world.[54] On this view, the *koinonia* of early Christian usage does not point to a reclusive, safe retreat, a great communal comfort zone. The life together of Christian community and Christian relations is actually no *koinonia* at all unless it really provides a space where 'blessed community', as Mudge calls it, really does become dramatically present, albeit partially.[55] Even if, to traditional thought, Mudge's way of seeing things is too universalist or hopelessly liberal, even reductionist, it does hammer home an essential point about Christian community. This is that the Christian *koinonia* is a 'mission' idea, a way in which an otherwise merely alleged salvation should become exposed to public view, even though it is 'fragmentary'[56] and imperfect. *Koinonia* exists to reach out to the world in word and being, in service, struggle, justice and peace. Advocates are clear that its purpose is not self-serving. Indeed much hangs on each local congregation's authenticity as a community reaching out far beyond its own internal life.

The discussion so far has aimed to see *koinonia* as free from introspection and self-serving agendas. Its unity connects with wider damage in human

---

51 Webster, p. 21.

52 Webster, p. 25.

53 World Council of Churches, *Nature and Mission*, p. 22.

54 WCC, *Nature and Mission*, p. 22.

55 Mudge, *The Sense of a People*, p. 30.

56 Mudge, *The Sense of a People*, p. 30.

relations. For, however else recent emphasis on *koinonia* is intended, it clearly does not imply cosy church, or insular and inward-looking church.[57] Similarly, local, internal power relations in a local church are significant for broader church interests, including politics, social ethics and economic theory.

Koinonia and Justice

So what of the second part of our guiding conception of local church as relating to power? We have suggested that it is a Christian community ordered by the way of Jesus. But one thing seems to be widely accepted, namely that Jesus in Luke 4 takes the Jewish hope of justice to be his own manifesto. Hence ecumenical thought on the *koinonia* includes a call to justice and truth.[58] Communion between people and with God widens in purpose, displaying this gift as available for the entire world.[59] Freedom for the oppressed leapt from the Hebrew ordering of its community and lodged in the new 'rule of love' which he came not just to speak about but to enact. This means that 'power' in every local *koinonia* potentially carries negative or positive destinies for itself and for wider justice. To the 'majority world', words like empowerment, liberation and freedom point to a world beyond their grasp. It matters therefore whether the adventure of local church as community in the face of power is fully connected in its practice to this global pain and longing. Church cannot be of help to others if it is colluding with privileged power and is corroding justice in its own practice. The excavations that follow suggest that power in local groups is intimately connected with the wider workings of power. Hence practices of church regarding transparency and freedom are more relevant to power in the wider world than might at first seemed obvious.

So we take seriously for church the Hebrew legacy of a covenant theology. This theme is at least the ensign of a radical view of power. For in both faiths it is a covenant that takes account of inequalities, disempowerment and genuine dangers of domination. This awareness keeps the *koinonia* awake to possibilities of power games, control, abuse and inertia even in its own community. The stakes are high. If power cannot be handled in productive and peaceful ways in a covenant community, hope wanes for those in the yet wider world who feel themselves victims of such power. So the concentration on the local *koinonia* and its relation to power really does relate to public theology. That is, local church's relation to power has to do with its authenticity and general fitness to be a sign of hope. And so at stake here is a local church's prospects for being a cause of action in the world, whether by kingdom words of truly good news or by good deeds of a truly new kingdom.

justice as way of Jesus

covenant – awake to power games

---

57 Alan Falconer, 'Introduction', in Tamara Grdzelidze (ed.), *One, Holy, Catholic and Apostolic: Ecumenical Reflections on the Church. Faith and Order Paper No. 197* (Geneva, 2005), 1–14, pp. 8–9.

58 WCC, *Nature and Purpose*, p. 13.

59 WCC, *Nature and Purpose*, p. 13.

Chapter 3
The Contested Concept. What is Power?

As we saw at the beginning, clarifications on power are essential for addressing the relationship of power to a local church. But answering the question, 'what is power?' is as daunting as attempting a crisp definition of music, poetry or religion. Consequently any desire to understand local church as community in the presence of power immediately comes up against the demands of twisting and turning philosophical debate. The complexity and inconclusiveness of such exchanges have led even the most skilled writers on church to settle for the ultimately 'contested' nature of power definition.[1] Coping strategies like this are not offered without good reason, for defining power has proven as slippery as an eel in a barrel of oil. However, this time such a route cannot be taken. A serious analysis of local church power really does gain value from a prior, determined attempt to account for power's various meanings. Fortunately, not every eddy of political and philosophical explanation need muddy the waters all the way down to the sea, though political thought about power tends persistently to leave its tidemark everywhere. Moreover, today there is a growing sense that power is not just a word for bare 'dominance', oppression or 'domination', as it is often wrongly assumed to be. For instance, the word might also describe such contributions to the stream of events as influence, resistance, permission, illumination, freedom, or strength to name but a few possibilities.[2]

Inevitably any account of the disputes will have to arrive finally at the extraordinary, upside-down genius of Michel Foucault. It seems as if the whole battle over 'political' power was a narrative designed to lead into his audacious revolution. He will turn out to have changed the scene on this subject for ever. As a result of his problematizing of matters, it has become clear that at least a basic process of classification is needed to distinguish major types of power. We will advance that process in some measure by a simple ploy, namely the association of varied prepositions in turn with the word power. That is, prepositions will mark subtle differences between types of usage, though these may be sometimes porous to each other. So for instance we can make distinctions between the options of (a) 'power *over*', (b) 'power *to*' and (c) 'power *with*'. Even though they sometimes merge or overlap, these key qualifiers of power should retain enough explanatory force for getting at the play of power in a Christian community. Further on, a few

---

1 As famously concluded by Steven Lukes in *Power: A Radical View* (London, 1974), and as cited and applied by S. W. Sykes, *Power and Christian Theology* (London, 2006), p. 7.

2 See Sykes, p. 1.

additional phrases will come into view theologically, such as 'power *from*', and 'power *through*'. And constantly evoked in the background is a plaintive question haunting all the prepositions: 'but the power of *what*?' And we shall reach this too in due course.

The Twenty-first Century as Turning Point

The only thing universally agreed about 'power' is that the subject must be obsessively important! So observes Kenneth Pasewark at the beginning of his provocative book in 1993.[3] His only lament is the tenacious grip of the political aspects of power on all debate. He complains that not even Foucault could shake off this obsession altogether.[4] This same leading approach, Pasewark regrets, remained dominant, not only in much specialist writing but also deep into the psyche of Western society as a whole. The point is well taken, yet revisiting the political model of power enables us to understand how we arrived at the more recent era of reflection on power. The review also helps us to uncover a surprising relevance and analytical value for current thought about church as community in the presence of power. But more than this, a review of twentieth-century roots of power-critique discourages easy and simplistic statements about power in church communities – of which we hear many. A pause to explore some distinctions in the puzzle which is power might steer us away from the sloppiness of thought that often blights intellectual spats about it. It also prepares us for the major shifts of emphasis from the end of the twentieth century and up to the present. It is this same period that has sparked reluctant recognition of 'power' as more complex and subtle than appreciated earlier. This awareness is crucial when at last coming to the subject of *koinonia*.

We also have the benefit of a handy, major publication which summarized the key milestones in last century's journey, namely the compilation edited by Steven Lukes[5] and representing the mature thought of the very period bemoaned by Pasewark. The collection brought together in the 1980's some of the greatest specialists of the period. So great is the constellation, stardust seems to fall off the page of contributors. Crudely put, the book's account of twentieth-century academic thought on power until the 1980s especially illustrated one consistent assumption. It is that conceptions of power mainly clarified around the idea of a particular player, or group, curbing the freedom(s) of another, or getting their way over or instead of another.[6] From now on this concept will frequently be referred to

---

3 K. A. Pasewark, *A Theology of Power: Being Beyond Domination* (Minneapolis, 1993), p. 1.

4 A judgement that may need qualifying in Foucault's case.

5 Lukes (ed.), *Power*.

6 Alvin Goldman, cited by Pasewark, p. 208.

as 'power *over*'. Although in a sense neutral in legitimated settings, say managerial or contractual ones, 'power over' mainly has to bear negative connotations.

Pasewark argues that this concept of power in political talk was limited. It mainly represented a capacity or potential that issued in an occasional action. Power was latent not pervasive. Power looked like an implement ready to hand, an available course of action or a sudden iron grip on a situation when required, rather than an inescapable, ubiquitous, ever present aspect of life. So for political thought 'power over' has been occasional and episodic. It is almost a utility, to be sprung as and when needed, perhaps frequently in some settings. In this sense it is 'external' – even when meaning only the mere potential or possibility of power's acting.[7]

For all the truth in Pasewark's critique, it is the political modes of thought into which people instinctively fall when speaking negatively of power. Hence, the truth is, if we are to focus attention on power in the shared life of the Jesus community, that traditional, familiar, political ground must briefly be journeyed. For when people talk of power in church their outlook has usually still not escaped from the subconscious limits set to the subject by political philosophy. In other words, the political preference for power as 'power over', is still alive and well in the popular mind. Hence it is worth exploring some of the more persistent themes right through to the more recent birth of new approaches.

A Brief History of the Political 'Power Question'

Power, Domination and Resistance

An account of intentional political treatments of power in the modern democratic world, say from the middle of the twentieth century, could easily break into the story at any one of several places. However, it is common in histories to note as a significant starting point, Bertrand Russell's spacious definition of power in 1938 (despite the prior magisterial work of Max Weber). For Russell, power is 'the production of intended effects'.[8] Even this unexciting, but flexible and accommodating, statement promises more than is at first obvious. With it, more

---

7 An appreciation of power understood as potential appears in the work of Peter Morriss, *Power: A Philosophical Analysis* (Manchester, 2000), pp. xii, xvii–xxx. See also Pasewark, pp. 1–2. Pasewark is in fact hostile to the common political habit of viewing power as potential as well as actual. But the practice has endured, right up to recent writing: Steven Lukes, 'Power and the Battle for Hearts and Minds', *Millennium: Journal of International Studies*, 33/3 (2005): 477–93.

8 Betrand Russell, 'The Forms of Power', in Steven Lukes (ed.), *Power* (Oxford, 1986), 19–27, p. 19. Also cited strategically by Paul Avis, *Authority, Leadership and Conflict in the Church* (London, 1992), p. 20.

sharpened and exacting political definitions immediately became likely and the formula has been variously adapted.

However, in the meantime, the vulnerability of the word 'intended' has invited scrutiny. For did not that degree of subjectivity, 'intended' effects in Russell's definition, lift the concept of power out of the reach of scientific and philosophical critique? In that case power was no longer an objective concept open to scrutiny at all and was of little political use in examining practices. Furthermore there was also the problem of *which* intentions were meant in 'intended effects'.[9] Did it not make any difference if the effects were intended upon people rather than things? And did it not matter if these intentions were from coerced intentions or from voluntary ones? More importantly, surely the whole matter looked different depending upon whether the intentions upon people were constructive and friendly or self-seeking and seeking to dominate. Hence a slight refinement by Dennis H. Wrong many years later (1979) was all it took to propel Russell's formula more clearly into the clear domain of 'power over'. Wrong's version needed to go only a little further to raise the stakes: 'intended effects *on others*'.[10] The term would then indicate that someone enjoyed 'power over' another, whatever the extent, method or result. The concept of power now was evolving into a hold enjoyed by one group or individual over other human agents and perhaps a superior action by one upon another, just as Pasewark later complained.[11] In other words, we now find ourselves in a domain of winners and losers. Power was in danger of always looking like a strategic game which could only rarely end in a draw.

For Lukes, the political model of 'power over' simply comes out more strongly in Max Weber's work in the first part of the twentieth century. We are reminded that Weber introduced people to the unavoidable presence of resistance in any use of power worthy of the name. In other words for Weber, power was only worthy of the name when it actually overcame resistance.[12] This stance was stronger, and more uncompromising, than anything offered later by Russell or Wrong. Robert Dahl's further insistence that the action in genuine power should be understood as actually controlling another player's behaviour is, in Lukes's view, a step too far. It falls foul of occasions when power acts mildly, say by a bare influence or accidentally. In fact Dahl tackled such difficulties by falling back again on introducing intention with all the problems associated with Russell's approach, already noted above.[13]

So then, we see that one key problem emerging is that of resistance. What is the degree of power enjoyed by one party over another in political formulations like Dahl's? Is any self-respecting power really a 'domination' without the possibility of effective resistance? The modern suspicion of power, and the constant expectation

---

9 Paul Avis, *Authority, Leadership and Conflict* (London, 1992), pp. 2–3.

10 Dennis Wrong as cited in Avis, p. 20.

11 See Chapter 7.

12 Steven Lukes, 'Introduction', in Steven Lukes (ed.), in *Power*, 1–18, p. 2.

13 Lukes, 'Introduction', pp. 2–3.

of an advantage gained by one player over another, has concentrated minds even more on these themes. The assumption has grown that power, under a political definition, must involve futile resistance. Resistance will somehow simply be crushed if all consensus and mild persuasion has failed. This is what we are dealing with when we utter the word power.

In Christian community a dim view should, on Christian principle, be taken of domination. And yet one player's crushing of resistance offered by another of course produces contrasting viewpoints. Both, however, are often interpreted through the lens of 'spiritual' values. For one side, the deed appears to be a necessary evil, maybe a needed discipline, perhaps even a deed of righteousness. But for the other party it appears a giant act of crushing injustice. Later chapters will explore how such perspectives might be anticipated, interpreted and handled. But, in line with Pasewark's concerns, we have to explore further complexities of power in order to grasp more clearly what to expect from power dynamics in church.

Money as Metaphor

A second development has generated much discussion. It is the 'zero-sum' view of power which was still driving debates at the time Pasewark's book appeared. The approach falls in line with that first principle of political definitions described above: the conquest of resistance. According to the theory, successful 'power over' one player by another always implies an equal and opposite loss of power or potency. One gains power and another loses it. A metaphor too tempting to ignore surfaced: the image of currency moving through society leaving a trail of gains and losses within an unchanging money supply. Talcott Parsons attributed the prominence of the zero-sum idea to H. D. Lasswell (during the 1940s and 1950s) and C. Wright Mills (the 1950s).[14] However, Parsons as a chief exponent of the money metaphor crafted his model with a very cautious approach to the idea of the zero-sum 'game'. For him, zero-sum type transactions of power were indeed a reality but they gave only a partial account of the nature of power in a political context. The complexity of both economic and political systems exposed the metaphor's limits. For instance, Parsons claimed, financial investment can indeed provide gain without essential losses within a rational system, a 'miracle of loaves and fishes'! Economies can expand.[15] However, it was to be Michel Foucault who became the real bearer of nemesis on the 'quantity theory of money' as an assumption in the political analyses of power,[16] and whose approach at first alarmed some feminists thinkers, as we shall see. Pasewark, too, was quick to

[14] Talcott Parsons, 'Power and the Social System', in Steven Lukes (ed.), *Power* (Oxford, 1986), 94–143, pp. 95, 126.

[15] Parsons, pp. 126–7. See also further comment on Parsons in Sykes, p. 101.

[16] Michel Foucault, 'Disciplinary Power and Subjection', in Lukes (ed.), *Power*, 229–42, p. 234.

spot the problems.[17] And since Pasewark wrote, Foucault's revolution has slowly spread and the zero-sum political analysis has come under further pressure, as we shall see later. And yet, even so, the political model itself has not yet withered away in academic circles. In fact Parsons's work, we learn, enjoyed a renaissance partly through discussion of the currency metaphor in Foucault.[18]

In its new form springing from Jürgen Habermas in 1987,[19] power was seen as circulatory like money but in a different way. Money serviced society without actually being 'embedded' in human organizations. Power, on the other hand was indeed so embedded. For power enjoyed some official positioning within those organizations – social organization was power's 'host' and its chief outlet.[20] A biological metaphor was here being invoked, welcoming the idea of power as continuous circulation but not necessarily taking on board an explicit zero-sum understanding. Though different in significant ways, Foucault and Parsons allegedly displayed 'family resemblances' which set them apart from the hitherto dominant approach to power based on the notion of agency. In other words for them, not all power needed conscious rational agents to ensure its impact on people or situations. It could take on an independent life of its own, as for example in bureaucracies or cultural norms and pressures. It could circulate and do its work in a seemingly rational process but without human supervision. Then power could be the complete possession of no one and the problem of everyone.[21] As Pasewark preferred, 'power over' was coming to be seen not just as merely potential within agents but also pervasive in systems.

Power through Strategies

'Power over' thus far in political thought seemed mainly a possibility or action where one party completely overwhelmed another. Not necessarily through violence or threat maybe. But still, 'power over' did stem from a commanding advantage of authority, status and/or resources. Hence its natural course appeared to be the crushing of resistance, and achievement of adverse effects upon another.

---

17 Pasewark, pp. 9–10.

18 Stewart Clegg, *Frameworks of Power* (London, 1990), p. 133. Clegg also argued, like Kroker, that Foucault shared with Parsons a 'circulatory' if more 'biological', or life-based, understanding of power, even though implicitly revising the money metaphor. Clegg was less in tune with criticism of Parsons by the nevertheless distinguished Anthony Giddens (Clegg, pp. 135–7).

19 Jürgen Habermas, cited by Clegg, pp. 133–4.

20 Clegg, p. 133.

21 Clegg, p. 239. Clegg is approving. Perhaps indeed he was even claiming postmodern credentials such as those which marked Foucault's era. Mark Haugaard, *Structures, Restructuration and Social Power* (Aldershot, 1992), p. 57. Haugaard, however, is suspicious of Clegg's claim to be postmodernist, holding that instead he has merely swapped some labels about. See pp. 57–9.

And yet this formidable 'power over' was not the *only* form of achieving intended effects over another. More gentle methods were recognized in the world. Hence effective influence could occur even through creative use of apparent weakness or serious disadvantage. This could be, say, through influencing an agenda decisively, or swaying participants (by fair means or foul), or excluding damaging issues from the schedule of key debates etc.[22] Hence ironically, in the modern, socially expanding world someone might get their own way, without domination, right at the heart of consensual decision-making.

It was lines of attack like this, and many more, that eventually caught the eye of Michel Foucault. In his later work he was eventually to focus sharply on them as he slowly loosened his dependence on conventional political and historical interpretations of power. These 'strategies of power' that could occur from positions of weakness, in his later view, came to be more useful to spotting power in the modern world than discussions about intellectual systems, class-struggles, ideologies, state manipulation and other grand canvas types of power. And it was such strategic angles on power that especially marked 'micro-contexts' (which we shall also call 'micro-communities') including that of church. A local church community might sometimes need to turn attention therefore from ideology, policy and conviction-politics to exposing the somewhat squalid arena of strategic power right there in its own midst. The sublime church of primal sacrament, supreme sign, faithful servant, body of Christ etc. is still capable of being the theatre of power strategies. In fact as a sociological reality, we recall, it could not avoid being so.

Power as Collective

By this time Hannah Arendt had questioned all the preoccupation with power as obedience and submission to a constraining authority, especially power as totalitarian rule.[23] While recognising that this strain in political thought had a rational history, she appealed instead to the Athenian city-state tradition. She called for new attention to a category of power that emphasized consent and 'concert'. Although for later critiques like Pasewark's Arendt marked a distinctive and constructive step forward, her defining of power still fell within that limited politico-philosophical framework. She stressed the fact that modern state power was, at least technically, dependent upon the consent of the people. It was then but a short step to her claim that power did not just refer to the ability to act but to act 'in concert'. She approved Madison's dictum that every government is really founded on opinion (that is, of the people, of a group).[24] So power cannot by

22 Lukes, 'Introduction', *Power*, citing the work of Peter Bachrach and Morton Baratz.

23 Hannah Arendt, 'Communicative Power' in Steven Lukes (ed.), *Power* (Oxford, 1986), pp. 59–74.

24 Arendt, 'Communicative Power', p. 62.

definition ever be the property of any one individual, however much it may seem so. The individual was always empowered by a group of some kind and this power remained in place just so long as the group did not withdraw its support or destroy that person. This applied even to the despot, though the consenting, supporting group may be an elite and small in number. Hence when subduing through terror, 'power' was no longer the appropriate term – perhaps the term 'naked violence' was now more appropriate.[25]

Habermas points out that Arendt's approach to power sprang from her attempt to give an account of true humanity. Her programme, he suggested, defined the nature of the person as above all an intersubjective, social being. This reality was marked foremost by *communication* (pre-eminently speech) within a network of relationships. The nature of power in the political realm was then read off from this.[26] Political power, for Arendt, existed to give expression to, and defend, the social reality of communicating relationships. It was therefore only legitimate power when it did both of these things. When it failed to do them it failed to be credible power.[27] In that case what claimed to be power displayed itself as no more than a form of weakness, now failed and frustrated. Habermas's fear is that the ideal of corporate communicative action (which we could call social solidarity on the move) focuses too much on a unity behind political power in modern democracies. Today thought, action, economics and politics are too complex and competing for them successfully to produce a single, harmonious community committed to a single heartbeat of power.[28] In addition Arendt's view could appear too whimsical and not to be taking sufficient account of political realities. In particular it needs to include strategies of obstruction and distortion – the political games that bypass the will even of the people.[29] Arendt has also received mixed reviews among more recent feminists. Amy Allen, however, has been hailed by Johanna Meehan as reviving interest in Arendt's work through detecting there an anchorage of political action in political and civil rights. This, it is claimed, is more securely grounded than a purely gender solidarity ('identity' politics), with its ambiguous norms of who is in and who is out.[30] At any rate, Arendt might yet turn out to offer significant light on power dynamics in community, and so in the local church.

---

25 Arendt, pp. 64–5.

26 Lukes approves Habermas's analysis and criticisms of Arendt: Lukes, 'Introduction', p. 3.

27 Jurgen Habermas, 'Hannah Arendt's Communications Concept of Power' in Steven Lukes (ed.), *Power* (Oxford, 1986), 75–93, pp. 78–82.

28 Habermas, pp. 82–3.

29 Lukes, 'Introduction', p. 3, giving an account of Habermas's criticism.

30 See her extensive review of Allen's book *The Power of Feminist Theory*, in Johanna Meehan, 'Review Essay: Feminism, critical theory, and power', *Philosophy and Social Criticism*, 30/3 (2004): 375–82 [electronic version], p. 380.

Christian Community and the Political Narrative

This has been a narrative of disputes among political philosophers concerning power in the modern political state, and there is no ambition at this point to offer uninformed mediation between the parties. However, this does not mean that the writers encountered are irrelevant to, or offer no help at all for, understanding the power in communities. For instance it simplifies things that in a local community context, the economic and administrative complexities of running a state do not apply. Accordingly, in such micro-contexts Arendt's vision of people working together is indeed realized. Moreover she stands as a link between classical discussion and the innovative approach of Foucault. Hence at least three lines of help to community can stand out from her work in particular.

First, Arendt's descriptions of 'power with', namely community power underlying centralized power, has a generic appeal. It plausibly describes what happens in any local setting and illuminates power patterns in such settings. For here it would indeed be true that any credible power would usually spring from a community of consent – energy through synergy. Of course, here too political strategies and smart moves by an influential activist minority could frustrate for a while the wishes of most members of the community. However, it would also be true that even the most successful strategic triumphs by politically astute players in a local community could fall apart if hitherto docile members finally found their voice or their feet. This is not a rare event in groups and any assessment of power in a congregation must take account of it.

Secondly, Arendt has specifically drawn attention away from command and obedience as the benchmark,[31] pointing us instead towards power as an achievement of consent towards common ends.[32] In other words it represents the possibility for a decisive shift from concentration on 'power over' (command and obedience) towards 'power with' (consent and cooperation).

Thirdly, the narrative's end highlights through Arendt the centrality of social communication. It is this that promotes a harmonious management of power in a community. Not only vast political states but also micro-communities like church are usually unable to achieve the ideal of an absolute and perfect consensus. But the communication and transparency that supports such a search for consensus seems a key way of maximizing 'power to' and 'power with'.

[31] Arendt, p. 62.

[32] Arendt, pp. 62–3.

The Day before Foucault

Safety in Vagueness

Lukes concludes that the great variety of angles on power in political writing prevented an easy agreement on what should be included when framing a definition of power. As already noted he sees political power as an unavoidably 'contested' concept.[33] He has identified the main complications. They include first the, albeit legitimate, qualities of 'intention' in power-action,[34] although this only raises such problems as how we can know what is in people's minds and how anyway we could trust even their own accounts of personal intention. Further, we face the ever-present problems with the concept of resistance. And finally we run into questions about the place of power's claim to change behaviour. Curiously, despite his criticisms, he acknowledges that empowerment as a co-operative venture (as in Arendt) deserves more attention. But he settles in the end with a starting definition safe and vague enough to please a Bertrand Russell: having power is simply the ability to bring about a difference in the world.[35] This of course dilutes the concept down to include almost every human action. In addition, qualifiers queue up once again to overwhelm such a definition. Is the difference made in the world to be a good or bad difference? Is the difference achieved precisely through overcoming resistance? Is it a difference made only in human society or anywhere to anything?

In fairness, Lukes has at least sought to rescue us from the subjectivity of intention that plagued post-Russell formulae. So it is not necessary that the person with power actually intends the precise differences made.[36] Rather, the outcomes must merely turn out to serve the interests of the more powerful party. However, fears have arisen over Lukes's view here, for it seems to reinforce simplistically negative attitudes to power, especially those found in Marxism.[37] In a recent return to the subject, Lukes shows that he has remained sensitive to the difficulties in his definition. These include the problem of how to escape value-laden decisions about what really are the best (long term or short term?) interests of the more powerful party. But he seems recently still to think it crucial to ask the question 'Whose interests were served?'[38] And this indeed is going to be an important strand later on in the discussion of power relations within a faith-group like church. The matter of whose interests are served remains at the heart of power-analysis. The difference in desired outcomes and actual outcomes within the dynamics of church

33 Clegg, p. 90, after a long discussion, agrees with Lukes on this score at least.

34 See also the critical questions of Clegg, p. 3.

35 Lukes, 'Introduction', p. 5.

36 Lukes, 'Introduction', p. 5.

37 Clegg, p. 128, even though Lukes clearly rejects strict Marxist ideology.

38 Lukes, 'Power and the Battle for Hearts and Minds', p. 483.

as sociological reality contains key lessons for all involved in its life. But more of that in due course.

One last comment is in order. Lukes, like Arendt, accepts that the interests of the powerful party may not even be selfish, but rather may even spring from generosity and in the service of community.[39] And Lukes remains committed more recently to this upbeat view of power's capacity to serve the interests of people other than the powerful. There is no reason to assume that the power to effect my interests always involves threat. In fact, sometimes power may even be on the side of everyone's good.[40] At any rate, here the chief point of power is not 'power *over*', the power of command-and-obedience. Lukes is letting power mutate into 'power *to*' – power to make an uncontested difference to the benefit of a whole community. The point here is that a new point of view has been emerging, and survives even within current political discourse. True it is not divorced from stone sober alertness to versions conceiving power as a strategy to subvert the true interests of others. For even 'power to' might also become difficult to distinguish from 'power over'. Pasewark trenchantly pointed out that 'power to' can simply be dominating power in disguise.[41] And yet such subtle changes that recognize the 'productive' or transforming quality of power (for good or ill) set up a crucial bridge to the new footings for the understanding of power built by Michel Foucault.

'Soft Power' – How Soft?

Still on this question of whose interests are served, Lukes turns to the impact and plausibility of Joseph Nye's theory of 'soft power'.[42] Nye's work, it should be said, is taken up entirely with international political strategies. He concerns himself with global tensions between Western values of freedom, equality and plurality over and against the values of sanctity and religious faith in, mainly radical, forms of Islam. Both are reaching out to European, immigrant Islam.[43] So Nye's category of power claims to work at a level deeper than merely offering inducements, threats or even persuasion. 'Soft power' then denotes one party's ability to draw a targeted people into embracing its values by means of 'attraction'. This means simply to aim at people wanting the same as you want yourself. It is successful when its target audience come to share a particular view of what is 'in their best interests' (for example, either shelter in the fold of Islamic certainty, or peace and safety from persecution in the culture of pluralism and freedom). The reasoning goes as follows: power is what can bring about something either against or for someone's best interests. But views will differ on what is actually either against or

39 Lukes, 'Introduction', p. 7.

40 Lukes, 'Power and the Battle for Hearts and Minds', p. 484.

41 Pasewark, p. 3.

42 Lukes, 'Power and the Battle for Hearts and Minds', pp. 484–92. See also Sykes p. x.

43 Lukes, 'Power and the Battle for Hearts and Minds', pp. 486–90.

for someone's best interests. One of these views must prevail through being more attractive, or seductive, than the other. This we call 'soft' power.

Lukes is suitably critical of this view for not sufficiently spelling out how human freedom remains intact in 'soft power'.[44] But he still does not point out that soft power itself only tumbles into the already vexed prior question of who, at some point, actually decided what is in the targeted party's interests and to which they must be drawn. Moreover there is also the yet deeper question of what standpoint governs that evaluation. 'Soft power' as described by Nye points to people coming round to a particular set of attractive or 'seductive' values (say, either pure Islam or Western equalities and freedoms). But on Lukes's own analysis neither side in this international struggle can claim objectively to know that their set of values is genuinely in the best interests of the targeted communities.[45] So it seems that transparent and credible evidence is paramount in revealing at least a minimum requirement: that the interests of the target audience, not self-interested politics, is truly at the heart of the wish to spread certain values. If not, then the power involved even in soft power regresses straight back into dominating power and a mere 'power over'.

Nye's relevance to power in the micro-context, such as a church setting, must be set out with care. All the same it has value for analysing internal local community politics. Accordingly, power conflicts arising in church must be resolved on the basis of a wish on all sides for everyone's good, *including that of the surrounding community to which church is sent in mission*. It must be recognized that sometimes one party does not really know (or care?) about what the other party considers its own best interests. The key lesson for avoiding conflict and domination in any form, is that a people on the way of Jesus turn tendencies towards 'hard' dominating power into sincere 'soft' power. This means that in its dynamics it fosters ongoing mutual understanding of each other's interests through genuine commitment to communication. This would be critical first of all to the shaking out of disagreements on worship, life and action as a community. But it would also be true in processes of teaching and group searching after authentic faith and behaviour. However, for a local church community, mutual interests are not even the priority: the mission of service to God and the world is that. It is in this field most of all that people's good, and their unforced freedom to choose such good, is paramount. So 'soft power' would be the hallmark of all decisions for mission and action in any church community in its mission and service to the larger community. It could even be one test of every mission strategy and proposed action for the wider world engaging a community in the name of Jesus.

[44] Lukes, 'Power and the Battle for Hearts and Minds', p. 492.

[45] Lukes, 'Power and the Battle for Hearts and Minds', pp. 482–4.

The End of the 'Political' Method?

Pasewark's summary of the situation when he wrote fifteen years ago was that little could be done to save the traditional approach from a merely external view of power, a vocabulary mainly of domination where power does not 'transform' its object with a life-giving efficacy but only controls it.[46] In traditional political thought, power was always to be 'exercised' by one over another. That was the bottom line. 'Power over' then even reached to the inner life of the person, as Foucault had demonstrated in his devastating critiques. For Pasewark, even the changing of the phrasing from 'power over' to 'power to' in a political context would not necessarily wash out the impurity of domination. For the new phrase might really mean power to do something to something which affects someone.[47] This in the end would be 'power to' through some form of 'power over'. Hence, for Pasewark political categories, even with humanized vocabulary, could not adequately conceptualize power for us. Even Foucault, he believed, had to be watched on this score.[48]

Pasewark himself was going to change the concept dramatically so that power was (in a slightly mysterious phrase) the 'communication of efficacy', a phrase that appears throughout his work. I would interpret that still as a form of 'power to'. But it was certainly intended as a particularly benign type of 'power to', that is I suggest, 'power to give life and good'. We shall in due course return to Pasewark's handling of power and its usefulness to power and the Christian community. In the meantime, however, a key thought is pushing through. If there is such a thing as benign 'power to' (give life) it is very likely that there underlies it something like the 'power of' – the power specifically of life. From now on we are always in the presence of the possibility that the desirable overarching power in Christian aspiration will be the very 'power of' (life), whatever contact it has with the other three forms (power, 'over', 'to', and 'with'). A fuller sense will emerge in the exploration ahead, opening out what power 'of life' might mean in Christian thought generally and for local church more particularly. For help we shall turn to Christian theology. But from now on it is towards this which the discussion is working even though the trail winds through some unlikely stops on the way.

46 Pasewark, p. 3.

47 Pasewark, pp. 2–3.

48 Pasewark, p. 5.

The Foucualt Moment

The End of the Beginning?

Michel Foucault was the big beast arriving to plunge into the settled pool of political philosophers.[49] He broke the 'narrative flow' on power.[50] The main tradition of political discussion had assumed a 'scientific' if contested sense of power. But Foucault depended much more on rhetoric, metaphor[51] and, we could add, parabolic description. He was casual by comparison with mainstream discussion of power, and bothered little to worry about clinical definitions and finely argued points.[52] A chastened political philosophy had indeed already begun to emerge. One can for instance discern in Stewart Clegg a shift from the endless exploration of 'power over'. Instead we hear talk of power as 'facilitating' and 'dispositional' (albeit with a key role for 'organization').[53] For this reason, he probably escapes the severest of Pasewark's criticisms. Clegg, at least, is one influential writer not trapped in a merely occasional and external view of power in the world. This suggests that Foucault had done his work and that discussion of power would never be quite the same again.

Why Foucault?

Evidence of Foucault's relevance to theology today appears from his presence there already in 1988. At that time a collection of writings about church by Roman Catholic writers bravely used Foucault's writings to sharpen Catholic self-criticism on power in the Roman Catholic institution.[54] This was pioneer work but an example not widely followed through. All the same, it illustrates that there are good theological reasons for calling at Foucault's door when exploring the complex relationship between Christian community and power. His work emerged self-consciously from Catholic France and displayed at many points a detailed knowledge of Christian thought and history. Indeed, though an atheist, he acknowledged his Catholic background without embarrassment or apology.[55] He sometimes showed remarkable courtesy and fairness towards Christian history at points that are hardly its finest moments. More particularly his later work focused on the strategies and meaning of power in smaller social units, and

49 See for instance Clegg, p. 2.

50 Clegg, p. 2.

51 Clegg, p. 3.

52 Clegg, p. 2.

53 Clegg, p. 239.

54 James Provost and Knut Walf (eds), *Concilium 197: Power in the Church* (Edinburgh,1988).

55 Joyce Schuld, *Foucault and Augustine: Reconsidering Power and Love* (Indiana, 2003), p. 1 citing an unpublished interview with Robert Bellah.

church community is surely one of these. So some important questions to church include the following: what kind is this power Foucault sees as always present in face to face social relationships? Which insights into such power should inform and perhaps guide leadership of a local church community in its shared life and decision making? What forms of power tactics and strategies should church expect to find within its own life and how much should they concern its members?

In addition to all this, Foucault is anyway already highly influential in many other disciplines, so why not in theology? True, in a celebrated but typically modest aside Foucault famously remarked that the twentieth century would probably turn out to belong to his erstwhile co-conspirator, Deleuzes. And indeed Deleuzes continues to grow as a subject of attention. But it is Foucault in the end who so far has dominated the last forty years on the subject of power as well as other fields relevant to a local church. In fact, there is probably no other writer whose thought on power has impacted upon so many surprising fields, including law, medicine, nursing, education, science, law and even geography. It would be hard *not* to conclude this narrative of disputes about power by giving special attention to him. It is even claimed that Foucault's writings single-handedly transformed critical work in the humanities and thereby shifted the fundamental way the academy handles the subject of power.[56] To appreciate what drove Foucault's thought, life and work, requires attention to the whole span of his astonishing intellectual career.

Foucault's Life and Personality

So far as Foucault's persona goes, Claire O'Farrell's introduction to his life and influence is easily the most accessible and engaging for a novice.[57] The great man, she reminds us, is a 'modern icon', the 'gay saint'. However, his name is still a shorthand way of indulging in intellectual pretension and being seen as a member of an élite club (as O'Farrell remind us, for example, in the Tom Hanks film, *You've got mail* and, yes, even a *Dr Who* short story). Among critics Foucault is also a byword for French jargonism, ephemeral trendiness and a newly arrived invasion of 'intellectual terrorism'.[58] However it quickly becomes clear, even in her own account, that he was a much more substantial and formidable intellect than these pop flatteries and sideswipes suggest.[59] The point need not be laboured here. As aspects of his thought on power emerge, it will become plain that we are

[56] Richard Wolin, 'Foucault the Neohumanist', in *The Chronical Review* (Electronic Version), 53/3 (2006): 1–5, p. 1. Peter Morriss must be tongue-in-cheek, or using a very particular definition of power, when claiming that Foucault doesn't really talk about power at all but only about *pouvoir* because merely denoting an action: Peter Morriss, *Power: A Philosophical Analysis* (Manchester, 2002), p. xvi.

[57] Claire O'Farrell, *Michel Foucault* (London, 2005), pp. 1–2.

[58] O'Farrell, p. 2.

[59] O'Farrell, pp. 3–4.

really dealing with a challenging and sometimes stratospheric thinker. And he is one who, if sometimes elusive, is often enough only too trenchant and clear for comfort.

Granted, Foucault is a most unlikely mountain guide for a church climbing towards self-understanding of its internal and external power-relations. Often seen as one of the high-priests of postmodernism, he hardly ranks as a Christian analyst. True, considerable discussion does move around the possibility of his subterranean spirituality and his alleged soft spot for Christian mysticism[60] as well as for his transferable value for Christian theology.[61]

However, as it happens, any use of Foucault on the religious front does not imply an entire alternative Foucauldian theological system.[62] Nor need it require seizing 'body-parts' of Foucault-thought and recycling these limbs of radical thought into revitalized systems of Christian theology.[63] As it happens, his varied takes on Christian faith do not greatly reduce his usefulness for our very specific task at this point. Formulations of power and church are mainly going to draw help from his extensive power analysis. As already noted, his dissection of the subject has transferred itself very comfortably into a number of academic disciplines. So we expect that theology too is well able to adapt for itself this one further catalyst among its many others, without surrendering its own specific character.

The consequence of all this is that reflection on power in church cannot with integrity ignore Foucault nor the controversy raging around him. And after engaging with his genius, it will be left with a much more complex, tantalizing and applicable set of concepts than before. All the same, this unsettling reality is easily missed, or lightly handled, by Christian theological writing on power. Foucault's contribution was about to open up new senses of power and to problematize, as well as deepen, old ones. He was to question easy assumptions about the main levers of power in human society and the manner of power's operation. With his challenges in the air, it was now difficult if not impossible to return to a simpler pre-Foucauldian age. That was a time when villains in power were always and predictably easy to pick off because of their tyranny and the only possible resistance to such despotism was some clear ideology or other.

Our narrative of discussion leading up to and away from Hannah Arendt traced power beyond simply '*power over*'. For it transpired that power might also assume positive, constructive forms latent or possible in the alternative phrase 'power to'. Now we can think of power as a freedom to act for the good of another. 'Power to' denoted a person's ability to engage their own capability, whereas 'power over' pointed to the exploitation of someone else's powerlessness.[64] It is true that

---

60 John McSweeney, 'Foucault and Theology', *Foucault Studies*, 2 (2005): 117–24.

61 McSweeney, p. 114.

62 McSweeney, pp. 120–24.

63 McSweeney, pp. 117–19.

64 Stephen C. Ainley, 'Mennonite Culture Wars: Power, Authority and Domination', in Benjamin W. Redekop and Calvin W. Redekop, *Power, Authority and the Anabaptist*

Foucault did not completely abandon an interest in the subject of power focused in traditional political language. But we do all the same see in him a gradual shift from political 'power over' to political 'power to'. 'Power' came more to denote streams of efficacy (though not necessarily good) coursing through society than to describe players controlling the game-plan. The 'power to' did not so much lie in the hands of dominant brokers (whether a group or individual) but in a less controllable and wider web of normalizing processes. Moreover, the small-time strategies that fed this larger web of life could be viewed more clearly at the grassroots in modern society. They inhabited the life of local communities and institutions, so were dispersed among many rather than marking out the few. This late twentieth-century eruption into the tidy world of political theorists caused seismic responses. Some feminists dryly observed that political theorists had anyway failed to recognize their own work already done in cultural studies and its capacity to nail forces for normalization in society as opposed to structured political activity.[65]

Significantly, Lawrence Kritzman claims that at the time of Foucault's death in 1984 at the age of fifty-seven no other intellectual in recent times was making such an impact on key academic domains such as history, literature, the social sciences, literary theory and for that matter medicine.[66] In fact one could add that his influence has continued to circulate further and wider ever since. Posthumous Foucault is everywhere.

Foucault the Person

As is well known Foucault's career started inauspiciously with his work as an assistant in a mental hospital. He began his hunt for the meaning of power by considering the extraordinary supremacy enjoyed by those who watch over the mentally ill and also over criminals. Powerful overseers controlled the reality in which these vulnerable humans moved, where every step of the inmates could be monitored. Under this penetrating scrutiny the inmates protected what rags of freedom they still had by a process of self-surveillance, ensuring that their behaviour met expected standards. However, Foucault also detected forces for evoking self-surveillance elsewhere too, for example in such modern state spheres as education, health and social policy. The institution (mental, educational, penal)

Tradition (Baltimore, 2001), 138–44, p. 139. This is foreshadowed by Spinoza's distinction between *potestas* ('rule over') and *potentia* (creative power), a point for which I am indebted to Professor Chris Norris. Foucault seems to be part of this shift.

65 See for example, Susan Hekman, 'Feminist Identity Politics: Transforming the Political' in Dianna Taylor and Karen Vintges (eds), *Feminism and the Final Foucault* (Urbana, 2004), 196–213, p. 206.

66 Lawrence D. Kritzman, 'Introduction: Foucault and the Politics of Experience', in Lawrence D. Kritzman (ed.), *Michel Foucault: Politics, Philosophy, Culture: Interviews and Other Writings* (New York, 1988), i–xxv, p. ix.

internalized self-security

served Foucault as a microcosm of civil surveillance generally and for the practice of self-surveillance. Through such internalized practice of self-scrutiny, the body became the site of domination and normalization. We shall return to these radical ideas later.

Meantime, Foucault did not lose his instinct for supporting struggles towards freedom and justice. He began his academic work in the environment of the French radical Left and demonstrated that fact by a full-blooded involvement in the 1968 student demonstrations. This was how Foucault became the darling of revolutionaries. Yet at the same time he began a searching critical evaluation of the great trends of intellectual thought, especially of those on the Left.

So on the one hand, he did indeed take the side of student revolutionaries in the campus revolutions of May 1968 and of the overthrow of the Shah of Iran by the Revolutionary Guard in Tehran in 1978–79. Equally he took his stand for humane treatment of mental patients and prisoners, along with Deleuze and others, starting a movement which led in turn to major political reform. On the other hand, he himself denied any connection between his particular campaigns and his theorizing on power and freedom. In fact he mocked the notion of an intellectual who solves problems. He denied having any special intellectual status as a revolutionary or activist. He sometimes wrote his work anonymously, winning the title of 'the masked philosopher'.[67] Intellectuals did not step forward as prophets, he chided. Intellectuals are not there to tell others what their moral duty is. Even less should intellectuals try to shape a person's political will. Rather their role is to disturb people's mental complacency.[68] The intellectual had ceased to be an oracle or the protector of the masses from deception or error.

Especially, intellectuals should no longer serve as the thought-wing of revolutionaries like a Marx or Lenin. In the age of the individual, the intellectual's task is to provide the software, the tools that will enable individuals and groups in their actual struggle for freedom or in their search for voice.[69] All the same he could *sound* like a prophet. More than once, at different stages in his career, he chewed up liberalism's mantras even though they often fed the cry for justice.[70] In addition he conducted a fitful relationship with the intellectual vanguard of the French Left, not to mention the dominant French existentialist camp led by its high priest, J-P Sartre. Mere logic ought to demand that activists for freedom

---

[67] Lawrence D. Kritzman, 'Introduction: Foucault and the Politics of Experience', p. ix.

[68] Michel Foucault (Interview), 'The Concern for Truth', in Lawrence D. Kritzman (ed.), *Michel Foucault: Politics, Philosophy, Culture: Interviews and Other Writings* (New York, 1988) 255–70, p. 265

[69] Lawrence D. Kritzman, 'Introduction. Foucault and the Politics of Experience', p. xii.

[70] Hubert L. Dreyfus and Paul Rabinow, *Michel Foucault: Beyond Structuralism and Hermeneutics* (Brighton, 1982), p. 202.

would take all the allies they could lay their hands on, especially these allies – but Foucault did not always do so.

At the same time Foucault did not shirk the paying of respects to those who had influenced him. Sometimes it was Heidegger he honoured as perhaps the major influence. On other occasions it was Nietzsche, especially Nietzsche's concern with truth – the history of truth, the 'will to truth'.[71] Although the mark of Nietzsche is widely detected on Foucault's work of the early 1970's Foucault was plainly not a Nietzsche clone.[72] Commentators have indeed detected Nietzsche mainly in Foucault's criticism of Western thought and his attacks on what he called the attempt to separate out 'truth' from power. Nietzsche and Foucault alike did not think that the function of knowledge (=truth) was to tame the excesses of power.[73] However, unlike Nietzsche, Foucault identified with the weak and vanquished, the mentally ill and the deviant.[74]

Starting with Pocket Foucault

An account of Foucault's view of power has to include at least three major approaches to the meaning of power in human society. Arguments have raged about whether he moved clearly on from one to the other in definite phases with sharp breaks and departures or whether he managed to incorporate each previous stage in his evolving world-view. The three main variations of power in his thought are well known: (1) classic '*sovereign power*', or the rule of monarchy and total government, (2) '*disciplinary power*', pointing to a systemic conditioning of thought by culture or state policy (probably including for tidiness' sake, a branch that he called 'bio-power')[75] and (3) '*micro-power*', denoting smaller, sited settings of power such as state institutions, family and smaller interest-groups. These are all sites of local face to face 'power relations'. It seems reasonable to include here the local church community and comparable groups.

It is time to summarize these three types of power and then give attention to some details.

Sovereign power in Foucault was the power of 'bare life'[76] present in the times of monarchs and tyrants. It simply operated in the 'realm of death'. It contained

---

[71] Michel Foucault (Interview), 'Critical Theory/Intellectual History', in Lawrence D. Krizman (ed.), *Michel Foucault: Politics, Philosophy, Culture, Interviews and Other Writings* (New York, 1988), 17–46, p. 32.

[72] Dreyfus and Rabinow, pp. 106, 108–11.

[73] See J. D. Faubion, 'Introduction' in J. D. Faubion (ed.), *Michel Foucault: Power* (London, 2002), pp. i–xxvi.

[74] J. Bernauer, Michel Foucault's Force of Flight: Toward an Ethics for Thought (London, 1990), p. 180.

[75] For a recent account see Mike Ojakangas, 'Impossible Dialogue on Bio-Power. Agamben and Foucault', *Foucault Studies*, No. 2/May (2005): 5–28.

[76] At least as controversially interpreted by Agamben, cited by Ojakanagas, p. 5.

ultimate power, the sanction of life and death, the absolute negative. It wielded not only a threat to take away life itself but even to crush the present means of life. True, its power was less absolute than seems at first sight, but it still was very great. Certainly domination pervaded the harsh realities in the period of monarchs, brutality made bare in punishment mechanisms, law and institutions.[77] But it also survived alive and well in various forms even later, not just through law but through regional and local settings and their institutions.[78] Controversy rages over Foucault's own political philosophy. This includes his call to 'cut off the king's head'[79] and his apparent resignation to politics being a 'war continued by other means'.[80] We are not going to be diverted by this debate but it suggests that at least fairly late Foucault still feared sovereignty as a single centre of dominating power.[81]

However, in *disciplinary power* Foucault pressed beyond discussion of 'legitimated', sovereign might and considered power as taking on new life through subtle techniques and mechanisms. This power beyond the reach of legal questioning was more interesting and significant.[82] To understand domination in this scenario, one must not be sidetracked into seeking guilty villains of oppression, let alone dissecting their intentions. What mattered now was not *who* but *what* subjugated people. The answer could be many things: publicly correct knowledge, remorseless processes, norms of behaviour, influences on our very gestures etc.[83] Now it was not so easy to draw a line between dominator and dominated, but instead we found ourselves in a more fuzzy domain of power relations or multiple strategies of power.[84]

It seems natural to see this second major form, *disciplinary power*, could enfold *bio-power*, making a single stream. Certainly both contrasted with 'juridical' power, the power of law and right, or with naked political force. For Foucault 'disciplinary power' started up the production of 'norms' to define humanity, and

---

77 Michel Foucault, 'Two Lectures' in Colin Gordon (ed.), *Power/Knowledge: Selected Interviews and Other Writings 1972–1977: Michel Foucault* (Brighton, 1980), 78–108, p. 95.

78 Foucault, 'Power, Right, Truth', in R. E. Gooden and Philip Petit, *Contemporary Political Philosophy: An Anthology:* (Oxford, 1997), 545–50, p. 96.

79 Michel Foucault (Interview), 'Truth and Power' in J. D. Faubion (ed.), *Michel Foucault: Power* (London, 2002) 111–33, pp. 122–3, reaffirming his earlier verdict.

80 Foucault, 'Two Lectures', pp. 90–91. Was this his wish for a society freed from the restraint of a governing civic value?

81 Reignited in the publication of lectures: Michel Foucault, *Abnormal. Lectures at the College de France, 1974–1975 and also 'Society Must Be Defended': Lectures at the College de France, 1975–76* (New York, 2003).

82 Foucault, 'Two Lectures', p. 97.

83 Foucault, 'Two Lectures', p. 97.

84 Lawrence D. Kritzman, 'Introduction: Foucault and the Politics of Experience', p. xvi.

eliminate the 'abnormal'. It established an authoritative 'science' or knowledge which subtly reinforced ideas of normality.[85] For such reasons Foucault's 'bio-power', according to some, especially belonged in this category and concerned itself with nurturing life in society, by promoting a healthy social vitality. Now that the state did not threaten with death all the time, we were left only with subtle governmental nurture and control. Control in bio-power worked through mass public channels, health and education. Its norms had a way of including certain citizens but excluding others. It normalized cultural and social processes so that such 'truths' became internalized in each citizen. Bio-power was a fruit in democratic society of 'technologies of power' over the human subject, the 'self'. Thus bio-power was a form that power took in our era and existed for a social end: to ensure the fullest possible life for 'society' and to enlarge it. To this end bio-power's method was to subject society to precise and comprehensive regulations.[86]

Bio-power functioned not to threaten and destroy but to enhance and generate *life* (even though centres of domination may remain).[87] Accordingly it did not merely *react* to individuals. It actually *produced* individuals, or selves, in a continual process of shaping and forming through public norms, namely what we have come to call 'normalization'. People were usually unaware of this process, according to Foucault. They continued to labour under the illusion that this self was somehow transcendent and prior to the workings of bio-power upon them. Bio-power did the graft of disciplinary power in creating mass self-surveillance, subtly guiding people's lives and conditioning their view of themselves. It shaped a person's self-consciousness and behaviour. Such was the work of liberal modernity and completely in line with its quest to maximize the greater social good. 'Norms' conditioning people replaced laws pressing down on them and this was now the chief means of social control.[88] Bio-power replaced sovereign power for the enforcement of conformity.

Whether sovereign power with its brutalities could now be deemed a relic of the terrifying past or not, bio-power was itself quite frightening enough. Many critics found it to be pessimistic, positing a docile, helplessly passive population even in modern democratic society. For even here in Western society, in a democratic environment, resistance against bio-power would not be easily mustered. How could it be otherwise, since bio-power did not merely repress

---

85 Although we note the cautionary comment that Foucault was not so often targeting the hard sciences as the 'human sciences', social and political (some would say 'near-sciences', or 'soft sciences'). See Dreyfus and Rabinow, p. 177.

86 Ojakangas, p. 1.

87 Michel Foucault, 'Power, Right, Truth', p. 549.

88 Aurelia Armstrong in 'Foucault and Feminism', in the *Internet Encyclopaedia of Philosophy*, (http://www.iep. edu/f/foucfem.htm), p. 1. Her article is a rare example of a quality website article: a technically excellent and lucid summary of Foucault's relation to feminist thought [accessed 1.01.07].

subjects. Far more radically, it *produced* and *shaped* them in their very being as subjects. It crafted the very assumptions and motives that would have led to resistance.

As mentioned already, it was a contentious issue whether Foucault intended to divide sovereign power and bio-power cleanly into different eras, or whether in fact he always expected a residue of the first latent in the second.[89] There was, as we have seen, that famous moment when Foucault argued vigorously that we must 'cut off the king's head'. But he probably meant only that we needed a political theory of power that was not built just round the issue of sovereignty alone.[90] Rather we must today mainly see power as 'capillary', that is, not externally and formally enforced from above, but pervasive and inescapable. Power/knowledge did not just lie on the surface but also lurked as invisible within society.[91] It was circulatory, coursing through the whole of society.

The *third* strain of thought about power in Foucault is '*micro-power*', power in a localized context yet tied in to large-scale disciplinary power and bio-power. We find this idea associated more closely with Foucault's later or middle writings (mid-1970s to the end of that decade). I suggest that out of Foucault's various angles on the subject this one most touches church as face to face life together in the presence of power. Foucault found power to be not just a static dead hand of sovereign might pressing top-down on micro-societies as in relatively recent European history. Nor was it only a process of all-encompassing norms circulating through the whole body of society, as set out by himself. A form of power also pulsed away as '*micro-power*' right down within smaller groupings (families, local institutions etc). And here power did not usually install itself in any one central point of the smaller social unit. Instead it harboured a wide variety of forces, influences and effects in each place, a microcosm of wider workings of power. So power was automatically present everywhere – and everywhere resistance was present in specific forms of local interaction. For power was even made known through meeting and absorbing resistance.[92] Accordingly, local power was a process that was fluid, even unpredictable, and an unavoidable by-product of relationships. It centred on people in their real concrete, direct, face-to-face relations.

Hence, as with lessons taken from Nye, power-analysis is particularly relevant to local church and its character as a common life as well as its wider life and mission. Here too the character of the church that embarked on mission would first be known in its innermost power relations. So how should Foucault's analysis of micro-power be understood for managing power in church life together? To answer this question and clarify what is involved, we face yet deeper, more sustained reflection on the Foucault narrative. For his thought about power can

89 The burden of Ojakangas's article, 'Impossible Dialogue on Bio-Power'.

90 Hekman, p. 203.

91 Foucault, cited in Hekman, p. 203.

92 Richard A. Lynch, 'Is Power All there Is? Michel Foucault and the "Omnipresence" of Power Relations', *Philosophy Today*, 42/1 (1998): 65–80, p. 65.

only be understood within a broader understanding of his life and the changing pattern of his thought. We now turn to this.

Mercury or Marble? Continuity in Foucault

It is clear by now that Foucault was a mover and shaker. It procured him the right to confuse readers frequently. He did this by moving on unpredictably, carried along by his own originality. Some commentators have simply given up on expecting to find in him progression of historical processes. Some simply ignore history in Foucault and cite him randomly as if evolution in his thought were irrelevant.

What did Foucault himself say about his helter-skelter of novelty? He sometimes seemed to be in defensive mode about it. But in any case what critics condemned as erratic departures, he saw as a zig-zag slalom-like progress.[93] He saw radical shifts as stages in a roughly detectable single direction.[94] He even lamented his failure to change radically *enough* or to fulfil his own stated ideal which was nothing less than constant new developments of thought. Hence, late in life he bewailed that his final major works sadly differed little from earlier ones even though some critics and reviewers saw only dramatic change. So, he teased, don't look for that much difference between the earlier and later books.[95] This disingenuous remark has to be taken alongside another famous jibe of his not to ask him who exactly he was or expect him to stay the same – for he would leave it to the miserable bureaucrats and police to see that his papers were in order.[96] Certainly there is a tongue firmly in the cheek with the protest that he was never interested in analysing power but rather subjectivity, the study of the self.[97] The fact is that exploring the way selves are shaped immediately required analyses of power and he has admitted that he became quite involved with the concept.[98] After all, the human subject was positioned at the centre of complex power relations.

So did he progress in a discernible way, retaining throughout his career a simple foundational concern with freedom and subjectivity as he himself claimed? Or was he always in flight from his own inconsistency and provisionality, stumbling into new problems as he went? One influential view supported his own version in some measure in 1982 with the theory that his work always implicitly contained key concepts that developed later even if the weighting and conception sometimes

---

93 Foucault, 'Two Lectures' p. 94.

94 Dreyfus and Rabinow, p. 205.

95 Michel Foucault (Interview), 'An Aesthetics of Existence', Lawrence D. Kritzman (ed.), *Michel Foucault: Politics, Philosophy, Culture: Interviews and Other Writings* (New York, 1988), 47–56, p. 48.

96 From Foucault's *Archaeology of Knowledge*, cited by Kritzman, 'Introduction', p. ix.

97 Michel Foucault, 'The Subject and Power', in J. D. Faubion (ed.), *Michel Foucault: Power* (London, 2002), 326–48, p. 326.

98 Foucault, 'The Subject and Power', p. 327.

varied.[99] On this account it was an uncomplicated matter. Foucault had progressed more or less naturally from one related theme to another. It would be easy enough to reconstruct that famous slalom with an eye to the continuous central concerns. Hence, Foucault's earlier outings traced sovereign dominations in history which crushed the self, together with the power-drenched institutions that covertly directed and coerced individuals (sovereignty). He then, moved on to unmask forces shaping our selves/subjects in the modern era through the sway of power over 'truth' (disciplinary power and bio-power working especially through the human sciences). Later he developed from this 'capillary' approach a yet more penetrating view of power as it works locally and much nearer to home for all of us. Finally, approaching his untimely end, he calmly picked up the cause of the freedom of the subject once more in his 'aesthetics of the self'. All sense, reason and consistency! An arrow's flight, a straight trajectory.[100] Perhaps too, Foucault tackled the subject of power before he focused on the actual word.[101] In this period of Foucault anyway, it is argued, power issues really did pervade his central question for the late twentieth century, namely the progressive organization of life and society.[102]

Other views of Foucault sound out a contentious note on his logic of progress. They puzzle over an allegedly erratic feel to his staged departures of thought. Some suggest a quintessential 'pluralism'. In a middle way, Eric Paras suspects that some commentators have masked the plurality of ideas by reducing them to a false harmonization. This could be done by cherry-picking Foucauldian themes in a text-referencing fashion without listening to the whole of his journey.[103] On the other hand an over-concern with chronological continuity is bound to be a hazard when chasing a specific theme all the way through Foucault's writings. The effort to find consistency can fall prey so easily to a synthesizing that ignores him as an intellectual on a long quest in a busy academic and political environment.

At any rate, there is an adventure and novelty in Foucault that impresses, and most critics are forced to speak at least in some sense of 'early', 'middle', later' and even 'final' Foucault, though the complication can plainly stick in some throats. On this approach, the Foucault slalom-run proves very contorted indeed, sometimes distinctly off-piste in its twists and runs, travelling far and wide in a

---

99 Dreyfus and Rabinow, p. 104.

100 As Paras interprets this view typically from Ferry and Renaut in Eric Paras, *Foucualt 2.0: Beyond Power and Knowledge* (New York, 2006), 157. For the sake of focus we have left aside here Foucault's 1960s environment of structuralism with its earlier dispatching of the transcendental subject, but see Claire O'Farrell's lucid introduction to Foucault's phase in structuralism: O'Farrell, pp. 26–9.

101 O'Farrell, pp. 64–5.

102 Dreyfus and Rabinow, p. xxii.

103 Caroline Ramazanoğlu, 'Introduction', in Caroline Ramazanoğlu (ed.), *Up against Foucault: Explorations of Some Tensions Between Foucault and Feminism* (London, 1993), 1–27, p. 8.

series of diametrically opposite turns. Paras warns that nothing could be more unreasonable than flattening down Foucault's thought into a single, uninterrupted, coherent programme. He argues instead that it is a succession of near-independent questionings that, for the moment, had captured the philosopher's imagination.[104]

Paras's version is carefully considered and has the advantage of paying attention to the varied influences upon Foucault. It cannot be ignored. More particularly he claims to find in Foucault a social intellectual, responsive to the changing circles in which he moved.[105] He detects a shifting scene of world politics and the series of social and political concerns that drove Foucault in his activism. Hence crises affected Foucault more than abstract, detached and subtle refinements on subjectivity. So in opposition to the hidden mechanisms of surveillance and control, his early work railed against what he called the myth of human progress. He attacked complacent and over-optimistic liberal humanism and Marxism. Intellectuals had sleepwalked right into the illusion of rapidly improving species and society. Faith in the myth of human progress sedated them to an insidious shaping of ideas and selves that went on in 'liberal' and so-called 'emancipated' Western democracies. As Foucault saw it, talk of human rights failed to make any dent on this creeping, nameless power.

According to Wolin, Foucault's early work was 'a manifesto of anti-humanism' which rejoiced over the 'death of man' (man being overrated) and he saw the world as better off because of it.[106] No, the needed revelation was more radical. It exposed and interrogated the subtle tactics and techniques of power rather than buying into them. On this score, liberalism and Marxism fell short. Meantime, the pressing action demanded by the 1968 student movement only temporarily eased Foucault's impatience with Marx, for he was drawing the worst conclusions from Marxism's human rights record in Eastern Europe, China and South East Asia. He had now departed from Marxism. But he remained a passionate supporter of human rights in a manner commendable but difficult to square with some of his critical conclusions.

Paras highlights the difficulty of splicing the Foucault narrative cleanly at any given place. All the same, there appear to be key notions from each stage that are retained or recycled, and the evidence of Foucault's final writings certainly betrayed no regret or retraction. This brief summary of Foucault brings a number of reminders to the foreground.

Foucault's wrestling with the power in society remind us that theories of power should not be detached from experienced dynamics of social behaviour. Power is not a subject to be reduced solely to abstract and detached dissection. In addition it is probably safest to hear Foucault's programme as always telling a tale of continuity mingled with change. Recognition of novelty still seems to leave intact his earlier insights into power. And many departures are really only expansions on

---

104 Paras, p. 152.

105 Paras, p. 152: Foucault was receptive, 'permeable'.

106 Wolin, p. 2.

an original theme. Finally, Foucault's statements, by his own wish, must be read in context and not too much weight of eternal truth hung upon them. In line with his dislike of systems, he wished his work to be a tool rather than a doctrine.[107] This get-out will be all important when we tackle individual themes of his thought and try to re-contextualize them in the world of Christian community. But what does it all mean for power in the community of church and its 'life together'?

The Foucault Story and Church Community

So what has Foucault's developing thought on power to do with *koinonia* in the presence of power? There is much more to come, but already it is emerging that any engagement with local church's relation to power would be helped by paying attention to modern developments. More recent ones in the narrative of debates dispel any easy and exclusive definitions based crudely on 'power over'. Hence, for clear insight into what goes on in churches, we need first to recognize a complexity in the uses of the word 'power'. In addition, Foucault himself was drawn from a focus on 'power over' into a grappling with 'power to', and even he could not make a clean transition. Leadership of church has to be acutely sensitive to these distinct but overlapping domains. They might help to disentangle interests when power strategies break out in a community. The worthy motive of 'power to' easily drifts into the more dubious method of 'power over'. Moreover, an analysis of church in the presence of power is not a flight into the realm of useless theory. It is a pressing and challenging topic confronting church's claim to be sent on mission. The streams of 'power over', 'power to' and 'power with' will dominate every project.

Finally, introducing church to Foucault with an eye on power likely involves some serious contextualizing activity. It is best here to remember that church, like any faith community, has a distinctive life which will inform responses to discoveries about power. The containment and easing of power safely for a church community is only going to happen through applying distinctive Christian lubricants to the machinery of power for particular Christian ends. Much theology will be needed to address the workings of power inside a church community from within a radical Christian framework. Foucault's passion for freedom with honesty hands on to leaders in a local church a compelling standard for all their applications to a life together of the Christian family. For this reason theological resources will increasingly press to the fore as this narrative and analysis now moves on.

107 For example see O'Farrell, pp. 109, 120.

Chapter 4
Church and the Environment of Power

In our account of political thought, the ongoing debate showed most writers to be preoccupied with 'power over' which they exercised at the expense of someone else's power. However, a helpful distinction was emerging between 'power over' and 'power to', as well as the entanglement of these two. The temptation now is to leap straight from this historical background to tackling power dynamics in social groups and the applications of this for *koinonia*. But unfortunately other hurdles need to be cleared first. For although Foucault eventually began to concentrate on micro-groups with their face to face relations at grassroots, yet he did not renounce his earlier belief in 'subjectivization' going on in wider society. Even with regard to small social groups it was significant that large-scale power continued to influence the population through 'knowledge' and norms. Systems of thought, culture and government continued to manufacture individuals ('making up people' as Ian Hacking termed it[1]) throughout society. It is necessary therefore to persist with the subject for a little while yet, though we are beginning now to need some specially minted terms such as 'endemic power', 'pervasive power', 'encompassing power', 'web of power' and 'circulatory power' to try and capture Foucault's way of thinking. This selection enables us to avoid using only a purely spatial metaphor like 'top-down'. Though 'top-down' is appropriate, it cannot quite convey the versatility of Foucault's approach. Armed with this wider vocabulary we explore power's grip further and what we unearth will be closely related to power patterns in groups like church.

Disciplinary Power as a Key Term

Foucault introduced his unusual use of the word 'discipline' (and 'disciplinary') in 1972.[2] It signalled work in progress between his writings on knowledge and power, and the fuller, more famous, account in *Discipline and Punish*.[3] 'Discipline' in this

---

1 The title of Ian Hacking's 1986 essay, cited by Steven Lukes, 'Power and the Battle for Minds and Hearts', *Millennium: Journal of International Studies*, 33/3 (2005): 477–93, p. 491.

2 Michel Foucault, 'Power, Right, Truth', in Robert E. Goodin and Philip Pettit (eds), *Contemporary Political Philosophy: An Anthology* (Oxford, 1997), pp. 545–50.

3 Michel Foucault, *Discipline and Punish: The Birth of the Prison*, 1977 (ET), Originally published in 1975 in France under the title *Surveiller et punir: Naissance de la prison*.

new power theory did not carry the usual freight of the word. So it did not denote a severe regime, or form of punishment, or an institution. Rather it pointed to a technique,[4] a creative and productive process with a superficially benign function – that of producing a well-behaved and prosperous society by shaping universal norms and values for individual persons. It did so, he maintained, with a high hope of success.[5] The governing code that it carried was not that of oppressive monarchy and juridical rule, nor that of law but of 'normalization'.[6] That is, this power generated 'norms' by which people came consciously or subconsciously to feel assessed for their normality rating in society. And it was not too strong to call these norms 'coercive forces'.[7]

Discipline and Punish showed Foucault at his most provocative and challenging. Perhaps more than any other work it won him infamy in some eyes. Power is pervasive and unavoidable, forming our consciousness and even affecting our thoughts of resistance so that we cannot escape its omnipresence. It is this work that created the suspicion that he had now given up on the possibility of a busy and docile population offering genuine 'resistance'. The historical research it presented ended at nineteenth century history. But Foucault, intentionally or otherwise, convinced many readers it was really about the present modern era by identifying a dream of total order for society, and highlighting control in institutions still with us, especially schools, factories and the military.[8] Taking this assumption as not exactly denied by Foucault, we can therefore see in recent democratic times a population of modern societies still seemingly docile and passive.

So despite the apparent arrival of our choice-laden, modern autonomous individual, the real picture was that of a social order guided silently by a culture of authoritative knowledge. And this knowledge was itself shaped by subterranean power interests, often fairly summarized as the *status quo*. It was not just prisoners and mental patients who had their 'normality' assessed and rated. Nor was power something that only occasionally reared its head on memorable and unpleasant occasions. To believe so is to collude in the deception and lose sight of the hidden continuous permeation of power through all social life, a power expressed in public

---

4 Hubert L. Dreyfus and Paul Rabinow, *Michel Foucault: Beyond Structuralism and Hermeneutics* (Brighton, 1982), p. 153.

5 See Claire O'Farrell, *Michel Foucault* (London, 2005), p. 133, for a useful range of approaches to the subject in Foucault beyond simply *Discipline and Punishment* and also for the ways in which the idea metamorphosed.

6 Foucault, 'Power, Right, Truth', p. 549.

7 Foucault, 'Power, Right, Truth', p. 550.

8 Stewart R. Clegg, *Frameworks of Power* (London, 1990), p. 16, laments the lack of a modern sociological training in Foucault and many of his followers, yet acknowledges that Foucault links well into Talcott Parsons's approach and the existing 'labour process' debate in English-speaking sociology.

'knowledge'.[9] This process encircled society as a whole. The tone was set by the appearance in *Discipline and Punishment* of Jeremy Bentham's famed Panopticon (a circular prison building with cells grouped around a central tower) mentioned earlier. The Panopticon made its appearance as more than just an extreme example or illustration. It also became a cherished metaphor for a modern system of total subtle surveillance to replace crude 'sovereign' government (which, we recall, belonged to brutalizing, totalizing monarchies and military regimes of previous ages). Pasewark reminds us that up to this point Foucault himself had thought of power almost entirely as repressive and reactive. But now it was much else besides and had metamorphosed into a new strategy.[10]

Bentham's design of a prison where the surveillance came from the centre and reached to every corner described in metaphor the workings of an entire 'disciplinary' society. In fact it was more. It was a dream about the efficient society resulting from a comprehensive 'productive' power in the modern world. It advocated a 'gaze' that penetrated in every direction and caught everyone in its sights, not just the obviously dysfunctional. Such a gaze, of course, was not altogether born at the coming of democracy, despite Foucault's narrative. For already in small micro-communities, especially rural ones, 'surveillance' was always a formidable fact of life.[11] Allegedly the dream of this nineteenth-century government was that through systems of examination, individuals were categorized as normal or not normal and shaped by the scrutiny accordingly. By establishing norms for the well adjusted and properly functioning society and all its members, a process of shaping individuals came into being.[12] Norms etched the lines between 'normal' and 'abnormal' into both consciousness and bodily behaviour.[13] Self-surveillance naturally helped things along.

Pasewark helpfully summarized *Discipline and Power* as highlighting the omnipresence of power rather than its merely occasional and repressive irruptions. As a result we have a shift from the question of 'who represses whom' to one of mechanism, of 'how' power works, and a new profile of the depth to power's presence.[14] Normalizing power was in a dubious sense 'productive', transforming

9 Michel Foucault, 'Two Lectures', in Colin Gordon (ed.), *Power/Knowledge: Selected Interviews and other Writings, 1972–1977: Michel Foucault* (Brighton, 1980), 78–108, p. 102.

10 K. A. Pasewark, *A Theology of Power: Being Beyond Domination* (Minneapolis, 1993), p. 16.

11 See O'Farrell, pp. 42–3.

12 See as typical O'Farrell, pp. 104–5. See also, 'Afterword', in Colin Gordon (ed.), *Power/Knowledge: Selected Interviews and Other Writings 1972–1977: Michel Foucault* (Brighton, 1980), 229–59, pp. 252–5, where he seems to attribute to Foucault the belief that technologies of individuals take on a life of their own and becomes the real source of the disciplinary process.

13 Lukes, 'Power and the Battle for Hearts and Minds', p. 491.

14 Pasewark, p. 18.

people, not just prohibiting them.[15] And all in the name of cohesiveness and society's health.

Much feminism welcomed this theory of pervasive, multi-faceted nature of power shaping human identity.[16] Many feminist writers had already held patriarchal culture subtly to determine the nature of female roles in society and the freedoms or otherwise of the female body. They tended to welcome Foucault's confirmation of this insight. For feminism, differences between male and female were not benignly neutral but from early times formed the basis for injustices and oppressions. In addition muscular and other physical powers provided the natural male criterion by which to judge the relative worth of women against men. Moreover, there was a tendency to judge women entirely under their attributes of physical attractiveness.[17] Foucault's view was felt at first to be supportive of these critical insights. For it supplied details to the case, holding that 'discipline' and 'bio-power' boldly determined how humanity in the modern state might flourish. And it did this most specifically in the local domain of sexual and family values. More specifically, that meant disciplinary power's creation of norms for family (hence 'sexual' norms and body-identities) in the fledgling industrial era. Even amid the first feminist doubts about whether Foucault was a mixed blessing they still found in him a soul-brother in this territory of norms, bodies and identities.[18]

Nevertheless, difficulties have dogged the Foucauldian and feminist notion which ascribed individual traits, especially gender markers, to all-encompassing, norm-making disciplinary power. And yet despite the problems that it raised, the theme persisted.[19] Equally, feminists concerned to inspire resistance to power might take comfort from one of Foucault's concessions. He admitted that disciplinary power's circulatory, normalizing influences did not quite completely 'saturate' the whole of society. Normalizing power, Foucault conceded, was patchy and more

[15] Foucault (Interview), 'On Power', in Lawrence D. Kritzman (ed.), *Michel Foucault: Politics, Philosophy, Culture: Interviews and Other Writings* (New York, 1988), 96–109, pp. 104–5.

[16] See, for example, Susan Hekman, 'Feminist Identity Politics: Transforming the Political' in Dianna Taylor and Karen Vintges (eds), *Feminism and the Final Foucault* (Urbana, 2004), 196–213, pp. 203–4; Aurelia Armstrong, 'Foucault and Feminism', Internet Encyclopaedia of Philosophy http://www.iep.utm.edu/f/foucfem [accessed 10.01.07], p. 1.

[17] As typical of many comments: Aurelia, 'Foucault and Feminism', p. 1.

[18] See Susan Bordo, 'Feminism, Foucault and the Politics of the Body', in Caroline Ramazanoğlu (ed.), *Up against Foucault: Explorations of Some Tensions Between Foucault and Feminism* (London, 1993), pp. 179–202. See alternative feminist perspective in M. E. Bailey 'Foucauldian Feminism: Contesting Bodies, Sexuality and Identity', in Ramazanoğlu (ed.), *Up against Foucault*. The most sustained programme to discuss this within feminism, however, is the very substantial writing of Judith Butler (see below). Also see the key player, Sawacki, from 1998, cited in Aurelia, 'Foucault and Feminism', p. 1.

[19] See especially Judith Butler, 'Bodies and Power Revisited', in Dianna Taylor and Karen Vintges (eds), *Feminism and the Final Foucault* (Urbana, 2004), pp. 183–96.

constraining in some situations than in others.[20] What's more the 'self' co-operated quite freely (unconstrained) when internalizing the 'norms'.[21] These alleged concessions would certainly be necessary to save Foucault from reckless denial of all resistance to normalizing power.

What of discipline's 'gaze' then, of its surveillance and internalizing of norms right now in the twenty-first century? Ironically, since Foucault's death technological revolutions have completely vindicated his perception that we are becoming a world of surveillance, under a relentless 'gaze'. Privacy and freedom are emerging as major concerns. The coming of electronic records, CCTV surveillance, computer hacking, over-informative blogs, prolific message boards, profiles on free websites and ID theft all vindicate Foucault's cry to those who tread uncritically through the forest of disciplinary power's surveillance and subtle pressure to conform. The point for us, however, is that we also meet within this big picture an even more arresting fact, that surveillance has a history in micro-groups such as faith-communities. In other words it has a special potency at the local level in micro-groups. Power relations within small groups like this, including church, thus live under the double jeopardy of all-encompassing influences from above upon its members and the possibility of micro-group observation from within. This could stir up serious cross winds of power in a community's common life together, influences all the more dangerous for not often being recognized.

Disciplinary Power and Local Groups

We have seen then, that Foucault continued to develop the notion of disciplinary power, a wider circulatory type of power which spread out, infiltrating society and affecting smaller groups. In due course we shall examine how he moved on to concentrating upon power and behaviour out 'on the periphery' among such local groups. Foucault's conviction was that no micro-group existed in its own safe, protected environment. All who belonged to such human associations were in interaction with assumptions and norms served up to them by wider influences.

So it seems worthwhile to take account of Foucault's more mature attempt to relate grand, circulatory power to localized knots of power in institutions or smaller social groups. One way to get into Foucault's later ideas on power relations in groups is to take a brief digression into two key terms appearing earlier (namely 'archaeology' and 'genealogy') which relates so closely to disciplinary power. This pause will also offer new insights into power patterns in groups and therefore for 'life together' in a church community.

---

20 Dianna Taylor, 'Foucault's Ethos', in Dianna Taylor and Karen Vintges (eds), *Feminism and the Final Foucault* (Urbana, 2004), 258–74, pp. 264–5.

21 Taylor, 'Foucault's Ethos', p. 264. We leave aside the problem this notion presents for Foucault's denial of the existence of a free prior subject.

Key Slogan 1: 'The Archaeology of Knowledge'

Foucault came to employ the word 'archaeology' to sum up the practice of delving into the past with a view to power-spotting (though not yet of course having discovered local 'power relations'). This typical, novel hijacking of a common term like archaeology aimed to use the past purely as a background to present-day forms of domination. Such historical intellectual digs, unearthed 'subjugated knowledge' which had been deliberately controlled and covered up in the past and present. But it was not an arid, historical exercise. He wished to fuel his strident analyses of how power works right here and now.[22]

With the term 'archaeology' he attacked the Enlightenment's simple trust in knowledge as scientific, objective, neutral and transcendent above the squalid world of power. He upbraided philosophers for so driving apart 'truth' (or 'knowledge') and 'power'.[23] For him, this rather convenient artificial division invented by modern liberalism hailed truth as the defender of freedom and of higher realities. Truth then sat in judgement on that rogue called power. But Foucault claimed to have unmasked this simple picture, exposing it as an elaborate and compelling illusion. In reality, at worst, 'truth' itself also lay under the shadow of power and at best the two were symbiotic partners. For truth was a product of power. Power determined what would be accepted as public truth. This fact now made power even more dangerous, precisely because it was wearing truth like a disguise. Blatant, oppressive power had been easy to spot and straightforward to deal with. But truth's alleged secret pact with power allowed power-drenched knowledge to reign above suspicion, its covert power covered by a 'royal dress'.[24]

Gone now was the reverent cherishing of pure and eternal truth unsullied by power and useful as a trusty blade against power. And banished also were all those theories of steady human advancement in pursuit of truth, whether liberal, Hegelian or Marxist-revolutionary. That myth no longer deserved house space. So while science for instance might indeed contain repeatable and applicable theorems it still took its momentum, purpose, discourse and application from the very power swimming around in society's political and social setting. These social conditions were, even in modern times, the womb of power![25] There was an ideological goal to all science in any particular phase of history and the scientific knowledge was rooted in these social conditions with their possibilities, though the human sciences were the main butt of his attack.[26] Foucault's way of doing history has long since suffered criticism and many no doubt would argue that it is discredited. We would be digressing to discuss his reputation here let alone to grapple with his earlier talk

22 O'Farrell, p. 68.

23 Michel Foucault (Interview) 'On Power', p. 106.

24 Pasewark, p. 9.

25 Gordon, 'Afterword', p. 243. He goes further and insists they actually form conditions of existence.

26 O'Farrell, pp. 96–7.

of the 'episteme' (his word for a set of relations that tie together scientific subjects differently for each major historical epoch).[27]

The main point, which is still influential, was his growing disenchantment with theories of the ascent of the human species. He attacked the famous 'myth of human progress' whether liberal, evolutionary or Marxist-dialectical. Granted, he had not abandoned the revolutionary and activist urge. Nor was he really trying to make his name as an anti-Marxist historian. But he was seeking to dispel the vapours of a dream – a dream blind to power's repeated, underlying presence at every new feast. History, in fact, was the story not of the grand progress of our species but only of varied power reversals.[28] Rather, subjection, domination, and combat were to be found everywhere in every era, today not so much in individuals or ideologies, but more in embedded 'rituals of power'.[29] So the myth of human advance lay under yet more questioning.[30] This myth naïvely treated history as an unsupervised social shaping of people through prevailing 'truths' in various epochs of power.

Key Slogan 2: 'Genealogy': The Genealogy of History

In 1971 the word 'geneaology' had appeared in Foucauldian thought to strengthen yet further the attack on a grand narrative of the human march toward the heights of history.[31] The Foucault campaign continued to unmask 'hymns' to human progress[32] and the work of genealogy searched out the many dead ends in history where power reigned. Genealogy's special insight beyond that of archaeology has been variously fought over. Maybe for Foucault, genealogy contained a more explicit description of power, or proved a sharper tool for criticism. In this way it

[27] Foucault, cited in Dreyfus and Rabinow, *Michel Foucault: Beyond Structuralism and Hermeneutics*, p. 18. See Dreyfus and Rabinow also on 'archaeology' in pp. 98–103. In addition, see J. Bernauer, *Michel Foucault's Force of Flight: Toward an Ethics for Thought* (London, 1990), p. 145. Compare O'Farrell, pp. 64–73.

[28] Foucault, in 'Nietzsche, Genealogy and History' cited by Dreyfus and Rabinow, p. 110.

[29] Foucault in 'Nietzsche, Genealogy and History', cited by Dreyfus and Rabinow, p. 110.

[30] O'Farrell, *Foucault*, p. 68. See also Bernauer, p. 143: the works that followed *Archaeology of Knowledge* were continuous but offered new rules complementary to the earlier ones only because two things had changed: the field under analysis and a new level of labour.

[31] Foucault, in the essay, 'Nietzsche, Genealogy and History' quoted by Dreyfus and Rabinow, p. 106. The germ of Foucault's work in the 1970s first crops up in this consideration of Nietzsche, it is claimed in Dreyfus and Rabinow, p. 106. On the other hand we should read it with caution since it contains a number of ideas that Foucault will go back on very quickly. O'Farrell, *Foucault*, p. 68.

[32] Dreyfus and Rabinow . p. 106.

would have brought clearer insight into how power might determine what is 'true' and 'false'.[33] But at the very least genealogy also claimed to show how science and knowledge in our own era strengthened power's influence 'over' a human population.[34] Power drew strength even from its own production of 'knowledge'. But how did educated people like us become deceived by this growing influence? The answer is that people came to embrace such partly manufactured knowledge as truth gradually. First the knowledge appeared useful, then it became entrenched and revered, and finally it circulated as a proven wisdom throughout society.[35] Wider culture embedded new knowledge in many social practices which then in turn governed human thought. The practice of genealogy intended to expose all current, prevailing knowledge as no more than a construct from these processes, though not necessarily deceptive right down to the last detail.[36]

Foucault may have proven too much at this stage. For it now became impossible to rely on any truth, including his own. And now cannot the much treasured 'truth' of dissidents and human rights also be thrown into doubt because it is compromised by power drives?[37] We shall meet this lack of attention to normative 'truth' again shortly.

Implications from Archaeology and Genealogy for Christian Community in 'Truth'

Even with the maturity of later reflection, Foucault himself still stood by allegedly important results from his work of genealogy. He did not abandon his suspicious stance towards a disciplinary, circulatory, all-encompassing power.[38] His labours had highlighted the existence of marginalized voices outside the domain of intellectuals and lent support to these voices. He praised such recently

[33] O'Farrell, *Foucault*, pp. 68–9. Or perhaps we should think of its tracing of the laws of domination, so Dreyfus and Rabinow, p. 110. See also James K. A. Smith, *Who's Afraid of Postmodernism? Taking Derrida, Lyotard and Foucault to Church* (Grand Rapids, 2006), pp. 86–7.

[34] Dreyfus and Rabinow, p. 110. See also Bernauer, p. 144: in the idea of genealogy Foucault was still correlating the 'true' and the 'false' in relation to historical analysis and political critique.

[35] Jon Simons, *Foucault and the Political* (London, 1995), p. 43.

[36] Wendy Brown, 'Genealogical Politics' in Jeremy Moss (ed.), *The Later Foucault: Politics and Philosophy*, p. 43.

[37] Lawrence D. Kritzman, 'Introduction. Foucault and the Politics of Experience', in Lawrence D. Kritzman (ed.), *Michel Foucault: Politics, Philosophy, Culture: Interviews and Other Writings* (New York, 1988), i–xxv, pp. xxi–ii. Hence Kritzman calls France to embrace final Foucault's call to self-government by resisting the sovereignty of any one system of thought: Kritzman, p. xxv.

[38] S. W. Sykes, *Power and Christian Theology* (London, 2006), p. 102.

recognized forms of knowledge. For 'subjugated' forms of knowledge represented a welcome insurrection and 'transgression' against intellectualist, conventional knowledge, a knowledge created by power. In a return to his early concerns for human freedoms Foucault became an advocate for custodians of these 'subjected' types of knowledge. Critical studies should especially have been standing up for knowledge that was low-ranking, unqualified, and even disqualified. His point of view partly sprang from his campaign on behalf of psychiatric patients (and is an approach wonderfully illustrated in the celebrated novel and film, *One Flew Over the Cuckoo's Nest*[39]). It was through recovering these scattered fragments of disruptive knowledge, he argued, that criticism really did its work.[40] So these trampled-down gems of knowledge, buried for long enough, carried memories – memories of struggles which society's bank of privileged knowledge should now recognize. If honoured and added to the expertise of intellectuals, such truths could still be of use to us today.[41] In fact, Foucault often took pleasure later in holding that these excluded forms of knowledge were indispensable to real 'truth'. He had not deserted the merits of genealogy even when well into his later projects on power. And once he had released the demon critic from the bottle, it would be not easily stuffed back in again.

Whether one adopts the full Foucault here or not, even a fragmentary acknowledgement of his ideas must disturb any complacency in Christian community today. This is the first, unsettling discovery of power theory from Foucault for church when considering the dynamics of power in its community life together. What if such subjecting of valid knowledge goes on in the comfortable corners of church? What if local leaders from articulate and intelligent professional classes have managed to so focus on leadership as a rational practice that they have, albeit unwittingly, silenced other voices? These voices could be entrusted with memories of pains and struggles without which no church as community should surely dare move forward. In that case, it does not matter if Foucault is a poor historian or if he exaggerated the play of power upon public knowledge. At the heart of Foucault's highly contestable work there was a nugget of truth (if perhaps he would have indulged us the naïve use of this word 'truth' for once). And it is truth crucial for life and action together in church – even for church's very being (that is, of its *esse* [being] not just its *bene esse* [wellbeing]). The super powerful apostles in the Jerusalem church of Acts 15, humbly shared decision-making with the ordinary members of church, the poor, despised and downtrodden (Acts 15.22).

So what about broader webs of knowledge and power impacting a church here and now? We have to face the sociological reality that power and privilege can

---

39 The acclaimed 1975 film directed by Miloš Forman, and adapted from the 1962 novel, *One Flew Over the Cuckoo's Nest* by Ken Kesey.

40 Michel Foucault, 'Two Lectures', p. 82.

41 Foucault, 'Two Lectures', pp. 80–81, given, we recall again, in 1976 well after Foucault offered his account of genealogy in 1971.

drive the circulation of systems of knowledge. Hence relatively affluent, Western partakers of life together in the way of Jesus might be very easily blinded by their culture to the poverty and burdens of the majority world. They imagine they are themselves poor. This is a conditioning by circulatory 'knowledge', by a culture of wealth that encompasses and shapes people, in the case of church working against their true calling in the world. Such all-encompassing, disciplinary power could not simply bypass people in churches, precisely in their life together as community. And it is not just widespread, secular cultural norms with which a faith community has to reckon with either. For there are also powerful, internal sub-cultures, often imported from 'success' merchants elsewhere. We think here for example of legalistic forms of spirituality, fashionable techniques for church growth, shallow or intellectualist theologies, know-all superior theology and other bids for empires. It is hardly high philosophy to suspect that these influences will inflame diverse, even conflicting, standpoints in local church community and contribute to cross currents and power patterns there. Foucault's contribution has simply been to concentrate minds rather powerfully on the matter.

Knowledge and Power: Siblings, Singles or Ciphers?

Towards the end of his life, Foucault indulged himself in an ironic slip. He hinted strongly that he could after all slide a piece of paper between knowledge and power. He commented that at the end of the day he did indeed recognize truth as a distinct value that was not totally compromised by powers driving it. Truth was after all the only way of deciphering the world (though political power may all the same yet 'destroy us').[42] Power and truth might even pull still further away from each other and go their separate ways. It was a grudging concession. However, he at least seemed to plead, in an interview close to his death in 1984, that his earlier phase of interest in knowledge and power only meant to show that quite different forms of 'knowledge' can arise from otherwise comparable power sources. This urge to clarify things at least probably means that he did not actually intend to merge power and knowledge into one thing, as some alleged. Nor did he plug knowledge into power as in a scientifically determined, inevitable process of cause or effect.[43]

---

[42] Michel Foucault (Interview), 'The Minimalist Self', in Lawrence D. Kritzman (ed.), *Michel Foucault: Politics, Philosophy, Culture: Interviews and Other Writings* (New York, 1988), 3–16, p. 14.

[43] Michel Foucault (Interview) 'The Concern for Truth', in Lawrence D. Kritzman (ed.), *Michel Foucault: Politics, Philosophy, Culture: Interviews and Other Writings* (New York, 1988), pp. 264–65. The interview was with Francois Ewald, first appearing in May 1984 in Magazine Littéraire, so close to Foucault's death.

Hence for Foucault knowledge and power were not synonyms, or even two sides of the same entity.[44] They were different enough to evoke and form one another. This symbiotic relationship, each producing the other, is alleged to be one of Foucault's keys for understanding power and knowledge.[45] He simply saw alleged truth as looped in with systems of power. One fed into the other. In one late interview Foucault conceded that he was in the end a kind of sceptic about the matter of knowledge, but used philosophy to sound a caution and set some boundaries to received public knowledge.[46] We leave aside the great man's unwarranted privileging here of philosophy which also, one should note, claims to be 'knowledge' or 'truth' of a kind and seems to be the one form miraculously protected from determination by power! We simply turn to a rephrasing more useful for practical purposes. It is plain that he intended mainly one thing by his probing of truth and power. That was to ask what the 'truth' means for today's world, how it was frequently adjusted by power and whether as a result resistance might be possible.[47]

So Foucault left a warning that has a recurrent value for all discussion of truth. He also urged his audience always to live within sight of three forces by which one became an individual. These are: first, concepts, then practices or rules, and finally one's relationship to oneself.[48] This is a set of themes that unfolds further at a later stage but does not here display a level of disenchantment with truth that some have come to expect. Hence Foucault himself finally cast doubt over his originally uncompromising statements about unavoidably power-shaped knowledge (culture and policy-shaping public norms) and knowledge-shaped forming (of people by the norms). Perhaps it is best to see this supremacy of power over human souls and bodies as mixed in its potency and its impact. He may have, unknowingly, already left space for an individual's resistance and freedom which he failed to exploit.

Softened claims in later life

'Truth', Church and Power in Society

One could be forgiven for now wondering what all this could possibly have to do with a Christian community seeking to work together in a common life of worship, for service to others and in being a voice for the oppressed. Surprisingly, much of this is relevant. For one thing, the new angle on 'truth' could confront some

44 Dreyfus and Rabinow, p. 203.

45 Dreyfus and Rabinow, p. 204.

46 Michel Foucault (Interview) 'The Return of Morality', in Lawrence D. Kritzman (ed.), *Michel Foucault: Politics, Philosophy, Culture: Interviews and Other Writings* (New York, 1988), 242–54, p. 242.

47 Deleuzes cited by Kritzman, 'Introduction', p. xxiv.

48 Michel Foucault, 'The Battle for Chastity', in Lawrence D. Kritzman (ed.), *Michel Foucault: Politics, Philosophy, Culture: Interviews and Other Writings* (New York, 1988), 224–41, pp. 21, 253–4.

embedded patterns of thinking not always challenged in churches. The formation of dubious 'truths' might well infect power behaviours of a micro-culture like church. For instance any local church community in our culture is likely to be unconsciously a mix of levels and advantages. These may stem from class, gender, professional status, health or ethnic conditions. And any bias arising from these may be as deeply concealed to its participants as the power that Foucault sees quietly at work in public customs and norms. This makes it even more urgent that a church seeking power relations filled with integrity must pay attention to 'the telling of the truth' in every recess and the impact of that upon the shaping of human persons and power relationships.[49] If sound, this comment raises several unsettling considerations.

In the first place, suspicion has fallen on the notion of 'pure truth' unsullied at all by struggles for power whether on the large scale or in a local group such as church. This is not the place to change topic and launch into dissection of faith-truths, confessions of beliefs that bind Christians together. This is not about questions of doctrinal authority and of basic beliefs about the words, life and continuing presence of Jesus in church life. Rather it is about perception of the situations that spark power strategies in churches. In these, the expectation for an eventual pure, complete, unanimous consensus in 'truth' for every situation in every moment has been one of the major jagged edges of life together in a local church community. 'Conviction politics' is exquisitely focused in the micro-political setting of church. A solemn truth can always be manufactured to justify a leadership initiative, a new rule, the sacredness of the *status quo* or the value of endless activism. The term 'time honoured ways' springs to mind as a way of conjuring an aura of 'truth' around wilful inertia. Hence the sacredness of a basic church value sometimes transmutes into the sacredness also of particular strategies chosen to support or express it: 'We believe in God's mission of love and just as certainly believe in this policy as the only true way for this local church to express it.' Here a strategy has the same status as a non-negotiable value. The sacred values themselves are often key ones like worship, mission, spirituality or community … but the strategies are often suspect ones like privileging, secrecy and distracting verbiage.

Secondly, even Foucault himself eventually acknowledged that his own starting point and assumptions in *Archaeology of Knowledge* could hardly be free of prior influences. If even he can be open to this admission then so can church communities and particularly leaders or those with influence. Within the situation of competing local 'truths' (viewpoints) in a community like church, it is all too easy to raise one's own point of view to the level of a politics-free 'moral' or 'doctrinal' truth. In face to face conflict, one person's (or group's) claim to be holding a viewpoint of 'pure' truth should meet intense scrutiny. Any claim

[49] As Michel Foucault claimed, this was always his focus in contrast to Deleuze. Foucault (Interview), 'Critical Theory/Intellectual History' in Lawrence D. Kritzman (ed.), *Michel Foucault: Politics, Philosophy, Culture: Interviews and Other Writings* (New York, 1988), 17–46, p. 33.

from a leadership (especially such ones as 'we have been led by the Spirit' or 'it comes from the leaders' authority') if not opened up to discussion, could ignore the interpreted nature of all strategies offered to a community. The vantage points influencing these strategies are in some measure a fruit of knowledge produced by various power sources. Of course, only excessive scepticism insists that one viewpoint is always as suspect, vulnerable and fragile as another. But it is also naïve to assume that one's own is always pure, unbiased truth and that it is unique in this regard. Of this stuff, church splits, or at least church tensions, are made.

Thirdly, what is really required is to treat any conviction about church action, worship or life not as 'pure truth', but as participating in truth, though perhaps to a high degree. It is always the product in part of reflection and personal values. It most likely draws on values widely shared in the community – but also expresses a personal 'truth' shaved and shaped in some measure by a distinct background in the speaker. We may be looking at such social elements as class, family, education, experience (bad and good) and religious ethos. And in addition these will all have emerged battle-scarred from the various wars of dominations that have disfigured so many human lives. We can almost say that a conviction cherished and expressed now, is itself a pock-marked survivor of past conflicts. The position taken, whatever else it is, cannot lay claim to be simply 'pure' truth drawn from the untainted well of ideal Truth. This, as it happens, does not invalidate and relativize all views on contentious situations. After all, Foucault did not deny the working efficiency of the suspect human sciences even when he portrayed them as the fall-out from social and political big bangs. What his insight does achieve is to lower the stakes. He puts heated and overconfident (or overstated) convictions into proportion. Most of all his approach planes down élitist intellectualist claims to take possession of all 'truth'. This especially speaks to those who claim to be academic theologians.

Lastly, there is a further more pointed lesson. Community systems frequently, though often unintentionally, blank out the minority voice: the inadequate, the eccentric, the loser hanging on for dear life, the confused, the doubting, the voice from the fringe, the one paralysed with pain. Foucault has a profound lesson to teach church about the special contribution that the cry of suffering makes in touching the bedrock of reality and speaking from the experience of the excluded, the subjugated knowledge. Confident power, professional self-assurance, competence and even clear thinking might all unwittingly tread down these forms of knowledge.

However, in Christian thought all is not as relative and untrustworthy as it seems. Love welcomes truth, Paul argued (1 Cor 13.5,6). None of the challenges raised above destroy the roots of the community walking together on the way of Jesus. The Jesus narrative itself offers an instance where Foucault's allegedly viral power over truth did not apply. Here in the life of Jesus power did not determine truth. Instead truth really did judge and undermine power. That is, in his own choices the truth about himself determined a relinquishing of power. In John's account Jesus says to Pilate, 'You could not have this power over me unless it was given you by God' (Jn 19.8–11). But of course we are talking of a special truth here, that of divine love. We are looking at the acclaimed self-giving of Jesus which was sourced in his relationship with Father and Spirit and then enacted on the human stage in self-emptying and self-humbling. In this one place, for Christians, power was not self-serving and did not manufacture a convenient truth or knowledge to serve its self-interest. Of course the Christian story here does not consequently privilege all the words of those also who happen to belong to the Jesus-way. Rather it leads a church community also to wrestle with that divine order: the truth of self-denying love which modifies all power relations among followers of the way.

Power and Being your True Self in Church Community

Tracing the relation of knowledge to power in Foucault has revealed a further theoretical principle that very much startled his first readers: his idea that power was not merely a constraint and prohibition, an intervention. As we shall see with the later notion of bio-power, it was also productive and even in its own way contributed to order, welfare and economic development. But then again, we meet unappealing words like disciplinary, totalizing, normalizing and subjectivizing. Despite their 'global', or encompassing range the intended essence of these words still raises challenges too for micro-societies such as the church community, the *koinonia*. And some of the unsettling issues they raise will carry weight here in local groups as well as on the larger scale. The issues appear at first as very abstract and theoretical but then their implications and applications for church community life grow clearer and more profound as we think further about them. The terms in Foucault also easily merge into each other and into a general vague sense of all-encompassing power. It seems useful, then, to separate out two in particular and so clarify the ideas here.

Encompassing Terms (1) 'Subjectivization'

As many have pointed out there is a deliberate word play in Foucault's connecting of the 'subject', the self, with a subjecting of the self to a process. His word usually gets translated 'subjectivization' (more effective in its double meaning in the French *asujetissement*). This process formed people into subjects, centres of action and aspiration that they perceive as their own inner selves. To recall the phrase from earlier discussion, power was working away at 'making up people'. 'Subjectivization' described a profound cultural and political process that affected what people became. Here it was unlike the old sovereign power of prohibition or constraint.[50] Normalizing power actually formed people as 'subjects', individuals, selves. Even a person's perception of herself as a 'person', had actually been manufactured from outside of her by public 'knowledge'.[51] This chief, all-encompassing 'power' in society created and moulded people as subjects with an eye to the common good of society. The emergence of an individual was really down to this work of subjectivization.[52]

Hence, in Foucault's view people in modern society can be called 'subjects' in two distinct senses. First, is the sense that people are *subjected*, perhaps unconsciously, to the formative influence of public knowledge. Secondly, they then actually become *subjects*, with a resulting identity and self-awareness.[53] Of course, Foucault first criticized the process as it appeared in the clinical, psychological and psychiatric disciplines. And, despite defences offered, it is occasionally conceded that modern 'individualization' in psychology was indeed working in the very way Foucault described it. For instance psychology, it is admitted, really has sometimes been about managing human life for the greatest possible prosperity and fulfilment, just as Foucault suggested, though not in a coercive and repressive way.[54]

But a startling refinement further followed this theory – something that proves highly relevant to church community in more local or networked settings, and so also to *koinonia* life together and to its processes as community. To understand what was going on with subjectivization, the making up of people, one should not begin with this all-encompassing subjectivization at all. One should start instead from the many and varied local mechanisms of power, from small social networks, for power circulated everywhere. Only by beginning at the extremities of power could you then track inwards to disciplinary power. Then it was possible to see how together these local clusters of power connected up and interacted so as to strengthen the more all-encompassing, disciplinary power. The joined up clusters of power could thus assist the process of normalization, reinforcing from the ground up what also came at people from circulatory power. For the wider web of subjectivization through disciplinary power utilized the many local techniques, or 'technologies' of power.[55] And 'local' here denotes a wide range of sites and agencies such as family, voluntary groups, social movements and channels of

---

[50] Reasserting this as late as 1978! Michel Foucault (Interview), 'An Aesthetics of Existence' in Lawrence D. Kritzman (ed.), *Michel Foucault: Politics, Philosophy, Culture: Interviews and Other Writings* (New York, 1988), 47–56, p. 48.

[51] Foucault, cited and explained by Ian Hacking, 'The Archaeology of Foucault', in David Couzens Hoy (ed.), *Foucault: A Critical Reader* (Oxford, 1989), 27–40, p. 36.

[52] Foucault, 'Power, Right, Truth', p. 546.

[53] See the summary by Steven Lukes, 'Introduction', in Steven Lukes (ed.), *Power* (Oxford, 1986), 1–18, p. 11, for Foucault's late, persisting thought here.

[54] Nikolas Rose, *Inventing Ourselves: Psychology, Power and Personhood* (Cambridge, 1996), p. 114.

[55] Foucault, 'Power, Right, Truth' p. 550.

communication.[56] Of interest to us is that it therefore includes a local group like the church community.

In addition, the wider all-encompassing process of person-making, disciplinary power, was not a secret and inaccessible world. Rather its claims were always open to scrutiny in the human sciences and in forms of public 'knowledge'. Hence it made its impact on society precisely by appearing harmless and more benign than the controlling force of legal imposition or coercion. The normalizing process enabled apparently natural and obvious 'norms' to operate alongside the juridical world so they could be easily internalized by each individual.[57]

Admittedly the power of norms was sometimes buttressed by the continuing presence of sovereignty in the domain of law.[58] Yet subjectivization did not itself work through legal processes of oppression. But by the same token, neither could people look to legal processes to rescue them from this incessant intrusion of subjectivization. After all, the law had been one of the key constraining features of earlier 'sovereign' forms of political government.[59] So one would gain little help from sovereignty or legal 'rights' in seeking to awake from the dream and resist this process of person-making. Sovereignty and rights would not prove a spur to resistance and freedom.[60]

Responses to the New Thinking

Some feminists have taken with gusto to this invitation to track power beyond merely its life as sovereign, political and juridical. Judith Butler in particular carries through the theory of subjectivization. On the one hand the body's identity really emerges from formation by disciplinary power, yet on the other hand the same identity is also an acting perceiving self or 'subject'. We know this second fact because the self redirects and 'transvalues' power.[61] The difficulties such a paradox present do not seem to be completely resolved in the challenging, and brave, attempt that follow in Butler's own work, a discussion which is too detailed to digress into here. But perhaps we can take some insights away from her discussion for our own quest after the meaning of power with regard to Christian community.

First, difficulties seem to persist in the Foucauldian implication that human selfhood is entirely the result of prevailing norms 'making up people' (Hacking's turn of phrase, we recall, not Foucault's). For other realities might also be in play. After all, surely a human individual is more than a temporary, docile social or cultural construction. That is, surely person-making always implies a corresponding

[56] Jean Cohen and Andrew Arato, cited by Hekman, pp. 205–6.

[57] Foucault, 'Power, Right, Truth' p. 549.

[58] Foucault, 'Power, Right, Truth' p. 549.

[59] Foucault, 'Power, Right, Truth' p. 550.

[60] Foucault, 'Power, Right, Truth' p. 550.

[61] Judith Butler, pp. 186–7.

reality – that of a rational and active individual, able to host normalizing power, able to internalize it and so to be transformed by it. So the most flexible theory of self emerging from Foucault's rule could be that of a (maybe rudimentary) self, agent, or subject which forms the constant basis for the emerging 'subject' of social (re)construction. Social power, or subjectivization, in other words, can only adapt a continuous personhood perhaps developed from the most primitive personal past. It does not actually call that personhood or self into being.[62]

That possibility of an essence or self, probably prior however, perhaps sends up alarms for feminists. It revives the old spectre of a fixed human 'nature' ('essentialism') and natural gender roles, rather than preferences shaped by social, environmental nurture and external social differences. Essentialism might seem to legitimize all kinds of inequalities and injustices (especially gender ones) because they are 'essential' to each person, fixed in our identities by nature. For feminists these preferences do not spring from nature or DNA. They really arise from an unjust, conditioning environment which is not 'essential' and can indeed be changed. But maybe the theory of a pre-existing self does not imply an unchangeable person, impervious to liberation or possible new identities. It could be more the case of a core identity shifting around between different states,[63] both a stable nature and a developing self. At least this is more true to self-experience than an identity envisaged entirely as the ever changing self prey to subjectivization. The more flexible view of the subject here is certainly in line with certain Christian anthropologies which respect from birth the individual with rights and needs. More to the point it is the continuous self that comes to 'conversion', whether religious or not. If Christian this would be conversion in the Spirit to the mind and way of Jesus as 'Lord' and as archetypal human. At any rate, this balance between pre-self and formed-self suggests feminists need not necessarily fear the overthrow of radical critiques of social conditioning often basic to their programme.

Secondly, as Butler herself suggests, there are glimpses of freedom and resistance possible even within Foucault's own theory of a circulatory, normalizing process. The body as a site of conditioning power and its many circuits, still managed in her view to redirect and, 'transvalue' that power.[64] So the human subject, or 'self', could still convert or divert circulatory disciplinary power into new individualized possibilities. It appeared to Butler from Foucault's essay, 'The Subject and Power' that a subject that is 'produced' by power could also become a new form and conduit of power. So her work suggests that Foucault missed a chance here in his most famous phase. He could indeed have shielded the principle of freedom

---

[62] See the approach of Alistair I. McFadyen, *The Call to Personhood: A Christian Theory of the Individual in Social Relationships* (Cambridge, 1990), pp. 101–2, concerned specifically with Foucault's approach.

[63] Michel Foucault, feminism and identity, in a useful website http://everything2.com (accessed 15 February 2008), author not stated but with handy outline of Foucault on identity and key feminist responses such as Nancy Hartsock and A. Sawacki.

[64] Butler, pp. 190–92.

even by his own lights. He seemed in his middle work to have overlooked a ready wormhole to freedom,[65] though how this would have worked without a prior free subject is still a puzzle. Margaret A. McLaren argues similarly. According to Foucault she notes, we cannot escape all those social norms sent down upon us by the subjectivizing process. But all the same, she holds, we should also create forms of existence and relation to others which are not like that but are non-normalizing.[66] It is these possibilities that lie at the heart of the idea of a church in community, journeying together on the way of Jesus. The principles of community on the Jesus way involve escape from a normalizing moulding of the self. Furthermore there could be a disturbing of received norms that is based on the way of Jesus and a new set of counterintuitive norms which spring from 'true' freedom. So it matters whether Foucault's account should be taken as complete.

As it happens, Lukes offers a sober response to the onslaught by 'subjectivization' theory. He traces the roots of the concept along a line from Max Weber, through J. K. Galbraith, highlighting the 'monopolistic power' which offered only the illusion of a free self. In addition he sees Foucault's contribution on 'normalization' as still lying within the classical political discussion.[67] To the insights in Lukes we would want to add that the person-shaping process in Foucault lacks a sense of the diversity of influences playing upon people in the day of information deregulation. If exploring forces for formation of people now, we would probably think of, say, such varied forces as visual media, information technology, political correctness, celebrity and market seductions. These belong to the many 'forces', 'energies' and 'materials' that Foucault said can create people's selves. These are what shape a society. And this very fact questions how watertight is Foucault's theory of disciplinary power. For the presence today of so varied a range of influences, raises questions about whether there is such a prominent, directing public knowledge that does the job in so total a way as Foucault alleges. And yet we can admit that all the same, normalizing does go on around us, as the power of political correctness illustrates. It suggests that there must be some serious residual truth in his analysis.

A final point deserves mention just here. 'Subjectivization' today seems to stem from the market as much as from bureaucratic, social or political control. It is not difficult to see how we consumers are being shaped by external market forces. Consumerism thus takes its place at the high table of all-encompassing power which is 'making up people'. 'Normal', or normalized, people want goods instantly, buy big, risk debt, extend beyond their resources, and compete hard both to sell and

[65] Butler, pp. 188–9.

[66] Margaret A. McLaren, 'Foucault and Feminism: Power, Resistance, Freedom', in Dianna Taylor and Karen Vintges (eds), *Feminism and the Final Foucault* (Urbana, 2004), 214–34, p. 224.

[67] Lukes, 'Introduction', *Power*, p. 11. In the wake of Foucault's giant contribution, Clegg, drawing on Bauman, illustrates this subjectivizing power over the individual from the rise of the consumerized market: Clegg, pp. 273–5.

buy. We need everything as new and live out our denial on issues of sustainability. Consumption is all. Accordingly, consumerism seems to assume 'seductive' and frightening new features.[68] Hence the consumer's demands from the market turn into their own opposite, namely the market's domination of the consumer. We become enslaved to the market's rhythms and projects.[69] Accordingly the reach of consumerism stretches even into the power streams of local social groups. Therefore 'person-making' and 'community-making' unavoidably make their presence felt in the power patterns of a church community. As a result the market acquires a voice in the power relations and behaviours of church. That voice of the market may be felt for example in competitive rather than collaborative impulses, or in expansionist motives for church growth or influence. Such traits can naturally inscribe themselves on power relations in church all along the way and even upon friendships within a company seeking to walk the Jesus way together.

Encompassing Power and the Christian Community

There are already implications becoming evident, from this extended discussion, for *koinonia* as church community. The main lesson is that church can hardly remain untouched by the far-reaching effects of Foucauldian and other types of normalization, for these naturally touch local groups. In addition to what is suggested above then, further comments might be relevant.

First, as suggested already, local church is not immune to nagging norms from the wider power-environment that tend to a shaping of its members. These norms could be those that dehumanize and anaesthetize people to inequalities or injustices, including those evils safely out of sight overseas in the majority world. Being shaped by such norms naturally fosters such traits nearer to home such as narcissism, individualism, competitiveness, selfishness, secrecy and thoughtlessness. These are the stuff of power streams locally as well as more widely.

Secondly, Foucault's power theory implies that church community might need to take care over the 'transforming' of its own members whether for service to God or action for the good of a wider world. The challenge a church faces in its norms is to remain intentionally self-critical in the light of the Jesus way without being legalistic and oppressive.

Thirdly, the local community, of the *koinonia*, like other social groups, could measure its health in part by how well it nurtures a community of 'transgressive voices'. These voices may occasionally disrupt accepted, widespread norms including those unfortunate ones that dehumanize people or contradict the way of Jesus. The voices of dissent might tell subjugated truths for the community born of hurts or secretiveness. Or maybe the truths protest at external concerns: the poor, the vulnerable and the alien. The distinctiveness of these voices in the *koinonia*

68 Clegg, p. 274.

69 Clegg, p. 275.

springs from their faithfulness to the life and mission of Jesus. But for local church that surely implies a value not just in transgressive *speech* but also of transgressive *living*, a quest to reflect Jesus-like deeds.

Fourthly, church community naturally seeks to be prophetically self-critical before commenting on whatever it perceives outside as webs of powerlessness and helplessness. Church positively pursues empowerment within its own midst and only this way hopes to find its own transgressive voice for others in the world. It does so as a fellowship of the way without looking all the time for help from the lost 'juridical' world of sovereign power.

And finally, the people of the *koinonia* ultimately turn towards a number of distinctive faith-resources for help in resisting normalizing power. Pre-eminent here is the power-renouncing life and person of Jesus which is the only transforming standard for a *koinonia*. Discussion later will also highlight the power of the Spirit and the notion in Christian tradition of a divine self-emptying and vulnerability.

In summary, life together would seem to require humble attention, as a community, to how far its shared life contains spoken and unspoken 'norms' which cannot be justified from the Christian Scriptures or from shared values present in Jesus. For example, Lydia Harder testifies to at least one bad experience of community norms in her native Mennonite origins. She laments narrowly based truth-claims exchanged in a rigid, normalizing set of rules and the ability of one maybe to deliver the 'knock-out blow' that transferred power from one combatant to another. In this setting one could not much hope for an ongoing renewal and transformation.[70] If considerations like these carry any credibility, it would seem then that 'disciplinary', normalizing power is only too relevant to the local life together of church.

Encompassing Terms (2) 'Bio-power'

Foucault's *History of Sexuality* appeared in 1976, only one year after *Discipline and Punish*, and was badly reviewed by some critics (perhaps feeling cheated that the title was a little misleading – just like many of Foucault's titles). All the same, its many short narratives and general accessibility made it a suitable university undergraduate text and multiple copies may be found on many a university library shelf. However, the appearance of this book did not mark an erratic departure from earlier thinking. Many Foucault watchers have regarded the publication as simply the peak of a systematic phase in Foucault's thinking, even though this writing focused now on power relations in local groups rather than disciplinary, all encompassing power and took sexuality as a case study just as promised some time

---

[70] Lydia Harder, 'Power and Authority in Mennonite Theological Development', in Benjamin W. Redekop and Calvin W. Redekop (eds), *Power, Authority and the Anabaptist Tradition* (Baltimore, 2001), 73–94, p. 93.

earlier.[71] After all, this new book remained in touch with wider, normalizing power through a mysterious term. 'Bio-power', as we noted earlier, governed bodily life. This category of power was not just about sex but also about birth, mortality, health, life expectations etc. These two, body as machine and body as life, were indeed contrasting concerns but still connected by many links.[72] Together they contrasted even more sharply with the old total power of 'sovereignty' that mainly breathed death.[73]

Foucault's account of sexuality, then, appeared as part of the story of bio-power. He gave one chapter the title: the 'Incitement to Discourse' as he set about modern liberalism once again. Through him, the great Freudian 'repressive hypothesis' was about to be overthrown. According to Foucault, sexuality was not after all repressed and censored in the nineteenth century. No, we were looking at quite the opposite process. Foucault called it a 'discursive explosion' of sex.[74] Sex-chatter over-ran our modern, Western culture, though with a polite, scientized vocabulary, properly policed.[75] We fell prey eventually to a determined effort by various agendas to ensure that sex was constantly spoken about, a result achieved by endless explicitness and detailed repetition. The result was to be the emergence of norms and regulations about sex.[76] Foucault believed he was showing us that all this sex-chatter in the modern world was really just the final triumph of bio-power. For bio-power presented itself as nothing less than the truth about ourselves, about our identities. And our sexuality, now lifted out to the surface, would expose to view the greatest depths about each of us.[77] Here lay the key to 'technologies of discipline', the techniques by which norms effect changes on a docile population. By such a narrative Foucault made sexuality just a convenient topic for exposing bio-power's shaping of our identities.

Hence Claire O'Farrell sees bio-power as really just another view on normalizing power.[78] Or perhaps it was *one* 'pole' of such power.[79] At any rate, for Foucault, his later attention to micro-contexts like school, family and church did not challenge bio-power's presence.

True, bio-power fostered life in the human world within a framework of 'norms', though even Foucault questioned its success sometimes.[80] But bio-power

---

71 Bernauer, p. 143, noting a promise in *Archaeology of Knowledge*.

72 Michel Foucault, *The History of Sexuality, Vol 1: An Introduction* (London, 1979), p. 139.

73 Foucault, *History of Sexuality*, pp. 139–40.

74 Foucault, *History of Sexuality*, p. 17.

75 Foucault, *History of Sexuality*, pp. 17–18.

76 Foucault, *History of Sexuality*, p. 18.

77 Dreyfus and Rabinow, p. 175.

78 O'Farrell, *Foucault*, p. 106.

79 Dreyfus and Rabinow, pp. 134, 140.

80 Foucault, *History of Sexuality*, p. 138.

especially helped in adapting the population to economic developments.[81] For it made the social body viable, by centralizing it and managing it,[82] and so the development had political and demographic functions. For instance bio-power could curb such threats to society as famines and plagues through management of the population. Using power-inspired public knowledge as a tool, such 'political technologies' proliferated, concerning themselves with this adjustment of population to economy.[83] They inserted themselves into the overlapping domains of health, living conditions, the body, and strategies of survival.[84] In addition the new harvest of 'norms' colonized society and so outflanked even the intimidating power of the law. A society of ever multiplying norms was the result.[85]

Nothing could help illustrate bio-power's work better than the case of sexuality. Hence the categorizing of 'normal' sexuality became part of the process arising from a politics of populations.[86] Foucault was unrepentant about his gloomy analysis when he was interviewed in 1977.[87] When specifically asked about bio-power, he made clear his view. Bio-power's control of sexual norms shaped the culture from which we are able to recognize ourselves, in which we are let loose and shaped.[88] Audaciously, Foucault concluded that sexuality was not natural. It was invented to spread bio-power, the power to adjust and modify society for economic purposes of life and survival.[89]

More Responses to Foucault

In philosophy and politics, not all have rested easy with Foucault's account of the wider concept of bio-power. In this phase of his thought, he has been reckoned to describe society in impersonal, non-social terms,[90] almost as if there are no free human agents driving power. Bio-power, after all, could indeed look just like a machine or organism running without direction. For Foucault it only took on life in state bureaucracy, liberal norms, freewheeling social science etc. True, Susan Hekman senses that bio-power did indeed treat people as living beings, but only in

---

81 Foucault, *History of Sexuality*, p. 141.

82 The context here is the 'social body'. See Foucault, *History of Sexuality*, pp. 140–41.

83 Foucault, *History of Sexuality*, p. 143.

84 Foucault, *History of Sexuality*, pp. 143–4.

85 Foucault, *History of Sexuality*, p. 144.

86 Foucault, *History of Sexuality*, pp. 145–59.

87 Michel Foucault (Interview), 'The History of Sexuality' in Colin Gordon (ed.), *Power/Knowledge: Selected Interviews and Other Writings 1972–1977: Michel Foucault* (Brighton, 1980), pp. 183–93.

88 Foucault (Interview), 'The History of Sexuality', p. 186.

89 Dreyfus and Rabinow, p. 168.

90 Paul Patten, 'Foucault's Subject of Power' in Jeremy Moss (ed.), *The Later Foucault: Politics and Philosophy* (London, 1998), 64–77, p. 66.

the sense of being slightly more than bare legal entities.[91] Richard Wolin complains that bio-power is so inescapable and all-encompassing of humanity that one is still left in a quandary about whether anyone can resist or escape it.[92] Bio-power as part of disciplinary power's work seems so determinative of every action that any attempt to 'transgress' or defy it might itself be merely an outcome of bio-power itself silently colonizing all our thoughts and aspirations.

More Challenges for Koinonia *from Bio-power*

The earlier discussion on disciplinary power provoked the question of how such heady political doctrines could be relevant for the life of Christian community. Even more is such a question raised over the implications of bio-power in particular. And once again it is possible to see issues confronting the life of the *koinonia* community. Two stand out. First, the way of Jesus challenges the *koinonia* community to resist any purely utilitarian view of human society present in bio-power. This resistance would start close to home with attitudes of mutual respect within the common life together when encountering power patterns. So a resistance to bio-power refuses to shape people for a merely economic purpose. A true life together on the way of Jesus can resist more and more a purely functional view of people in relation. For mature community in Jesus offers a humanizing sanctuary to correct even its own internal power conflicts since its members no longer view each other only in terms of usefulness to the community.

Secondly, a community of believers may become skilled in recognizing the power of the norm within its own ranks. That is, it may succeed in finding out whether its common life harbours spoken or unspoken 'norms' just like bio-power. And it might be able to detect that those norms are derived from popular perception, rather than from the Christian Scriptures and the common life of *koinonia*. These norms often spring from cherished traditions or betray negative attitudes to the world. The key question is this: are these norms truly constructive and positively productive in the life of *koinonia* or do they belong merely to random tradition, long practice, trendiness, superspirituality or even legalism. And key here is whether they really do take their lead from that *koinonia* life rooted in Jesus.

Power and Freedom

The passion for freedom has dominated modernity since the sixteenth century. But what it really means for Christian community belongs in the same counterintuitive world as a Christian view of power on the shared way of Jesus. We have come to see that power in Christian community should not centre on 'power over'

[91] Hekman, p. 202, citing Foucault.

[92] Richard Wolin, 'Foucault the Neohumanist', in *The Chronical Review* (Electronic Version), 53/3 (2006): 2.

(… others), but 'power to' (… enable and transform) and 'power with' (… others in synergy working to enable and transform). In due course we shall encounter 'power from' (… the Spirit of service) and 'power through' (… vulnerability not privilege). Freedom too is going to move among the prepositions and so become transformed from its particular individualist form in classic and late modernism. The question that faces us now is whether that freedom in Foucault's epoch-making ideas turns out to be a delusion. And should freedom also emerge in a different dress for church just as power has?

Encompassing Power and its Limits

Some critics of Foucault found the earlier talk of all-encompassing power in Foucault just too negative. Granted, Foucault's portrayal of power's irresistible reach was intended to spark activism not despair. The dangerous character of power's products simply called for extreme intensity of activity. It appears that originally he only meant to question the grand illusion of liberty which enchanted the great Enlightenment project. However, in the process he seemed for many also to have written off all individual freedom, the very fort he was protecting. The mesh of conditioning power appeared so fine that no sight of freedom was possible through it. The technologies of normalization had even cut down the bourgeois class itself before storming on to master the even weaker working classes.[93] Such rhetoric as that on 'capillary power' simply appeared to rob people of the rational power of choice that lay at the heart of freedom.[94]

As we have seen, for Foucault the so-called rational subject remained stuck as a product of all-encompassing, circulatory power. The person was exposed (or "subjected") to such limits on personal choice and freedoms right from early childhood.[95] Even the liberal struggle for freedom itself turned out to be adept at excluding and normalizing. It clung to abstract, narrow, humanist ideals of what a 'normal' humanity looked like.[96] Hence Foucault claimed that liberalism had

[93] Dreyfus and Rabinow, p. 186.

[94] So complains Lukes, 'Power and the Battle for Minds and Hearts', p. 492. However Lukes has his eye here on the Foucault of the 1970s and that message was not so strident in the final phase of Foucault. Stewart Clegg charts the rise of a debate about the relation of individual agency to endemic determination from Lukes's *Power* (1974) through to Anthony Giddens's wrestlings with power from 1976 onwards: Clegg, *Frameworks of Power*, pp. 129–30. Is it just coincidence that this is the issue for Foucault also in the 1970s?

[95] Richard Wolin, 'Foucault the Neohumanist?', *The Chronicle Review*, 53/ 2: B12, pp. 4–5 (electronic version): p. 1.

[96] Compare as just one representative example, Hekman pp. 198, 207, and her insistence that liberalism fails to recognize the socially constructed character of the self, assuming a universe of identical abstract subjects. This approach, she argues, tends to deny difference and to support stereotyping, pp. 210–11.

both masked and extended the pervasive presence of disciplinary power.[97] Modern Enlightenment thought had bought right into the constraining, modern surveillance of society. It had rested too securely on clear and systematic philosophies such as Marxism and humanism which were all too sure about causes and outcomes. For this modern liberalism was committed to bio-power. It would improve the species and manufacture individuals worthy of the acclaimed new 'society'.[98] Foucault challenged international socialism, especially activists of the French Left, not to dodge the horrifying implications of the Soviet prison and concentration camp. Specifically, they should not put inverted commas around Soviet socialism to act as some kind of disclaimer. Instead they should listen to the heroic sufferers of the Gulag rather than settle for singing some old love songs for the revolution.[99] The question this indirectly raises for ecclesiology is once again whether the believing community too prefers to sing a little love-song for church, deliberately blanking out the realities of church as a sociological entity, a flawed social grouping and a power-cluster.

The truth in 'middle' Foucault was that these big-story accounts of human society had aided and abetted the shaping of every self in modern society by bio-power, so that even the sense of resistance itself could not be trusted to be one's own. Power in Foucauldian thought, according to Joyce Schuld, went right down to the inner person and the competing micro-relations which racked the individual self.[100] So could human freedom really survive, given such withering summaries of the self by Foucault? One precious vestige of freedom remaining in place was critical reason, developed and honed from the Renaissance to the final flourishing of liberalism.[101] So the power that shaped and made a human self was not for Foucault always completely totalizing. It was omnipresent but not omnipotent.[102] Because of this, despite everything, a certain kind of freedom had indeed survived in Western society and even he had honoured it. Granted this was not the grand, transcendental, galloping freedom of the Enlightenment promised in Kant. Rather it was limited, specific and partial.[103] Foucault's residual freedom resembled only a sense of balance or an internal technique of gravity holding out against the cross winds of power relations and influences.[104] In this way, freedom was always

---

97 Johanna Oksala, *Foucault on Freedom* (Cambridge, 2005), p. 182, in line with Sawacki.

98 Foucault, cited by Oksala, p. 182.

99 Foucault, 'Power and Strategies', Colin Gordon (ed.), *Power/Knowledge: Selected Interviews and Other Writings 1972–1977: Michel Foucault* (Brighton, 1980), 134–45, p. 136.

100 Joyce Schuld, *Foucault and Augustine: Reconsidering Power and Love* (2003, Indiana), p. 15.

101 Oksala, pp. 186–7.

102 Schuld, p. 25.

103 Oksala, p. 187.

104 Schuld, p. 29, 229n.

theoretically present. Theoretically indeed, we could always use our freedom to modify power. So everyone had multiple options to alter relations of power by changing tactics and shifting the balance of power regarding people, groups, or policy. It was possible to reposition and await a new configuration, or even reconfigure power patterns ourselves by the use of yet smaller micro-triggers.[105]

So could there really be a springboard today to a freedom of any value? Foucault came in hope to herald critical questioning as the condition of new possibilities of freedom. To question critically was to give a place to the unexpected as opposed to the inevitable.[106] So he pointed to this capacity for questioning and self-criticism as useful for renovation carried out on the self.[107] At least this far power and freedom were not exactly opposites. They related to each other symbiotically. For in Foucault's thought new relations of power were to be kept in check by such practices of freedom as self-critical enquiry.[108] He conveniently overlooked the point that such self-criticism requires the existence of a prior subject![109] Moreover, the freedoms that he wrote about late in life mainly served only the self and were aesthetic and individualized, as we shall see.

So could a freedom of this kind actually be, or lead to, what we call 'ethical' action? For the moment we comment on the idea that freedom (though partial) stands out itself as *the* ethical value adopted. In that case of course any accompanying actions are bound to be assessed ethically accordingly to this somewhat limited standard. And for Foucault ethics was indeed all about the practice merely of freedom for its own sake.[110] Only in this very particular way did it challenge and change anything in anyone – by exploring new freedoms (experiences), relationships, pleasures etc. But surely such beautiful and appealing qualities, deemed freedom by Foucault, hardly deserve to be called *ethical* practices at all.[111] For many people these descriptions would seem more to signify the shallow narcissistic manifesto of consumer aspirations, evidence that perhaps even Foucault could be bewitched by norms.

At any rate, calling this ethics could be deemed far-fetched. It might even be the exact opposite of ethics by endorsing self-absorption, which by definition remained the sure and certain enemy of a social ethic. Issues such as human rights, social development and anti-militarism seemed not to disturb the Foucauldian

105 Schuld, p. 28 perhaps catching Foucault in an optimistic mood. See also her drawing on later Foucault, pp. 72–3, 244n, 246n.

106 Oksala, p. 188. The body too might be capable of resistance and 'overflowing' the limits set it by prevailing norms (p. 189).

107 Foucault cited by Patton p. 73, from Foucault's 'What is Enlightenment' (German version 1978). Patton himself, however, points out that this presupposes the prior existence of possible subjects of such activity!

108 Schuld, pp. 26–7.

109 Commented on by, among others, Patton, p. 73.

110 Oksala, p. 190.

111 Oksala, p. 190.

ethical theory of freedom. So on the matter of all-encompassing power and the free individual, the most we could say in favour of self-criticism at this stage is that it may leave open a window for freedom, though not all are hopeful here.[112]

Christian views of freedom, rooted in the Scriptures, differ considerably from Foucault's approach. And this has implications for power relations in church community. The history indeed goes right back to Hebrew faith since in the Exodus narrative, a people are not freed just for freedom in itself but also to 'serve God'.[113] This result indeed spelt freedom,[114] for it included rescue from the conditions of slavery and offered peace to work, associate and enjoy life. But it was also all bound up with a freely chosen covenant of life which engendered peaceful relations. In the Christian Scriptures this went further and became the freedom to love, indeed to love so much as to bind oneself to the liberating service of others (Gal 5.13).[115] Hence freedom means becoming 'disposable for God' and available for others, in other words to be freed from self-seeking and liberated for the life of selfless love in a new community. Walter Kasper typically represents this strain, interpreting freedom not as enlightenment autonomy but as the freedom to participate in the self-giving freedom of the Trinity.[116] Equality on the way of Jesus in this way challenged to its roots the very assumptions of a slave-based society (Gal 3.18).[117]

So the meaning of freedom in the Christian *koinonia* is not that of liberalism's 'freedom to pursue your own good'.[118] Rather it is freedom for self-giving to others, the supreme and most unlikely freedom of all. A community on the way of Jesus assumes that this is the gold standard for liberation. Yet at the same time self-giving is balanced, even in early Christian thinking, by robust principles of fairness and justice which disallow oppression of the weak. Hence Paul expects that a church established under his mission work will have the capacity to judge with complete fairness where disputes arise and he clearly assumes that such eruptions are inevitable (1 Cor 6.1–6). Nicholas Lash argues that the time has come for adulthood when we transcend autonomy in favour of community.[119] It

---

112 See Foucault's claim: Michel Foucault, 'The Subject and Power', in James D. Faubion (ed.) *Michel Foucault: Power* (London, 2002), 326–48, p. 342, but also his own doubts: Michel Foucault, 'Power and Strategies' p. 142. Here he concludes no spaces of freedom within the fine mesh of power. See Oksala, p. 191.

113 For the many biblical references see Richard Bauckham, *God and the Crisis of Freedom: Biblical and Contemporary Perspectives* (Louisville, 2002), p. 9.

114 Bauckham, pp. 9, 10.

115 Bauckham, p. 15.

116 For example as in Walter Kasper, *Jesus the Christ* (London, 1976), pp. 158, 214 and *Theology and the Church* (London, 1989), pp. 69–70.

117 Bauckham p. 14 cites this but also handles the issue as it arises in Ephesians 5.

118 J. S. Mill, cited by Bauckham, p. 20.

119 Cited in Bauckham, p. 44.

needs little imagination to reflect on the difference this value would make to power strategies within the *koinonia*.

It seems then that the logical possibility of freedom managed to cling on in one Foucauldian principle at least, namely each individual's capacity for self-criticism. Out of such ability perhaps could surface transgressive voices and healthy collisions of varied free, mutual actions. Hence autonomous action in the teeth of seductive normalizing seemed just about possible. But whatever this meant, it could not compensate for the Foucauldian mistrust of the Enlightenment's 'ideal' of 'normal' humanity and a wariness of 'transcendental' subjects of moral action.[120] The Foucault mind was still haunted by the difficulties of holding to freedom in a world of bio-power, of culture conditioning, of big government and of disciplinary norms.

Possibilities of Resistance?

The account above has laid out a sobering Foucauldian view of subterranean power in society. So what of the problems Foucault's gloomy theory of endemic power presented for any hope of resistance to disciplinary bio-power? Positively, in these earlier writings, Foucault still expected that centres of resistance to endemic power could lock into place and link up into a new chain of revolution.[121] Any epoch could give away only too clearly the location of the real centre of power, leading to possible resistance to it.[122] It seemed, then, that perhaps forms of resistance could rise up after all through the unmasking of encompassing power.[123] Further brief points of resistance flared here and there in Foucault's world, strong enough to cause upset to the tidy world of all-encompassing disciplinary power. In fact the work of such all-encompassing power actually still implied a measure of cooperation from the person being shaped, if often through an unconscious collusion.[124]

In *History of Sexuality* he attempted to offer more hope for resistance by switching attention to the local picture and its more fluid internal power relations. Here resistance was more conceivable, but mainly as part of a whirlpool of power strategies and tactics.

Foucault was interviewed in a journal feature by the philosopher Bernard-Henri Levy in 1977 (just one year, of course, after the appearance of *The History of Sexuality*). Levy asked Foucault about his claim, now famous, that resistance is always present along with power. Of course, taken literally it is hard to see how the dictum makes sense. But Foucault was actually talking about power relations in local groups where he particularly held power to be fluid and open to challenge.

[120] Patton, p. 73.

[121] Foucault in Bernauer, p. 157.

[122] Foucault in Bernauer p. 157.

[123] Foucault in Bernauer p. 150.

[124] Foucault in Berneuer p. 150.

With regard to these anyway he made it clear that he was not posing a substance of resistance against a substance of power.[125] He was just saying that as soon as there was power in a familiar group, there was born *a logical possibility of* resistance. It was always possible to oppose power's grip, given favourable conditions and with a strategy in place.[126] This is a tantalizing statement and many readers must have regretted that his interviewer did not further draw out Foucault on the point, despite its subsequent fame. Perhaps the claim is milder than at first appears. It is about ever changing, conflicting strategies in modern institutional social settings. It might also partly be adding a mere unhelpful truism: for there to be a 'power over' there must have been a resistance that it overcame.

However, whatever Foucault meant we see no promise of the rising up and triumph over normalizing power's seductive captivity. But Foucault's assertion must be carefully contextualized. Not all belong to Foucault's world in the first place. The trodden-down poor of the majority world, especially women, have to accept not seductive power-knowledge but unrelieved tyranny even in family, home, village or faith-group. There is no room for resistance or freedom here. Foucault's switch from considering past sovereign domination of society to present dominating seduction of it should itself be suspect. It appears conditioned by typical Western insularity to the majority world and the minimal existence of many of its population.

Not surprisingly, the response to Foucault's wrestling with resistance is mixed. Susan Hekman at least takes some heart from it. Because the forces that determine our identities are everywhere, then resistance must be pervasive as well.[127] But Margaret McLaren is not well pleased with Foucault's clumsy examples of what forms this local resistance might take for women when confronted with domineering men in the marital situation. She rightly jibs at the options for freedom flatteringly called 'resistance': stealing their man's money and refusing sex![128] Her own example proves more successful, that of the Mothers of Plaza de Mayo in Argentina, and perhaps she even rescues Foucault's claim.[129] They were the mothers who protested daily against the disappearance of their children during the 1970s and 1980s, provocatively defying tyrannical domination. All the same much suspicion hangs over the claim that resistance for Foucault is possible to real personal situations of domination, even today.

---

125 And he could have added the jibe, 'as liberal and Marxist systems mistakenly do'.

126 Foucault, 'Power and Sex', pp. 122–3.

127 Hekman, pp. 211–12.

128 Margaret A. McLaren, 'Foucault and Feminism: Power, Resistance, Freedom', in Dianna Taylor and Karen Vintges (eds), *Feminism and the Final Foucault* (Urbana, 2004), 214–34, p. 221.

129 McLaren, pp. 221–3.

So resistance was simply *given with* power. It was intrinsic to the very nature of power relations, most notably in a local group of varied people.[130] And to worry that one power would always be an overwhelming outright winner misunderstands the nature of power in such dynamics.[131] That is, it does not pick up how power relations generated a multiplicity of power ploys and points of resistance present everywhere in the power network. So correspondingly there was no dead centre of revolt either, no pinpointed origin of every rebellion. Instead we would find only a plurality of resistance points under many different guises, from the vigorous back kick to a tactical passivity. So although there are occasionally head to head confrontations in local power situations, more often we find shifting, transitory points of resistance. Like the network of power-relations itself, the local points of resistance cannot be contained in any one place but may spill over and colonize this or that community.[132] In any case, Foucault argued that domination was only a particular and unappealing type of 'power over', one where power had hardened into a fixed form. Here there would reign a constant advantage to the dominant with few margins of freedom for the dominated.[133] This was rarely the situation.

Sharp-eyed feminist writers, however, were only too well versed in the actual conditions of domination where resistance was faint. But even then feminism itself proved divided over such things as the centrality of domination in power, the realities of inequality today and the critical status of resistance.[134] Foucault's later approach, however, simply reflected what he had come to see as the fluidity and mobility that marked face to face power situations. 'Power over' had now become more mutual and hence hard to work out. Here one could encounter an ever-changing landscape of local power interactions. And here you would find

---

[130] Foucault, *History of Sexuality* p. 95. Thinking that power was always the winner has already failed to see the reciprocal nature of relation in face to face groups.

[131] Foucault, *History of Sexuality*, p. 95.

[132] Foucault, *History of Sexuality*, p. 96.

[133] Duncan Iveson, 'The Disciplinary Moment: Foucault, Law and the Reinscription of Rights', in Jeremy Moss (ed.), *The Later Foucault: Politics and Philosophy* (London, 1998), 129–48, p. 129.

[134] See Margaret McLaren's dissent from Nancy Hartsock's view that Foucault imagines an equality of power in the modern world. On the contrary, political action and social analysis are still continually needed: Margaret A. McLaren, 'Foucault and Feminism: Power, Resistance, Freedom', in Dianna Taylor and Karen Vintges (eds), *Feminism and the Final Foucault* (Urbana, 2004), 214–34, p. 220. In addition, Amy Allen rejects domination as a suitable model for power relations: cited by Johanna Meehan in a full review of Allen's book, *The Power of Feminist Theory*. See an extensive review in Johanna Meehan, 'Review Essay. Feminism, critical theory, and power', in *Philosophy and Social Criticism*, 30/3 (2004): 375–82 (electronic version). For a view quite different to Allen's, one casting the position of women in particular in an initial reality of domination see Marsha Hewitt, 'Woman, nature and power: emancipatory themes in critical theory and feminist theology', *Studies in Religion*, 20/3 (1991): 267–79.

fitful forms of resistance whose tactics were sometimes influenced by wider, all-encompassing power but also sometimes weakened these same wider influences.

This account, it has to be admitted, does square neatly with the notion of bio-power that permeated the whole living mass of power-relations, constantly nurturing life (= alleged welfare) for the human participants. Perhaps here, Foucault also trained the spotlight on a widely neglected fact, quite critical to the life of any micro-community including the life together of church as community. He underlined the point that power in human society displays an unpredictable and disconcerting life of its own, as many politicians have discovered to their cost. Oppositions spring up from no apparent centre and go in directions not foreseen by anyone or intended by any party. Participants are swept along by the tide and so even those groups and figures with seemingly supreme power are carried away. The astonishing transformation of former communist countries in the late 1980s provides an illustration of the point and would have pleased Foucault. This almost Gaia-like, unstable and self-disseminating nature in 'power over' at least deserves the significance and attention that Foucault dedicated to it.

How much of the doubt about resistance here signals dangers for the shared life of a local church community? Certainly fuzziness over resistance does not seem in tune with a Christian prizing of justice and truth. Authentic community on the way of Jesus could not possibly remain relaxed over the thought that even mild resistance in society was relativized by a pervasive shaping of people. Even less could matters be considered healthy if the pursuit of 'truth' in Christian life together was limited to docile, unquestioning submission to one party's dogmatic utterances. Similarly church should not countenance the possibility of an abuse of power in a Christian community which faced no real questioning from any quarter. Here a barely logical possibility of a questioning voice could not be enough to grace a local church truly seen as community.

Social critics too, as we have seen, have agonized over Foucault's lack of attention to resistance. Admittedly, wherever there was regular power (not the 'absolutely total domination' kind) we may rest assured that there was the technical possibility of resistance. However, such forms of resistance already were always fragmented, conditioned and competing, despite the claim that wherever there was power resistance always came with it.[135] The fact is that possible resistance remained an underdeveloped theme in Foucault and we still have to strain hard to hear its songs of freedom.[136] In the domain of all-pervasive, bio-power there were instead only occasional flashes of enlightenment or brave deeds which for a moment transgressed the oppressive limits of normalization. There were no firm gains for freedom, nor sites secure from all oppression.[137] The reason for such dark assessments was simple. Foucault wanted to wake his readers up to the enchantment of power all around them and so he laid his message on thick. Hence

135 Simons, pp. 82–3.

136 Simons, p. 84.

137 Simons, p. 69.

he really did want to believe that it was possible to escape all-encompassing forms of power, perhaps even to come up with a winning response strategy[138] though in the end he did not achieve it.

None of this, however settles the more specific question of how much of any resistance was actually the subject's very own personal agency of freedom, or simply the 'freedom' of interplay between strategies and actions. Complaints arise that Foucault's 'thin' account of the subject provided only a bare minimum for doing justice to belief in particular, free and situated selves.[139] This problem remains significant for church along Foucault's wider thoughts on resistance and freedom.

Freedom and Resistance in Christian Community

The Scriptures of the earliest churches do point to possibilities of resistance, even though 'sovereign' power held complete sway in the classical world. Such top-down power was most obvious in Roman imperial might, but also in systemic slavery and in powerful forces against the education and political place of women, not to mention fearful superstition or legalistic forms of religion. True the Christian foundational documents sometimes seem to display apparent, relative conservatism towards some of these formidable forces. But then this despised movement of mainly the poor and slaves could hardly realistically campaign for, let alone achieve, early political change in such an environment. And yet Paul the apostle did indeed urge resistance to destructive norms in the culture, despite the entrenched top-down oppressive layering of society. Christians were not to be 'shaped' by such norms but to be transformed into forms of freedom (Rom 12.2, Gal 5.1, Jas 1.25).

The issues of power and resistance raised by Foucault and relevant to church in its community life are few but important. First, serious questions emerge about how far a Christian *koinonia* community might genuinely claim to be a community of freedom. The rush to see people 'transformed', 'spiritualized', initiated, catechized, inculturated or liturgized, plainly carries risks very similar to those influences operating on society through bio-power. If the result is a feeling of surveillance rather than liberation, the transforming process has already stalled and become counterproductive. For in Christ, only free responses in liberated faith count (Ro 14.22). The law condemns. The Spirit is freedom (Rom 8.1).

Secondly, self criticism and re-evaluation together by church communities have indeed turned out to be surprising channels to freedom – another Foucauldian revolution. This fact could pull many a church up short. For church can be impatient and irritable when called to reassess itself, even though that call is completely true to the Christian Scriptures. The pause for self-critical reflection seems to curtail freedom for some. For them freedom means unreflective spontaneity and

---

138 Simons, pp. 84–5.

139 Patton, p. 75.

action. Hence impatience with self-critical processes may stem from a feeling that the practice is a waste of time, even 'unspiritual'. Or critical discussion is seen simply as a hurdle in the way of getting on with a project. Yet self-criticism raises the human above other animals and is at the heart of freedom. The practice by church community surely is a major source of new freedoms and without it no transformation project is likely to succeed. After all, personal self-examination is all but universal in Christian piety, and so why not at the level of community too, if sensitively managed?

Thirdly, perhaps Christian church faces challenges brought to view by Foucault's wrestlings. Church has to find a way realistically to estimate the potential for domination in its community, while ensuring freedoms bending towards *koinonia* unity. Perhaps, with light from critical studies on power's workings it should be able further to make sense of power in community.[140]

Power Relations in Communities and the *Koinonia*

Plainly there was both consistency and forward movement in Foucault's conceptions of power. In the new world of the bourgeoisie many springs of power had come to operate. In an interview given in 1978 he also repeated his objection to perceiving power purely as prohibition, that which prevents people from doing things. It was, to him, much more complex.[141] For instance, it also positively 'placed' or 'located' people through a long process of 'techniques', especially of training that could constrain and condition them.[142] This notion in bio-power reflected Foucault's earlier determination to get at the vast web of unequal relationships that subverted and evaded the theoretical equality put in place through law and politics. All this said, at the same time his attitude to power underwent a development over time. The 'micro-physics of power' that reached right to the very bodies of individuals mastering and constraining them[143] may belong also to power's working in local settings. It was this complex nature of power in local communities that was to occupy Foucault now in his later phase and to beat up a storm of perplexity around him. It is at this point that his work most directly and practically raises questions for the Christian community and the imbalance of power relations and power-behaviours over against the distinctive levelling values of the *koinonia*.

140 K. A. Smith, pp. 96–7.

141 Foucault, 'An Aesthetics of Existence', p. 48.

142 Foucault, 'On Power', pp. 104–5.

143 Drefyus and Rabinow, pp. 113–14.

Chapter 5
'Power Relations' and Church

Chapter 3 revealed that the long quest of political philosophy for a clarification of power reached a crucial stage with the arrival of Foucault's ideas. However, at first, he too mainly focused on power's role in society as a whole. For, as we saw, he developed the notion of a disciplinary 'power over', a wide process of 'making up people'. However, in due course Foucault surprised everyone by deciding to scale down his power theory to the level of mundane, face to face grassroots politics. Accordingly, he now focused on figuring out the real meaning of power strategies in 'micro-groups' or 'micro-contexts'. Anything useful he says about that must obviously bear directly on the life of local church communities. Hence we now return to his concern with micro-groups, in the hope that to give it closer attention could throw light on neglected features. This further scrutiny might also throw light on how power relations, as well as their resulting power patterns, inhabit church communities.

Power Relations in Local Social Groups

According to Foucault, one could find power patterns and behaviours within all micro-groups, because these features arose naturally and unavoidably. They came with the territory, namely the inevitable diversity of levels found in any community. That is, power patterns sprang from the assortment of unequal power relations that were sure to feature in any local social group. These power dynamics flowed from a multiplicity of forces and what is more, any single centre of influence did not manage the whole movement. Rather a variety of power behaviours and forms of resistance emerged in any grassroots community, colliding and colluding to generate unforeseen results. As we shall see, his interest at first was on how this uncoordinated variety of influences fostered public norms, benchmarks for general behaviour, and how they so helped to shape people's identities without these individuals even being aware of it. But his writing eventually turned more to the actual workings of 'micro-politics' and their tactics, interested in them for their own sake and importance.

Foucault's focus, then, had changed radically from wider functions of power. He was now going right out to the 'extremities' of society and all the way down to local politics.[1] He did not envisage in these local groups any mastermind or ruling

---

1 Michael Walzer, 'The Politics of Michel Foucault', in David Couzens Hoy (ed.), *Foucault: A Critical Reader* (Oxford, 1989), 51–68, pp. 54–5.

party.[2] Rather, he argued that power came at us not from one dominating centre but instead from every direction. It worked as a complex, continuously fluid interplay of varied influences, though not all were malign. True, in face to face groups these cross currents might include strong bids for personal ends. But they might also harbour strategies of 'resistance'. And it will emerge that resistance could take many forms not just aggressive ones. They could include such moves as avoidance tactics, forceful silence, reconciling of hostile forces or even counter-bids for power. These influences may or may not constitute intentional plays for power but we should always expect a constantly shifting interplay of power behaviours, not always consciously intended.

As a social group in a micro-setting, local church fits neatly among the groups being described here. There is no reason to expect the naturally arising power patterns described above to be absent from a sociological reality such as a local church. This micro-power was always at work in face to face social settings, inhabiting strategies, mechanisms and tactics.[3] Hence, all the anxiety about power should now concern itself with probing varieties of interplay in these local power strategies and mechanisms. In other words the analysis must occupy itself with the techniques and ploys of domination at grassroots level.[4] Now it was worth adopting a new approach: 'ascending analysis' which started with social groups and worked upwards towards big, circulatory power.

Therefore the most urgent task was to concentrate on local social contexts.[5] There we might detect processes which actually affected our bodies, our immediate behaviour and even our very gestures. In order further to understand power we should uncover how people experienced real pressures locally through relationships and a host of immediate energies, agencies, desires and thoughts. This acceptance of a new focus would include recognition that power within a social group could only function as a chain,[6] for power was never channelled within a group by any one single party. Nor for that matter was it finally locked up inside that group, for power must travel and make itself networks.

However, the way this local power related to bio-power as a wider force was described somewhat darkly by Foucault and looks very complex.[7] At least it seems that bio-power was not now really concerned with moralities and ethical customs.

---

2 Walzer, pp. 54–5.

3 Michel Foucault, 'Two Lectures' in Colin Gordon (ed.), *Power/Knowledge: Selected Interviews and Other Writings 1972–1977: Michel Foucault* (Brighton, 1980), 78–102, p. 102. The second part also appeared with the title 'Power, Right, Truth', in Robert E. Goodin and Philip Pettit (eds), *Contemporary Political Philosophy: An Anthology* (Oxford, 1997), pp. 545–50,

4 Foucault, 'Two Lectures', p. 102.

5 Foucault, 'Two Lectures', p. 100.

6 Foucault, 'Two Lectures', p. 98.

7 Michel Foucault, 'The Subject and Power', in James D. Faubion (ed.), *Michel Foucault: Power* (London, 2002), 326–48, pp. 341, 346. It was originally published

Foucault saw it instead as feeding off the actual techniques at grassroots that gripped people and conditioned their thoughts. Bio-power came to colonize and use these local strategies.[8] It was now seen as itself dependent, for it was fed and sustained by these strategies working in local groups. That wider form of power in society would just 'dry up' without the nourishing life of these smaller domains of power,[9] such as family, small groups and other basic social units in society.[10] And on this basis we should resign ourselves to a state of endless mutual conditioning between big power and small power.[11] In addition, bio-power no longer appeared as a solid single weight pressing down on micro-groups, though it continued to circulate out to them. Equally, it was not monochrome and unvarying but richly diverse and layered. It was, in short, always a dynamic, shifting process.[12] The last hints of sovereign power in it, we might say, were dying.

Hence, Foucault now believed that to get a better grasp of power one should concentrate on understanding local practices, techniques and tactics. One had to search out how in addition they came to be adopted, colonized or 'annexed' for use by bio-power.[13] But this more sophisticated and mature theory of power also contained a further critical adjustment. The theory now suggested that various individuals, or selves, in society, were not only the products and targets of power but channels of it too.[14] And this meant that people in their local activities and grassroots relations constantly contributed to power interactions with unpredictable consequences.[15]

As we have seen, Foucault still believed in the existence of disciplinary power. He just wanted to say that another type of power also stalked the discussion. His 'Two Lectures', as late as 1976 (the date of *History of Sexuality*) made clear the continuing role of big power.[16] Hence, despite the startling new direction above, Foucault could concede that ideological power was indeed still out and on the prowl. According to Charles Taylor, pervasive bio-power remained for Foucault

famously as the 'Afterword' in Hubert L. Dreyfus and Paul Rabinow, *Michel Foucault: Beyond Structuralism and Hermeneutics* (Brighton, 1982), pp. 208–26.

[8] Foucault, 'Two Lectures', p. 99.

[9] Joyce Schuld, *Foucault and Augustine: Reconsidering Power and Love* (Indiana, 2003), p. 15. See her excellent summary of this relationship in pp. 14–17.

[10] Foucault, 'Two Lectures', p. 100.

[11] Charles Taylor, 'Foucault on Freedom and Truth' in David Couzens Hoy (ed.), *Foucault: A Critical Reader* (Oxford, 1989), 69–102, p. 85.

[12] Foucault, 'Two Lectures' pp. 96–100. We note the date: 1976. He was already in transition towards emphasizing power relations and mechanisms in local dynamics.

[13] Foucault, 'Two Lectures' p. 99.

[14] Foucault, 'Two Lectures', p. 98.

[15] J. Bernauer, *Michel Foucault's Force of Flight : Toward an Ethics for Thought* (London, 1990), p. 146.

[16] Foucault, 'Two Lectures', pp. 93–6.

alive and well, and possibly even more dangerous.[17] So it did not fade away in importance altogether. But a whole new era had arrived and it was the bearer of challenging questions for all social groups.

The Heart of Power Relations Theory

At the important maturing moment of Foucault's figuring through of power in a 'micro-context' he revealed his approach in *History of Sexuality* (in French 1976 and English in 1977). Here he took sexuality and identity as key illuminating themes and shaped them into a case study of power at the local level. He asked how power played out in local settings with particular regard to human sexuality. You had to leave disciplinary power out of the picture for the moment.[18] Ask instead through what tactics or devices power gained access to such a secure site as our sexuality (as he believed it surely did). Some critics seemed to overlook this very specific local setting for his probe. As we have seen, he seemed not to be denying all centres of power, or turning his back on bio-power or wider forms of power anywhere. Neither was he rejecting the presence of genuinely dominant players in either the wider or local interplay of power-interests. Rather he was just taking sexuality as a useful example, albeit 'a privileged one', to show how the presence and tactics of power operated from many points in local social groups. Hence power at this level emerged as a complex of multiple participants each contributing their unique, local cross currents of power sometimes leading to conflicts, transformations, agreements and reversals. The types of power involved were probably unstable.[19]

Power from Everywhere

Now at this point a famous Foucault adage was born: power may be found everywhere. This meant that power *came* from everywhere. For differences of power arose naturally in any set of living and dynamic relations that came along.[20] Social groups or institutions had the appearance of developing out of dominant intentional actions and strategies but in fact were only the interplay of various hidden, unpredictable levers and influences.[21] These could not be overthrown in order to set people free, because they did not issue from any one place. In fact,

---

17 Taylor 'Foucault on Freedom and Truth', p. 85.

18 Michel Foucault, *The History of Sexuality, Vol 1: An Introduction* (London, 1979), p. 90.

19 Foucault, *History of Sexuality*, p. 93.

20 Foucault, *History of Sexuality*, p. 93.

21 Eric Paras, *Foucault 2:0: Beyond Power and Knowledge* (New York, 2006), pp. 154–5.

the individuals or groups who *seemed* to be behind these mini-centres of power, were themselves in turn products of the system.[22] The word power also described the overall effect that resulted from these fluid relations. As we have seen, power seemed to Foucault a useful name for the outcome of a complex of unequal, diverse, unstable relations of power, especially if they had results on individuals.

Admittedly 'power' may seem to some an arbitrary choice of word for the effect of varied influences in interaction. But this is true of most other uses of the word 'power' that we have uncovered. Foucault's use was at least recognizing the complexity and plurality of meaning in power. It also tacitly conceded the limitations of the notion of 'power over'.

In just one page a unified theory of the local workings of power had taken shape.[23] Its main claims ran as follows. First, in face to face social groups, normally no single individual or group could seize or trap local power outcomes totally for themselves. This is true whether we are speaking of norms or of a group's direction and development. Secondly, actual 'relations of power', that is people's varied levels of status with regard to each other, these were simply unavoidable aspects of any local web of relationships. Relations between humans always included these natural, varied imbalances, inequalities and divisions. So power did not fall from on high, external and intervening as the voice of prohibition or as some kind of hostile watchdog. It was just there … in the lifeblood of social relationships. It was already integral to the very relations themselves. Where there were relations, there would be a random range of inequalities which we could call 'power relations'. Consequently, Foucault concluded that the local situations hosted a complex miniature power system, where differential power relations persisted.[24] These varied levels of power relations guaranteed an equally varied set of power behaviours within a group such as persuasion, tactical moves, avoidance, peace-seeking etc. These behaviours, in other words, would collude and collide creating ever new situations. We suggest that these dynamics could be called 'cross currents' of power, or 'streams' and 'patterns' of power.

Thirdly, to reiterate, such local power-complexes might individually or together end up feeding into the wider encompassing workings of bio-power. Soon after the publication of *History of Sexuality*, Foucault emphasized this. He was not at all now denying the existence of bio-power, big power. He was merely denying that power *only* took a particular all-encompassing form: arterial, pervasive and disciplinary.[25]

Fourthly, later Foucault tried to clarify the meaning of local 'power strategies' or power behaviours that stemmed from unequal power relations. True, the word

22 Paras, p. 154.

23 Foucault, *History of Sexuality*, p. 94.

24 Michel Foucault, 'Confessions of the Flesh', in Colin Gordon (ed.), *Power/Knowledge: Selected Interviews and Other Writings 1972–1977: Michel Foucault* (Brighton, 1980), pp. 194–228.

25 Foucault, 'The Subject and Power', pp. 346–8.

'strategy' could carry the connotation of getting one's own way in the 'game' of power relationships. Then, maybe it even appeared ruthless and Machiavellian. It was an action to deprive someone else of any reason to struggle against overwhelming odds. It was a strategy naturally aimed to end the possibility of resistance or flight. This would be domination and total victory. Then it succeeded in fixing inequalities so that they were permanent.[26] But mainly for Foucault a power strategy could have, for instance, merely produced a shift of advantage or established a level playing ground or even created a beneficial outcome for all participants ('power to' and 'power with'). It was not always badly motivated.

Finally, these assertions flowed into one celebrated yet contentious claim that power relations could be described as intentional and yet not strictly subjective.[27] A contradiction? Intentions without an intender? How could this be so? In the first place power relations and strategies were intentional in the sense that they were neither driven by pure chaos nor lacking rationale, aims and intentions. In other words he did not hold to mayhem group-theory. Power patterns were rational because they emerged from a mix of strategic actions, local knowledge and natural outcomes.[28] They displayed a certain kind of logic.[29] But at the same time no one single dominant centre ruled over their rationality.[30] Things tended to move towards a desired result but usually no one subject was doing all the pushing.

Consequently the actual cumulative outcome was not completely that intended by any of the participants.[31] Unpredictable outcomes emerged pretty much according to natural political laws from a multiplicity of inequalities, tactics and other assorted actions. However, these outcomes still defied prediction, even by the strongest player. Moreover, if there was no single centre of control in social groups, then neither was there a single centre of revolt either.[32] There existed no heart of a revolt, no headquarters of rebellion. The swirlings and movements of power patterns defied all such power monopolies. And what is more, the differential power relations behind everything were in fact the best hidden things in the social body.[33]

The great project had taken a lurch sideways, away from the grand, pervasive, disciplinary type of power. Now the analysis probed power on the ground, where we could sense its impact more personally and directly. It had become important to

---

[26] Michel Foucault, 'The Subject and Power', p. 347.

[27] Foucault, *History of Sexuality*, p. 94. See the customary lucid exposition of Foucault here by Charles Taylor: 'Foucault on Freedom and Truth', pp. 84–6.

[28] Bernauer, pp. 146–7.

[29] Dreyfus and Rabinow, p. 18.

[30] Foucault, *History of Sexuality*, p. 95.

[31] Dreyfus and Rabinow, p. 187.

[32] Foucault, *History of Sexuality*, p. 96.

[33] Michel Foucault (Interview), 'Power and Sex', in Lawrence D. Kritzman (ed.), Michel Foucault. *Politics, Philosophy, Culture: Interviews and Other Writings* (New York, 1988), 110–24, p. 118.

discover the truth about how power worked in micro-groups and what this meant for freedom. Hence *History of Sexuality* is interpreted soundly as an attempt to go yet deeper into the workings of bio-power and to show how it finds an ally in local settings of power – just where we might not have looked for it! One could identify power in a local setting's politics and analyse it, since such social units are renowned for their plots, plans and counterweights.[34] But even so this does not mean that everything could be expected to turn out as predicted by even the strongest participants and best-laid plans. It is not as if anyone could perfectly mastermind results from a local headquarters of battle.[35] Foucault wanted here to expose the illusion that the effects on people all go back to big fire-power, coming from the top down, and that nothing else needed to be watched. In fact 'technologies of power' demanded that we keep a careful eye on low-key local political settings including family and local institutions.

Foucault's approach has not passed without criticism. The likelihood of outcomes *never* squaring with a particular player's intention in local power settings remained controversial. Do surprise results always and invariably follow from mingled human actions? Perhaps this is so frequently, even in many or most situations, but surely not inevitably as an inescapable logic in all cases. More importantly, maybe anyway this lack of certainty can simply be put down to inherent weaknesses in a dominant player's scheming or to the 'hidden hand' of influence from a wider context.[36] But this perhaps would be close to Foucault's main point anyway. Bids for power in complex social settings, even small ones, will tend to come unstuck as a rule. However, the finer points of interpretation in this critical debate need not detain us. The key observation, now made by Foucault and here to stay, is that in modern micro-settings it is likely that no Panopticon-like centre controls all the action. The influence that any social group feeds into the wider web of power is most likely to come from a collision and collusion of varied strategies emerging in the group, not just one controlling strategy. Overall power strategies in face to face settings did not relate in a simple top-down way but rather constantly conditioned each other.[37]

This was not all good news. We may indeed like to see power fluctuating and moving about, to exclude domination and to allow new opportunities for change and liberation. And yet we may also want to replace prevailing norms with new ones, liberating and therefore hopefully enduring.[38] This is especially true for feminists and others believing themselves on the trail of liberation and justice. But this is simply one more reason for taking power relations analysis seriously and factoring it into realistic expectations.

---

34 Dreyfus and Rabinow, p. 187.

35 Dreyfus and Rabinow, p. 187.

36 Taylor, 'Foucault on Freedom and Truth', p. 85.

37 Bernauer, p. 146.

38 Dianna Taylor, 'Foucault's Ethos: Guide(post) for Change', in Dianna Taylor and Karen Vintges (eds), *Feminism and the Final Foucault* (Urbana, 2004), 235–57, p. 265.

A final, more mature reflection by Foucault on the minutiae of power relations confirmed the explanation above. Despite his earlier protests that he was not really concerned with power, he still returned to a sustained last assault on the tricky subject quite late in his life. In a few short pages in 1982, he ambitiously seemed to attempt a synthesis of his findings.[39] He offered a blend of classic suspicious views as set out by the Frankfurt school, his own earlier strident analyses and the later focus on local techniques of power and 'power relations'.[40] He went yet deeper into the subject in a way still relevant today to considering power patterns in a local church.

Power, Communication and Local Church

Techniques not Definitions

As we have seen Foucault turned his back on those who wanted an easy, simple theory of power. They were too obsessed with defining and capturing power. He especially meant Marxists and liberals though it applied more widely. Such people wanted to gain a quasi-scientific control over power's meaning so that they could gauge and anticipate its effects, even neutralize or overthrow power. But according to Foucault's later reflections that was not the real question in a world of bio-power.[41] After all, it may even turn out that power was not a thing in itself at all.[42] Hence the real question now concerned the observable techniques by which power managed to shape people. We saw that Foucault therefore wanted people to ask about strategies and subtle mechanisms of power. And the clue to these lay with live, local, face to face power encounters at grassroots. To discover the techniques of power that went about, we should trace how people in these groups were submerged and swept around in inequalities and towards norms that excluded some rather than others. Theories from Foucault's own earlier insights also reappeared, especially concerning the power of norms to seduce and subdue.[43] Power advantages did exist. For the games, strategies and tactics at play in local settings sprang from inequalities. Even in local settings unequal power relations ensured that some human beings after all wielded a measure of power over others.[44]

39 Foucault, 'The Subject and Power', pp. 336–7.

40 See however this taking shape in the 1970s: Bernauer, p. 146.

41 Foucault, 'The Subject and Power', p. 337.

42 Foucault, 'The Subject and Power', p. 336.

43 Foucault, 'The Subject and Power', pp. 336–9.

44 Foucault, 'The Subject and Power', p. 337.

The Crucial Nature of Communication in a Group

A further important claim surfaced now, this time concerning the centrality of communication to power games in a social group.[45] We should especially watch out, warned Foucault, for power relations that drew upon the trading of signs. A set of relations through communication played a key role in stabilizing power relations in, say, an institution or a group.[46] School furnished a useful illustration. Here a web of communication systems supported the goals of learning. Here clear power relations were closely tied to strategies of power through such things as 'training techniques' and other ways of obtaining obedience. Orders, procedures and coded signs of compliance held such societies together. And this exchanging of communication applied not only to formal institutions. It occurred not just in workshops, schools or hospitals, but also in any settings with a central discipline, such as the monastic or penitential. Probably, therefore, we can add that this included anywhere that follows a shared discipline of social behaviour – such as a church community united in following the way of Jesus.

We learn from this key technique of power that in micro-groups like church some power holder will always be able to maximize effectiveness by the privileged use of powerful communications systems. This brings the discussion right home to the Christian *koinonia*.

Power Relations, Communications and Christian Community

The relevance of power relations theory to a local community of the *koinonia* seems startling. A typical community of the *koinonia* cannot escape the positive and negative possibilities in power relations. A community ordered around the idea of the *koinonia* it may be but we have seen that it is still a sociological reality. This means that its circulation of communication reflects its power relations and their associated power patterns. Hence the widely varying influence on channels of communication often mirrors forms of inequality in a group, such as class, upbringing, gender, ethnicity, knowledge, age, confidence or wealth etc. Even a fairly monochrome social group contains this economic and cultural diversity, revealing varying backgrounds and fortunes with their consequent 'assymetries' or imbalances. As a result of those disparities, experiences of communication most likely would vary, whether in access to the means of communication (for example to the internet), or proximity to centres of decision-making, or native ease with the community's language and practices or confidence to speak up and question trends.

---

[45] Alistair I. McFadyen, too, is interested in communication in human social relationships but not so much with the role of power relations. All the same, an interesting intersection occurs in Alistair I. McFadyen, *The Call to Personhood: A Christian Theory of the Individual in Social Relationships* (Cambridge, 1990), pp. 140–46.

[46] Foucault, 'The Subject and Power', p. 338.

But do not Jesus-practices and the life of early church set a standard for the offsetting of such inequalities? This is very true in principle, but biblical accounts of early church and power theory equally still draw attention to the fact that power relations and exclusions are real factors in the life of church. And there can be no easy refuge in mere repetition of spiritual slogans simply to mask social reality, not even the celebrated banner: 'all one in Christ Jesus'.[47] For church can still turn out to be a stubborn complex of inequalities of many kinds with varied, subtle, maybe unintended, techniques of exclusion. Visual and formal communication signs, as suggested, might draw lines between insiders and outsiders to varying degrees. Those signs can extend to invitations and exclusions, restricted sub-groups, unconscious favouritism and specialized language. Even handshakes, compliments, hugs and smiles can be rationed out as unintended but meaningful gestures of exclusion.

Moreover, these communication practices may come to ensure or at least support conformity from members. They could even lend support to other features such as surveillance (light or heavy touch), rewards and obedience (obvious or subtle) or pyramidal hierarchy within the community (crass or unobtrusive). Communication practices may even prop up a leadership that seeks control and requires docility from members. These practices may not actually harden into regulations. There may be no written rules for them but they might nevertheless permeate the actual life of the community. In other words, they govern the church of the *koinonia* in its form as a sociological reality.

It seems unlikely that communication disparities will simply fade away by being smothered in 'spiritual activities'. It may even be that such activities will just become useful camouflage, covering up chronic, classic, social symptoms of power imbalances. The *koinonia* implies a participation together in one Spirit and a resulting shared life. A first step in cultivating the true social expression of this shared life is candid recognition of possible inequalities and communications. This is a concern to return to in due course. But in the meantime, we consider further the form that disparities might mean in reality.

Power Relations and 'Power Actions'

An unsettling dictum now appeared in Foucault. It stated that in micro-settings of face to face relations one cannot locate an actual essence called power. In this sense power did not exist! However the claim must be understood wholly in context. It meant only that there was no such thing as power outside of actual relations and especially outside of their concrete actions.[48] Power here did not exist in the

---

47 Compare Moltmann on this: Jürgen Moltmann, *The Source of Life, The Holy Spirit and the Theology of Life* (London, 1997), pp. 57–60, 66–7.

48 Foucault, 'The Subject and Power', p. 340. See John D. Caputo, 'On Not Knowing Who we Are: Madness, Hermeneutics and the Night of Truth in Foucault', in

abstract but only in one party's actions affecting another party's actions.[49] And so in power relations, power could only spring into being when action actually started up. Power occurred when actions affected the actions of others.[50] And all such actions, we remind ourselves, were called into being by natural, pre-existing, unequal power relations. The local setting was the best place to notice all this going on. It was intimate enough for people to recognize sources of influence and corresponding responses. Resistance in some form would always play its own part in the overall outcome of these patterns of power activities,[51] whether active or passive. Even the strongest play for power had to reckon with possible responses or avoidance tactics, perhaps even of inventive and effective strategies coming back at it. So what strong 'power' really amounted to here became plain only in each new interplay of actions and strategies with emerging results.[52]

This explanation pointed to a domain of fluid relations and freedom within a social group. Despite a group's potential devices of mutual inciting, forbidding or constraining, the strongest player was limited. That player only acted upon and through individuals capable of action and reaction. And then again, any superior 'directing', perhaps like that of a family or small group, may have been very modest. A superior maybe wished only to 'structure' the domain where others act, not to shape their very being as subjects. And such a directing conceded one crucial element: *freedom*. In fact, as we noted earlier, at the epicentre of each power relationship, and constantly evoking it, lay freedom for resistance from others and the stubbornness of freedom.[53] Such would be the case, however limited, since this was not a case of sovereign domination.

Earlier, we saw that the making up of people at a local level was for Foucault a sort of unintended by-product of rational yet unpredictable processes. Norms and identities resulted from the endless cumulative effect of influences upon people within the group. They could for instance, grow an unconscious attitude to race or gender. But another fruitful subject for enquiry came out of this. As we have seen the actual mechanics of all this was important and therefore also the meaning of local politics and a group's direction. The many, diverse 'actions upon actions' produce unforeseen results for a group's goals and achievements too, for there is no mastermind that can control everything. The conclusions to be drawn for analysis of power relations were simple enough for Foucault. They showed

---

James Bernauer and Jeremy Carrette (eds), *Michel Foucault and Theology: The Politics of Religious Experience* (London, 2004), 117–39, p. 130.

49 Admittedly, taken in isolation from bio-power this would support Pasewark's complaint against classical theory that it only theorized occasional power. But bio-power speaks of more.

50 Foucault, 'The Subject and Power', p. 340.

51 Foucault, 'The Subject and Power', pp. 342–3.

52 Foucault, 'The Subject and Power', p. 340.

53 Foucault termed 'agonism' a provocation between different influences and mechanisms rather than a confrontation: Foucault, 'The Subject and Power', p. 342.

that it was necessary to scrutinize the interplay of strategies emerging from local power relations.[54] This should be done without regard to personal motives. True, psychological insight would be enlightening but the theorist of power can only observe definite actions upon the actions of others along with actual observable outcomes, in other words, the behaviours, the strategies. This is all that concerns power analysis.

All in all, we are left with a beguiling, but probably overstated and over elaborate, theory of local power relations. It was not found to be without its problems. One alleged flaw is that this late focus upon local strategies without regard to moral ideologies or intentions was a strange feature for someone like Foucault to espouse. This was because it placed him alongside none other than the notorious Machiavelli, and like him showed an interest mainly in strategies and tactics not a moral end to power.[55]

Another obvious concern is that some power bids could be less neutral and so more devastating in social groups than his theory noticed. Sometimes a social institution, especially an extended family or a faith-group, can be completely integral to a person's happiness. Local power practices can therefore deeply damage the wellbeing of some members and indeed be dangerous. And what is more, in this setting any resisting strategies might well collapse before a well planned social coup. Nevertheless, it is probably often true that the final outcomes of power patterns and cross currents do differ from those intended even by a strong group, precisely as suggested by Foucault. Moreover, social groups probably do function most often as described in his power relations theory. It is easy to see this, once he has drawn our attention to its hidden character. And so we are brought to the key concern of this long analysis, namely the implications for church community.

Power Patterns and Church Community

We have seen that at first Foucault chiefly had his eye on how interacting strategies within groups inscribed norms within people's sense of identity regarding such matters as sexuality, gender or class. But equally we saw that in his later writings he followed through his claim that his real interest was not really in any particular norms but in the actual interplay of the strategies themselves. He was not just examining how the norms of local traditions connected with norms in a wider disciplinary power. Rather his main concern focused on *the very processes themselves*. We should start with the mechanism and strategies, he insisted, not with definitions or moralities.

That focus opens up fuller possibilities for insight into healthy dynamics for any local church community. Admittedly, question marks may still linger over

54 Foucault, 'The Subject and Power', p. 329.

55 Stewart R. Clegg, *Frameworks of Power* (London, 1990), pp. 5–6.

Foucault's power theory. For instance, he seemed to stray for a moment from his earlier belief in power as ever present and pervasive. He appeared to understate the place of constant subterranean power patterns by stressing occasional eruptions when stronger individuals actually act upon the actions of others. This was an episodic view of power, that Pasewark shrewdly lamented, and it seems too limited for understanding grassroots realities. For diverse power relations and their resulting patterns must surely lie continually below the surface in local groups if they really are intrinsic to social relations as Foucault suggested. They must surely influence thought and attitude not just in odd moments when stronger actions out in the open 'act upon the actions' of weaker players. Power streams and patterns, for instance, can lie out of sight for long periods, perhaps surfacing only when provoked. These streams, we know, are frequently hidden from view in secret attitudes such as deep prejudices about class, gender or race. Of course, many other unconscious attitudes can also be completely free of negativity or ill-intent in church life, taking the form, for instance, of admiration or even inborn deference. Moreover, these inner tendencies in members of the community might in the end only play lightly upon the relationships involved, but maybe only until reignited by a debate, crisis or conflict. Then they could show their true colours.

Similarly, Foucault's theorizing seems too relaxed about the real possibility of one stronger party or sub group finally gaining ascendancy over others. An effective centre of power is always possible, even in setting up the norms that mark a community. It is not perhaps like sovereign power or even bio-power but it can be a stranglehold all the same. Additionally, and more importantly, can it really be that these various power strategies, colliding and colluding, are all that there is in a group's social relationships? Are there no other possible sources and ingredients to these strategies in human relations?

This latter consideration brings us right to the question of principles integral to the notion of the *koinonia* community. Here we might find factors that could counterbalance other patterns and behaviours within a group. To be truly additional these factors would differ from power relations by not being immediately and naturally present to social groups in the same way differences of status are. But they would all the same acquire similar sociological effectiveness if they were learned, internalized and resulted in concrete actions. Then they would take their place alongside power impulses and perhaps strategically balance them. Status differences and resulting power relations tend towards discrimination, and strategies of conflict and disintegration. But *koinonia* principles tend towards deep inner unity and integrity on the community journey. When internalized, they foster a truly common, shared life and the softening of power relations. When they achieve this, it could be argued that at last ideal church and church of social reality have touched each other. Hence for Christian life together, patterns of the Jesus way set definite boundaries for the interplay of local power strategies and may be as central to the intrinsic nature of group dynamics as power relations are.

In summary, if churches are to be healthy then, they will surely attend carefully to at least three kinds of power which are ignored at a group's peril. First, we have natural, unequal power relations nestling right there in the midst of the community and which result from naturally arising differences in status. Secondly, there will be the resulting episodic but frequent actions of power. Experience suggests that these interplays of unequal strategies may be frequent and are often hidden to the casual eye. Thirdly, sometimes power relations can harden into domination and submissiveness, assisted by the feebleness or docility of an opposition. It seems critical for a faith community's leadership to take all these three classes of power seriously. If the third class of power in particular is mythologized, dreamt away or treated casually, the way is then open to the tightening grip of a stronger power strategy. The most sinister outcome of that result goes by the name of power abuse. Only the health of a fourth category, internalized *koinonia* principles, can counterbalance all these three and help to keep the feet of the community on the way of Jesus.

Conclusions on Foucault's Power Relations

For 'final' Foucault therefore, getting at what goes on in power relations requires concentration on a number of factors. These, of course, require translation from Foucault's theory into real life, and accordingly we make some suggestions. First, groups should be aware of the naturally varied status lines within any group, however egalitarian such a group appears. These lines undergird power relationships, and for example could consist of linguistic or cultural separators, disparities of competence or know-how, varying levels of wealth or health, levels of self-confidence, or differences of family and class background. In addition, certain motives heighten those imbalances, for instance desire for admiration, profits, privileges or celebrity. Moreover, only vigilance can spot actual strategies for lending aid to the continuation of imbalances, such as surveillance, regulations, social tactics, hectoring or other forms of speech. All this will be filtered through the special way power relations work in any institution, uniquely comfortable in its own home setting and culture. Moreover this account is credible only because 'power' is versatile, assuming as it does many guises and accommodating many adjustments.[56]

Surprisingly, Foucault's analysis did not imply freedom for modern local groups from the reach of disciplinary power. Such groups were still exposed to the wider, circulatory process of being 'governmentalized'.[57] Earlier theories remained of subtle state and cultural shaping by an all-encompassing bio-power found in every nook and cranny of organized life.

The application to a church community continues to be plain. As suggested, church cannot afford to pretend that it is immune to the sociological reality of underlying status distinctions. Nor can it assume that these do not set up any kind of power relations that will come out unconsciously or otherwise first in

56 All developed in 'Foucault, 'The Subject and Power', pp. 344–5.

57 Foucault, 'The Subject and Power', p. 345.

power relations, then in patterns of thought and finally in actions, behaviours and strategies. What is more, the wider chain of church practices and power strategies will be fed and determined by those active in the smaller world of local church communities. The health of the larger, representative *koinonia* depends upon that of the smaller. But a local community, we suggest, should have confidence in the *koinonia* principles of transparency, openness, care for the weaker and cherishing of a just unity. These too have an immense sociological power when internalized. *Koinonia*'s principles can thus enter the domain of internal power streams and of actual actions and strategies, counterbalancing or offsetting their natural forces.

Feminism and Power Relations

To understand feminism's relation to power theory, the earlier stages need to be visited briefly once more. Feminism's response first engaged with 'early' Foucault – or 'First Foucault' as Ivan Strenski calls his early writings.[58] For that Foucault it was power, we recall, that produced knowledge, determining what became publicly-owned knowledge or an established 'truth'. So Foucault, we saw, first fingered disciplinary power as the real producer or determinant of forms of public knowledge.[59] It was this knowledge and the 'norms' it created that becomes internalized by individuals in society. Although there was no single culprit behind the process there was plenty to be concerned about when thinking about this all-encompassing 'power over'.

Feminists welcomed the analysis. Wasn't this what the movement had been telling people all the time? The feminist project of identity politics was dedicated to exposing how gender identities were social constructs. But now these identities were moulded not just by the law and politics but according to Foucault from every direction in society.[60] This also showed that inability to discern gender inequalities and other inequities arose from the internalized knowledge manufactured by public institutions and from wider cultural conditioning. In this way different manifestations of 'power over' were understood.

For many women writers it could only be good to have such a state of affairs dragged out into the glare of the spotlight by a celebrated cultural critic. Others worried that now the self, the 'subject', perhaps did not exist because of such all-encompassing, identity-shaping power. But this was bad because the free 'self' was the only hope of resistance to domination and of struggles for freedom.

---

[58] Ivan Strenski, 'Religion, Power and Final Foucault', *Journal of the American Academy of Religion*, 66/2 (1998): 345–67.

[59] For instance, in Michel Foucault, 'Truth and Power', in J. D. Faubion (ed.), *Power* (London 2002), 111–33, pp. 130–33.

[60] Susan Hekman, 'Feminist Identity Politics: Transforming the Political' in Dianna Taylor and Karen Vintges (eds), *Feminism and the Final Foucault* (Urbana, 2004), 197–213 pp. 197–8.

If Foucault was to be taken seriously, this self now was maybe no more than a transient product of bio-power. Although that innovation itself was also to become honoured in feminism before long, some feminists felt alarmed, since any demythologizing of the self could only dishearten action for justice and freedom. The struggle seemed based on a fiction about selves. A relentless campaigner for the women's movement, Nancy Fraser was one of the more critical voices that called early Foucault to account. She complained that it was hard to swallow a disciplinary power that ensured nothing but docility and neutralized resistance in advance.[61] And with such disputes the matter might have lain. Many works on Foucault in fact give the impression that this is the abiding essence of Foucault's thought. But he was to speak again and once more to disturb the waters.

The Impact of Power Relations Theory among Feminists

Foucault's later turn to power relations at grassroots was for feminism both disruptive and exhilarating, for it proved a double-edged sword. As we have seen, being now concerned with local settings Foucault stated more explicitly that 'power' was subtle, fluid and dispersed.[62] As already explored above, it swirled around a variety of participations, mechanisms and strategies, having no command and control centre, and so no precise villain to resist.

As a result of Foucault's change of direction, Joyce Schuld[63] awarded him the well-earned title of 'reckless spoiler'. This seems an apt summary, for some sharp feminist viewpoints sensed a cause to fear not just for the feminist struggle but for all movements concerned with justice and liberation. Janet Ransom was typical, in observing apprehensively the passing by this time of the zero-sum political model.[64] Her hesitation was understandable. Of course, the zero-sum metaphor of power suited quite well Marxist and neo-Marxist critiques of power-capitalism.

---

[61] Nancy Fraser, cited by Aurelia Armstrong, 'Foucault and Feminism', in *Internet Encyclopaedia of Philosophy* (http://www.iep.utm.edu/f/foucfem accessed 10.01.07), p. 1. See also Foucault's handling of resistance and domination in Michel Focuault, 'Body/Power' in C. Gordon (ed.), *Michel Foucault: Power/Knowledge* (Brighton,1980), pp. 55–62. Also see the article in the same volume: pp. 109–33 (Foucault, 'Truth and Power').

[62] This language startlingly, is mirrored in quite different literature suggesting that local church power even hinders the proper dispersion of local church to the wider community. See for instance James Thwaites, *The Church Beyond the Congregation: The Strategic Role of the Church in the Postmodern Era* (Carlisle, 1999), and *Renegotiating the Church Contract* (Carlisle, 2003).

[63] Joyce Schuld, 'Augustine, Foucault, and the Politics of Imperfection', in James Bernauer and Jeremy Carrette (eds), *Michel Foucault and Theology: The Politics of Religious Experience* (London, 2004), 57–74, p. 61.

[64] Foucault cited throughout in Janet Ransom, 'Feminism, Difference and Discourse: The Limits of Discursive Analysis for Feminism', in Caroline Ramazanoğlu (ed.), *Up*

More importantly, for feminism it chimed well with attacks on hierarchy, patriarchy and consequently all exploitation of the humanity and nature. There was obviously a domination system at large and cultural critics must help to resist and overthrow its many-faced villainy. Campaigns must aim to sweep away the several encrusted levels of power and control still firmly in place. Ladders of class, gender and race must tumble into a new, liberal equality.

Varied theologies for liberation, too, assumed that the world needed a corrective disempowerment and re-empowerment with a resulting new, healthier balance for human relations and aspirations. These claims tended to remain anchored to a zero-sum view of power. To give up that proven framework for protest and advocacy was a big ask for many. This was especially the case for those with a partial debt to the Hebrew and Christian Scriptures and to a faith ethic, even more so where the welfare of the vulnerable and oppressed were at stake.

But Foucault had seemingly come to compromise the freedom and justice bandwagon.[65] Certain feminists had detected in his voice a destabilizing cluster of ideas. According to the new notion, the expression of power in these local settings was not about ideological battles for equality, nor could one spot the obvious heroes battling against clear villains.[66] Power in relations instead was pervasive, neutral and altogether natural. It freely flowed round and through all relationships as a necessary invisible aspect of it. It was a tag that linked one person to another. And the power relations themselves were dynamic, and so not predictably stable.[67] At such a micro-level this world of power relations produced an active network of forces flowing from no particular centre,[68] a noise of competing 'power-saturated' truths.[69]

---

against Foucault: Explorations of Some Tensions Between Foucault and Feminism (London, 1993), pp. 123–46.

65 Not quite surrendered according to the lucid arguments of Johanna Oksala, *Foucault on Freedom* (Cambridge, 2005), pp. 176–8. On this view dominations may be minimized.

66 Caroline Ramazanoğlu, 'Introduction' in Caroline Ramazanoğlu (ed.), *Up against Foucault: Explorations of Some Tensions Between Foucault and Feminism* (London, 1993), 1–27, p. 20.

67 James Bernauer and Jeremy Carrette, 'Introduction' in James Bernauer and Jeremy Carrette (eds), *Michel Foucault and Theology: The Politics of Religious Experience* (London, 2004), p. 6.

68 Susan Bordo, 'Feminism, Foucault and the Politics of the Body', in Caroline Ramazanoğlu (ed.), *Up against Foucault: Explorations of Some Tensions Between Foucault and Feminism* (London, 1993), 179–202, p. 191.

69 Ransom, p. 129.

Feminism Divided yet United

This one proposal from Foucault could now be perceived, potentially, to dissolve theories of the battle for power and empowerment (in fact 'dialectical theory' itself), for, to some, it dismantled neat domination scenarios. It dismissed ideological struggles for justice in local groups, and sidelined long-accepted processes of resistance, resolution, closure and fresh progress. As Susan Bordo summarized Foucault,[70] modern power should be seen as non-authoritarian, non-conspiratorial, non-orchestrated, especially on the ground in face to face group power relations. Hence simple and rigid claims, like those about male domination (patriarchy), suddenly fell under suspicion.[71] A revolution against revolution was taking place.

Theology seemed little interested in this further Foucault and in these developments from the influential world of critical studies. Even less had his work been seen as an aid to analysing power within church. However, feminist writers *were* wide awake and keeping watch, alert to new, perceived subversive implications of his work. Jeremy Carrette had already observed not only that Foucault had aggravated his earlier gender-blind analysis which already caused much concern and deliberation among feminists. Now he had also undermined the humanist platform upon which the liberal emancipatory politics of feminism stood, both ideological and in familiar social groups.[72]

The ideas of further Foucault were beginning to circulate in feminism. The post-Foucault feminist internal debate eventually burst to the surface with vigour in the important volume, *Up Against Foucault*, edited by Caroline Ramazanoğlu.[73] He already enjoyed the approval of many feminist writers, at least for his exposé of bio-power (for instance over norms of sexuality). Some now responded well to his further explanatory moves[74] and some even embraced the unexpected collapse of the patriarchy hypothesis that resulted. This latter amazing response arose precisely because power relations theory allegedly freed up feminists for action in joint local struggles.[75] The power that really mattered was the power of freedom emanating from more tangible relations in local situations. Dianna Taylor claimed that Foucault still conserved emancipatory politics, even in an age now stripped of trusted foundations for thought and action. Foucault thus offered a pragmatic approach to life in this new situation and so had not yet sounded the death-knell

---

70 Bordo, p. 190.

71 Ramazanoğlu, 'Introduction', p. 9.

72 Jeremy Carrette, *Foucault and Religion: Spiritual Corporality and Political Spirituality* (London, 2000), p. 64.

73 See references above to Caroline Ramazanoğlu (ed.), *Up against Foucault: Explorations of Some Tensions Between Foucault and Feminism* (London, 1993).

74 Ramazanoğlu, 'Introduction', pp. 21–2.

75 M. E. Bailey, 'Foucauldian Feminism: Contesting Bodies, Sexuality and Identity', in Caroline Ramazanoğlu (ed.), *Up against Foucault: Explorations of Some Tensions Between Foucault and Feminism* (London, 1993), 99–122, p. 119.

of conviction politics.[76] Hence, within the new Foucauldian age some feminists considered it possible to preserve old social and political valuables regarding power.

But other contributors were disturbed by the apparent sidelining in this Foucault of clear-cut language about the realities of domination, resistance and liberation. Within the same volume, Jean Grimshaw cited several critiques from feminist writers.[77] Her own concern was that the de-centring of power in the new Foucault undermined morale in activists for justice and liberation in their situations and networks. To see power as merely natural, would blur or even destroy the distinction between benign and malign exercise of power. At the same time, however, Foucault's bombshell had not completely wiped traditional feminism off the map. As late as 1996 Anna Hamar, as just one example, still recognized the claim that patriarchy was the root of all evils: a multi-layered system of subjugation and oppression holding all other such systems together, but oppressing women most particularly.[78] Although such doubts about Foucault are not in the ascendancy, they still represent an important point of view.

Christian Power Relations in the Light of Feminist Caution

This dilemma for feminism is the precise point where Foucault's later writing is problematic for church too as a community of equals in a life together. Authentic local church is caught up in wider justice agendas just as feminist communities are. Foucault's turn to fluid, indeterminate power seems to undermine clear-cut villains in such evils today as global exploitation, unjust trade, slavery and other forms of domination. Hence, what church seemed *not* to need was the intervention of Foucault seemingly announcing that a local church's activism in these matters was based on a myth.

Consequently a contradiction arises when church today looks back to the earliest Christian communities for a lead and example, because there it sees only a zero-sum environment. For the first churches belonged to an ancient world which revered chains of command and power as quasi-divine. Power as domination and hierarchy fully supported a socially and religiously privileged élite at the top of a pyramid of power. Zero-sum assumptions abounded. On the surface, it was difficult for churches then to imagine any other form of society in the Roman world. Hence, a fluid understanding of power relations such as Foucault's would

---

76 Taylor, 'Foucault's Ethos', p. 271.

77 Jean Grimshaw, 'Practices of Freedom', in Caroline Ramazanoğlu (ed.), *Up against Foucault: Explorations of Some Tensions Between Foucault and Feminism* (London, 1993), pp. 51–72.

78 Citing the Asian writer, A. Gnanadason: Anna Karin Hamar in 'Some Understanding of Power in Feminist Liberation Theologies', *Feminist Theology*, 12 (1996): 10–20, p. 12. She goes on to cite several other feminist writers in support.

have carried wildly unrealistic Utopian overtones in such conditions. The zero-sum nature of the world was barely open to doubt. Every possession of wealth crippled someone else, and power was absolute at many points in society. The fledgling communities did not and could not ignore the clear-cut domination picture of good and evil powers all around them, nor the sombre tones of that picture. Recent studies on the book of Revelation interpreted as a subversive criticism of the Roman Empire bear this out.[79] Obviously that 'badly-cut cake' model of power in an unjust world was a pressing reality in the early experience of churches. Leaders of the new community on the way of Jesus most certainly retained a clarity concerning absolute domination. A sense of heroes and villains prevailed only too clearly, and here mighty and impotent players engaged in the brutal Roman game of power. However, writers of the Christian Scriptures set themselves against giving house space to such a zero-sum world within the new 'households of faith', namely the communities of Jesus (1 Cor 6.1–8; 11.21, 22, Eph 2.19; 6.9; Col 3.11; Jas 2.1–7).

Koinonia principles for the community of Jesus were meant to undermine inevitability in the reign of dominative power. The early accounts of Jesus reveal glints of a coming quiet revolution in the new family of faith amid domination. Jesus endorsed in his own messianic calling the Jewish prophetic promise that the prisoner would be set free, the oppressed be liberated (Lk 4,17,18). Hopes for the more distant future belonged to this movement and were expected to shape it. The centres of power were about to be overturned, and subversive new disparities were soon to emerge, neutralizing the old ones. The rich and powerful, came the warning, would find it hard to enter the kingdom. Religious leaders claiming the high moral ground were in reality doomed unless first they humbled themselves. In the new kingdom, the first would be the last and the last be first. A new fluidity to power relations was already on the move in the community of Jesus. For example in the Gospel narrative, Martha seemed to represent a very traditional, female domestic role-model, but for one moment Jesus wanted her to experience the life of his rabbinical circle along with her already enlightened sister Mary, even though this was normally a male preserve. Jesus was mixing with and drawing to him disreputable and despised elements. True, the apostleship was male and formed a continuing inner group to be revitalized by the resurrection of Jesus. But in the most authoritative narratives of the early community, the prime witnesses to that resurrection were not the male apostles but women.

So a new fluidity of status was springing up in a mixed-gender inner group of 120 people on the Day of Pentecost, not to mention the Spirit's particular power descending upon 'daughters' as well as 'sons' in the dramatic narrative of Luke-Acts. Women began to emerge in key roles within the biblical narrative. It was a kingdom that would go not to the strong but to the vulnerable, the poor (Lk 6.20), those who served others. Everything would be turned upside down (Lk

[79] See for instance, Richard Bauckham, *The Climax of Prophecy: Studies on the Book of Revelation* (Edinburgh 1993).

6.20,21), disturbing a clearly cruel and unjust zero-sum regime. For the founding beliefs spoke of radical equality in the communities of the way of Jesus. A quiet revolution was bubbling away in the young Christian communities, one that could only be destined through the years to 'ascend' and to disturb sovereign power. The equality of slave and master in the community of Jesus for instance was surely a revolution difficult for Roman society to stomach. These new communities were being encouraged to receive hard readjustments of power and to let them mark its life together. The founding Christian Scriptures confronted the old world of layered society with new, apparently absurd values in the new community, including such ideals as humility, truth, equality and justice.

And so, new things were happening as the Christian way of the *koinonia* began to subvert the old dominations and balances of power. For in this way the communities of Jesus were gently beginning to loosen the rivets of the empire and subvert the norms of social hierarchy. Hence, the Hebrew prophets' concerns for justice remained in place but also a new, alternative, de-centring and fluidity of power emerged in the communities of the *koinonia*. Varied gifts and offices appeared along with numerous roles for all to play, even slaves. This much can be agreed with Antoinette Clark Wire[80] who is nevertheless critical of later turns taken in the early Christian communities.[81] We note that Sandra Polaski's carefully balanced estimate of developments is more positive than Wire's (see more in Chapter 9).[82]

And yet, church can be sobered by the sight of Foucault's onslaught being able to divide feminism. If a movement that is confidently and clearly addressing power relations becomes at first so unsettled by Foucault, then acceptance of fluid, complex power along also with a zero-sum model of power is a challenge for church too. And more important still, this is a challenge to face the reality of both classes of power and be prepared to think and act accordingly. Moreover, as we have seen, church must still seek ways to counterbalance natural power differentials within its community, using principles of *koinonia* that include: justice and freedom in the example of Jesus; a common partaking of the Spirit of Jesus; a Jesus-like ease with the fullest possible transparency in church life; a fully empowered and gifted community working together.

After all, then, without renouncing a true awareness of domination patterns in the world, the theory of power relations still speaks to a church's own life together. Local power relations and strategies are indeed as fluid as Foucault says and constantly in need of balancing qualities, just as we have seen. But then it would be important for churches to know this, and to know it very well. It would mean a less simple world than before, as well as learning to cope with the strong

---

80 Antoinette Clark Wire, 'The Politics of the Assembly in Corinth', in Richard Horsley (ed.), *Paul and Politics. Ekkleisa, Israel, Imperium, Interpretation: Essays in Honour of Krister Stendahl* (Harrisburg, 2000), pp. 124–9.

81 See further Chapter 9.

82 Sandra Hack Polaski, *Paul and the Discourse of Power* (Sheffield, 1999).

cross currents of power in Christian congregations using a more complex analysis than before of what causes conflict. Such enlightenment would also search for positive possibilities connected to power patterns present in local church.[83] And as we have discovered, additional strategies appropriate to the common life of a local church as *koinonia* may be internalized. These can then foster the health of authentic community by qualifying naturally driven power patterns arising from power relations.

Of course, later Foucault did not simply replace one type of power cleanly by another. If Paras[84] and others are correct, earlier, disciplinary and possibly sovereign power remained on Foucault's radar. We saw that disciplinary, all-encompassing power drew life from local groups and institutions. There must still have been heroes and villains, individuals perhaps or maybe sub-groups. And power streams were stronger and more widely based than mere ideological bias. These power streams represent subterranean interests, aspirations and fears, even in a church community on the way of Jesus. But now the dangers in such streams could be offset, we saw, by principles of transparency, justice and caring internalized in an authentic following of the way of Jesus.

Church and Power Relations

Power Relations: A Positive Adventure

It has been a long journey, questing after the shift of thinking on power in the mid 1970s. But it has spotlighted issues about power that interrogate our understanding of Christian community at a profound level. The first lesson, however, must be seen as encouraging for all groups, including faith-communities. Perhaps power relations theory has outlined a theory of synergy that turns out to be very useful for local church in particular. It is not a notion of perfect and efficient cooperation but the boosted effectiveness that comes from diversity, not to mention collision and collusion. The varied forms of 'power over' in a micro-community do indeed contain possibilities for self-destruction. But, if guided by internalized higher values and aims, 'power over' mainly feeds into positive 'power to'. That is, power as a 'communication of efficacy' leads to positive outcomes. Most of all, this synergy out of diversity might be most significant in various ventures of mission, worship and community. Effecting such 'power to' turns out to be a real adventure, true enough.

However, if Foucault is correct, the interaction of unequal power patterns is a process never quite fully predicted. And the final outcome itself, therefore, may not be completely managed from one centre, although perhaps it is more managed

[83] Schuld, 'Augustine, Foucault, and the Politics of Imperfection', p. 60.

[84] Subtly suggested by Paras, pp. 95, 154–7. See also Foucault, 'Two Lectures' throughout, appearing at roughly the same time as *History of Sexuality*.

than Foucault envisaged. For example, one can imagine a centre for serving the homeless or lonely somehow emerging from the clashing and combining interaction of power strategies in a church that is united otherwise in following the way of Jesus. Or again, a shared spirituality or set of worship patterns surfaces through the maze of taste and compromise. Or an agreement of words finds favour amid political exchanges, and becomes a united text on behalf of those who are oppressed and bereft of advocates. The question of course is: but how? And the answer, we have seen, is that a set of distinguishing values of life together on the Jesus way has provided strategies in addition to power plays. We have admitted that these additional values are counterintuitive, distinctive and perhaps carry a high price tag. They also depend in turn on equally distinctive theological resources some of which will occupy our attention later.

Despite the appearance of randomness then, leaders could conceivably still 'structure', or set limits to, 'fields of action' of members in the power games of the community. Power relations theory has predicted that power strategies will certainly arise with their conflicts and tactics.[85] The task of leaders would be to practise and extol the counterintuitive values of the Jesus way. This service at least requires injecting transparency, candour and opennness into the mix of strategies. These standards spring only from the established faith practices and deep beliefs of the whole community, to which the members have already committed themselves as followers of the Jesus way.

Perhaps on the wider front leaders will also grow more sensitive and practised in spotting a community's, sometimes unintentional, deference to the wider encompassing reach of bio-power. This can happen to any group through political, bureaucratic, media and cultural conditioning. Lapses here can be serious, affecting a community's commitment to the Jesus way, in indifference to injustice, suffering and complacency nurtured by the *status quo*.

Power Relations: Not Bad but Certainly Dangerous

Granted, power relations theory's chief flaw is to underestimate the emergence and possible ascendancy of any dominant party in social groups today. And if the theory were correct, splits from churches would be rare. In truth, when groups form with initially unequal power relations, several outcomes are possible including the nightmare scenario. The strong, through skill, class superiority, commitment or money for instance, really can take a hold on a local church. A sweeping result can equally arise from strong clerical masterfulness or campaigns from influential members. At any rate some power bids may become more or less successful. All the same, Foucault cautions us of something real: the apparent success for a dominant force in a church's life may not turn out to deliver what was expected. In modern,

[85] Foucault, cited by Barry Smart in 'Foucault, Levinas and the Subject of Responsibility' in Jeremy W. Moss (ed.), *The Later Foucault: Politics and Philosophy* (London, 1998), 78–92, p. 81.

'free' societies splits are always an option. The most powerful player is left with an empty victory or perhaps at least with something less than expected. Moreover, the domination strategy may have contained the seeds of its own destruction and implosion at a later stage. So power relations theory still has something to say to a *koinonia* community. It has still spotlighted the fact that every Christian community really does potentially contain a nest of possibilities arising from the many natural differentials between its members. And from these imbalances stem sometimes hidden unequal power relations which could easily trigger conflicting power strategies.

Leaders in church, it seems then, face pastoral challenges implicit in the unavoidable presence of unequal power relations in a community. It is just the very character of such inequalities to lie beneath the surface. They potentially host unpredictable power moves but also undefined forms of freedoms for resistance. And sometimes the power relations and power patterns stemming ultimately from diverse backgrounds never quite go away. The implication is that leaders at various levels in a church should not be taken by surprise at their presence. The unpredictable collision or collusion of forces, wills, and avoidance tactics confronts all leaders in every local church community and its sub-groups. Some, perhaps, will say that they become only too quickly aware of troublesome dynamics behind the façade. But maybe the sociological realism in power relations theory should help them further. With its help they might more easily accept why such factors are so persistent. It could also prompt leaders to take more seriously the resources of faith available for managing the cross currents of power, and more will be said about this later.

Earlier we recognized that a company of people journeying together on the way of Jesus could freely embrace some legitimate boundaries around its members' fields of action, suggested or urged by leaders. This move however requires that a leadership does not invent limits which explicitly go beyond a community's agreed values. Suggested boundaries would only be those essential to the community's declared commitment. They would concern only those voluntary intelligent matters of self-commitment which are intrinsic to their common faith. This may sound an easy canon to apply, but it is frequently breached by leaders in cunning and subtle ways – of which moral and spiritual blackmail is the most popular form of circumvention. It is breached by so-called 'heavy shepherding', the practice of monitoring and directing personal decisions in the realms of career, home and other major life choices. A similar offence occurs with overly explicit directions on church attendance, participation, financial contributions, conduct of rites such as funerals and weddings, appropriate dress and faith-sharing, to name but a few. Similarly the demand of ascetic requirements contravenes the principle. As even the formidable panoply of authority and power in Catholic renaissance times conceded, the ministerial authority was itself subject to legal codes and could not extend beyond the purpose of the Christian community for which it was originally designed.[86] In the ensuing reformation movement, where ministerial authority remained formidable, it was frequently only a limited field of authority, designed to serve the church community and valid only there.[87]

A yet further possibility remains for church. With the permissions of power relations theory before it, the whole community has opportunity to find its own, unique 'transgressive voice' that meets and disrupts the downward pressure of the 'norms' culture. On the strength of this encouragement a church community could rise up against local injustice, suffering and harmful complacency fostered by the *status quo*. It will become more practised in spotting a community's vulnerability to political, bureaucratic, media and cultural conditioning.

Foucault's theory of power's ever new configurations and incarnations also proves more or less correct regarding any particular church during its lifetime. The breaking of one imbalanced state of power in church often only introduces a new rearrangement of power imbalance. Power relations theory on the fluidity of power relations is confirmed by cycles of history in church life. They reveal a story of pendulum swings. Sometimes there are unstable, and therefore genuine, relations of power. And other times, as even Foucault is sometimes forced to recognize, imbalances become firm, if not exactly fixed, in a winning strategy of one over another.[88]

cycles

> The happy-clappy brigade have gone at last – but the dreary liturgists have taken over!
>
> Those stifling traditionalists have left – save us from the overbearing fundamentalists!

Power relations theory hence continues to strike a chord despite its flaws. We have seen that a community on the way of Jesus simply does not live above such power patterns as if power imbalances couldn't possibly touch something as holy and well-intentioned as church. Power theory suggests that such relations are inscribed deep in human relations, and they are invisible only to the stronger player. As a result, the healthy choice seems to be that of candidly recognizing the sociological facts of power relations. Only then is it possible to explore realistically what it is that shapes hidden power bids in a church. Hopefully, this way leaders can anticipate and balance power patterns by means of the overarching values of the Jesus way. Denial is hardly an option. Church, therefore, cannot afford to cloud the underlying truths of pilgrim church, namely church as a sociological reality. Even in the most exemplary church communities, the reality described here still applies, and shallow cosiness can obscure that reality. Church in the diverse world of modern Western society (possibly church anywhere) naturally harbours disparities of wealth, status, health, competence and know-how as well as possibly

86 G. R. Evans, *Problems of Authority in the Reformation Debates* (Cambridge, 1992), p. 230.

87 Evans, p. 230.

88 Foucault, 'The Subject and Power', p. 347.

linguistic and cultural differences. Paul's letters to Corinth betray such differences even in his time. And his outline of values of the Jesus way in 1 Corinthians 13 points the path to safety. But initially the key requirement is to recognize freely that power imbalances are functioning rather than being convinced by a sheen of superficial niceness. Frequently, instinctive denial of church's pilgrim character silently masks the dangers and gives opportunity for unnecessary irruptions and reconfigurations. A culture of gentle, fluid, honest and genuinely changing relations of interaction and influence are a church's best chance of staving off the rise of a centre of power.

Power relations theory also issues a caution against easy judgmentalism that often leads to power bids and triggers strategies. The theory urges that the actual *effects* of power relations (actions upon actions) should not be confused with the varied *motives* and intentions of the players. Outright victory, the theory concedes, could indeed be an intention. But not necessarily, since the outcomes of one person's actions upon another person's actions in the complex interplay of strategies may or may not be the one intended. Consequently there should be no overconfident speculation or overhasty deciphering of intended goals. The Christian community must disentangle these two questions of motive and outcome, in any journeying together. Care here, one imagines, would especially be important in crisis management, whether for reconciliation or for seeking out the truth behind tense relationships. And equally it would apply in more positive settings, for example the establishment of equality between members in a particular situation.

Power Relations: Passive Strategies

The notion of power in a face to face community as fluid, not easy to locate, and therefore without clear villains – this concept has no official status in most theologies of church order except sometimes to affirm freedom of conscience. Yet, recognition of it would be crucial. For surely much power in the life of a local community of the *koinonia* is just like that, simply *not* official. It is *not* organized or listed in any classification of church order. Accordingly when it takes the form of dispersed resistance it tends to be invisible except when its full effects are finally felt. People vote silently with their feet. Power may take its victims through non-intervention or abstaining, argues Steven Lukes.[89] Hence, proposed projects are welcomed officially but ignored in actual practice. Power and resistance (sometimes quite gentle resistance) are being quietly exercised. Apathy may strangely direct affairs through to their end. Docility becomes a mightier enemy than open revolt.

For the sake of argument, let's assume that the above survey of power relations theory has some merit. It would at least mean that sociologically it is always possible that the varied actions and strategies in a community could actually

---

[89] Steven Lukes, 'Power and the Battle for Minds and Hearts', *Millennium: Journal of International Studies*, 33/3 (2005): 477–93, p. 480.

converge where the new internalized values of honesty, humility and preference for the other softens power strategies. Collision and collusion are not the only possibilities. The presence of power relations born of inequalities thankfully need not always spell conflict and struggle. Yet churches have not always recognized this. Gillian Evans, after commending the sixteenth century reformers for their shift from clericalism towards the priesthood of believers, spots that still not all processes were a pretty sight thereafter. A negative view of authority as priestly-clerical, she argues, pushed reformers sometimes into a power struggle in resolving issues. Fluidity of opinion received short shrift. Ensuring decision in consensus among the faithful on occasion received only light attention even from reformers.[90] Inequalities, power relations and interplay of forces can, if qualified by *koinonia* values, indeed produce a common mind and responses free of hostility. The common mind can consist of these values just as effectively as it unavoidably includes assertions, plays for control and other dubious moves. But a wise leadership in a local group will assume the actual possibility for both.

It transpires, then, that healthy church lives from two principles: the simple fact of forms of 'power over' and the balancing and more final possibility of an outcome of positive 'power to', the power of a good communication of efficacy.

[90] Evans, p. 256.

Chapter 6
Strategies, Church and Freedom

Power, Care and Groups

We have reached a stage where we need to explore further factors that along with power patterns affect behaviour in micro-groups (such groups for Foucault ranging in size from schools down to families). We have already had reason to question the seeming claim that power relations can pretty well account entirely for behaviour patterns within any such modern grassroots community. We saw for example the possible impact of *koinonia* principles that are made personal and internal by individual members. When turning into active patterns of behaviour these values counterbalance and perhaps restrain power patterns. As it happens, the issue has already attracted attention elsewhere in critical thought. For in a lucid discussion and with careful reference to Foucault, Richard Lynch establishes for us that Foucault's wrestling with the subject of power in the 1970s does not require that he saw only power patterns at work in human relationships.[1] Lynch for his part does not even concede that power is the most important factor in all settings – although he is able to accept Foucault's claim that power relations are indeed 'omnipresent', that is, to be found everywhere through social relations. This at least allows for Foucault's rule that power relations in a micro-community inevitably stem in the first place from varied forms of status in any 'social landscape'.[2]

However, Lynch wishes to say much more than this. True, Foucault saw power as interwoven through all other features of social relations.[3] But, argues Lynch, Foucault did not see power dictating every single move, constantly barking its approvals or prohibitions. Nor were power relations totally the result of equalities in social relations. Rather they presented limits to social relations.[4] This should all be seen as an interplay. Certainly, Foucault reckoned that you do need to factor power relations into every analysis of social relations in order to provide an adequate explanation.[5] However, he did not assume that power streams *alone* could completely account for the way social relations work. Other triggers may be even more important, perhaps pre-eminent, as for instance pleasure, sex, friendship

---

1 Richard A. Lynch, 'Is Power All there Is? Michel Foucault and the "Omnipresence" of Power Relations', *Philosophy Today*, 42/1 (1998): 65–80.

2 Foucault cited by Lynch, p. 65.

3 Foucault cited by Lynch, p. 66.

4 Foucault cited by Lynch, p. 67.

5 Foucault interpreted by Lynch, p. 68.

etc.[6] Lynch's own example is not quite so obvious. It is something deeper than any of those above and underlies them all. It is the factor of *caring*.[7] This means for Lynch that not all relations may be reduced to either narcissism or power (or an interpenetration of these two). Genuinely altruistic motives are not an artificial construct or an illusion. They might sometimes truly underlie relations within community, despite a prevailing culture of suspicion. So cynicism is not the only possible verdict on 'caring relations'. On Lynch's understanding there can be a 'micro-physics' of caring to match the micro-physics of power.

Maybe, then, it is partly true that Foucault's approach is still indebted to a Nietzschean cynicism that exaggerates instinctive human hunger for power and self-aggrandizement. But, on Lynch's account, Foucault was not completely swept away by this verdict about humanity, albeit it is a very common one. He seemed to have left room in his system for the genuinely altruistic that lies at the heart of an authentic community aspiring to the way of Jesus. For church, such unselfish impulses spring from the life, meaning and authority of Jesus and a belief that the Spirit of Jesus can help everyone in the community to internalize the way of Jesus. The community of the *koinonia*, along with other communities of goodwill, is not, after all, predetermined to be nothing more than a twisted knot of power play.[8] High expectations for altruistic relationships in church life may seem ambitious, but they do not fly in the face of all critical thinking. As we shall discover, some serious sociology has also re-evaluated the cultivation of relationships and contemplated escape from the individualistic pursuit of power, wealth and pleasure. The trend marks a new path away from the detachment and aloofness that may lie at the root of anxiety in modern democracies.[9] The trend underlines the value in the search for points of intersection between power studies and the wider range of theories about human dynamics to which we shall shortly turn.

Meantime, Lynch's own stress on a micro-physics of caring would square well with a theology of church as communion and a fellowship of the common life. He is in line with what *koinonia* really means as one trait of a life together on the way of Jesus. And interestingly feminist writings may actually have further pointed the way to the power of caring, according to anthropologist André Droogers.[10] They

---

6 Foucault interpreted by Lynch, p. 68.

7 Lynch, p. 69.

8 Hence, we are not always confined to Social Exchange Theory as an explanation of human relationships as hedonistically based on the calculation of costs and benefits: e.g. Kelly and Thibaut, cited by Fraser Watts, Rebecca Nye and Sara Savage in their excellent *Psychology for Christian Ministry* (London, 2002), p. 68.

9 For the latter, see W. Miller and Glen Sparks, *Refrigerator Rights: Creating Connections and Restoring Relationships* (New York, 2002).

10 See André Droogers, 'The Power Dimensions of the Christian Community: an Anthropological Model', *Religion*, 33 (2003): 263–80. For feminist examples he directs us, for instance, to Carol Gilligan, *In a Different Voice: Psychological Theory and Women's Development* (Harvard, 1982), Nel Noddings, *Caring: a Feminine Approach to Ethics and*

have drawn attention to such settings as some base communities in Latin America, where Brazilian women exercise an alternative form of power to a political one, focusing instead on caring relationships. They appear to follow a praxis-inspired concept of power, contrasting, it is suggested, with prevailing male political and martial ones. Power in their language is the ability to influence behaviour, more particularly *to 'promote life'*.[11] Or to put it another way, caring is that power which nurtures mastery of life,[12] suggesting that power might interact with the caring relationship to promote empowerment. Caring here is not a tactic for gaining control but is itself a form of power and therefore a disinterested one. It is a genuine 'power to' rather than 'power over'.

This understanding could provide a further key to the disturbing of power patterns in a church community where disinterested love of neighbour is central to the way of Jesus. By adopting feminist suggestions on power, a community can offset the turbulence of its internal power patterns and strategies through the power of caring.[13] Yet more significantly, this insight into community would also mark yet one more shift from a focus on 'power over' to one more transparently concentrating on 'power to', that is, to transform positively. The 'communication of efficacy' now becomes more the preferred and coveted form of power rather than political 'power over'.

Now we have such a radical lead for re-evaluating power in the community of the *koinonia*, we can move to some sample findings from studies in social dynamics, to which we turn for further help. Group theory in particular offers yet more factors to balance power theories of group behaviour. David Johnson and Frank Johnson have offered a now well-known comparison of effective and non-effective groups.[14] This includes the following features of groups that really succeed in fulfilling their aims: (a) participation and leadership reaches to all group members and leadership is not based on authority, (b) power is equalized and shared, (c) controversy, and even conflict, are central to full involvement and is the source of creativity and originality, (d) stress falls on interpersonal activity, high levels of inclusion, affection, affirmation and extending of trust, (e) members assess their own effectiveness rather than being assessed from above, (f) innovation is encouraged. It is striking how much of this fits with Foucault's power relations theory but also goes well beyond its analysis. It is, perhaps, as near to Lynch's principle of care that a disinterested empirical group theory can be expected to go. It naturally blends well with a Christian view of group behaviour in church community and highlights aspirations of a healthy *koinonia*. Now, incidentally, we

---

Moral Education (Berkeley, 1984) and Joan C. Toronto, *Moral Boundaries: A Political Argument for an Ethic of Care* (New York, 1993).

11 E. Jacobs cited by Droogers, p. 273.

12 M. Jackson cited by Droogers, p. 277.

13 Droogers, p. 273.

14 David W. Johnson and Frank P. Johnson, *Joining Together: Group Theory and Group Skills (Second Edition)* (New Jersey, 1982), p. 11.

are ready to describe the aim of power in such a community as more than simply 'power to'. Now it looks more like a 'power-to-and-with'.

Church, Power and Group Dynamics

We have now to turn back and concentrate once again on the Foucauldian power patterns engaged by other types of strategies. To help us understand more clearly what it is that other strategies such as caring, have to offset we need to get at the practicalities. What can we learn from wider writing about power's actual workings? We leave aside for the moment what is called social psychology (whether classically from the psychologist's viewpoint or very differently from that of a sociologist's) or any branch of any cognate disciplines.[15] The discipline of group dynamics is of more immediate interest because of its relevance to power's implications for practice in Christian community. The category as such, originates as recently as the middle of the twentieth century, and so is younger than social psychology. Moreover, its literature is not so prolific as that in psychology and sociology. There are just a few recently written textbook introductions, but enough writing exists to show key popular concepts about the way face to face groups, such as a healthy church community, might work at their sociological level. In a leading textbook by Donelson Forsyth the argumentation is well and convincingly supported from considerable, diverse empirical research.[16] Much of the material, like the discipline generally, is designed for use in politics, management, education and industry. However, the key iconic situation around which Forsyth and many others organize their reflections is a religious one: the ill-fated People's Temple of James Jones and the tragic mass suicide of its members in 1978. Consequently one gets the feeling of painfully direct relevance to power in a faith community. The event has prompted many questions about how power works in groups (and not just religious ones).

Forsyth's fruitful chapter on power makes no reference to Foucault,[17] but much of what he gleans, squares with the Foucauldian 'strategies' of power. Forsyth works principally from the famous and oft-cited work of experimenters French and Raven, who have expanded and categorized power beyond its standard political meanings. True, Forsyth does recognize standard classifications. He

15 The term 'social psychology' is not usually what it sounds to the layperson. It actually focuses either on the effect of social interaction on an individual psychology or on how people particularly mediate perception of each other into their own personal actions or interactions (as in 'social-interactive sociology'). These, and the scholarly debates surrounding them, are not directly our interest here. However, in due course, some notice will be taken of social psychology in passing.

16 Donelson R. Forsyth, *Group Dynamics: Second Edition* (Belmont, 1990). It is splendidly clear and now published in a recent Fourth Edition.

17 Forsyth, pp. 180–210.

speaks for instance of 'coercive power', which for him is usually the threatening of punishments, not just physical but also social, psychological and emotional. In addition he speaks of 'legitimated power', referring to legitimation from a group, an agent, or a qualification. But he adds three further categories, of which he argues we must also take account. He labels these as 'reward power', 'referent power' and 'expert power'. James Jones, it is explained, maintained his grip on his followers through combining all of the above five types in a complex ring of control. According to Forsyth 'reward-power' can take many forms, from pay rises to social approval. 'Referent power' especially highlights the influence of a 'reference group', which provides standards by which members can evaluate their own behaviour and beliefs.[18] In addition, referent power, in the form of a model for self-evaluation, might also emanate from a key figure who generates admiration or respect.[19] 'Expert power' springs not necessarily from actual know-how but from the *appearance* of being expert.[20] On this account, expert power may be no more than massive audacity or plausibility, though it might also genuinely flow of course from know-how. But with regard to local church community, these categories also have a wider usefulness in highlighting a menu of power strategies available in group situations of conflict.

The key point, however, is not that such strategies bolted together can concentrate power in a single powerholder in a local group, though this is certainly a possible outcome. The main lesson, rather, is that all strategies in varied guises are available in principle to all interests in a group. Moreover the range can be broadened to include indirect tactics such as avoidance, hints, ingratiation and disengagement, as well as interactive ones such as negotiation and trading. Certainly unappealing power tactics also populate Forsyth's list, especially a kind of nagging (reiteration, return, and repetition) which tabloid vocabulary now calls 'pester power'. Additionally mention is made of manipulation tactics such as deception and hints.

In Forsyth's account reiteration, persistence and repetition appear to be a significant way in which a minority exerts influence on a majority.[21] Minorities, as well as majorities, we are reminded, can be coercive too, even if not always successful.[22] One example where this has proven to be a winning strategy is in take-over campaigns run by highly conservative or fundamentalist sections in faith communities. Here the closed and stubborn minority view can win out from its blind certainty, patience and persistent mantras rather than through persuasion,

---

18 Forsyth, p. 184.

19 Forsyth, p. 184.

20 Forsyth, p. 186.

21 Hedy Brown, 'Themes in experimental research on groups from the 1930s to the 1990s', in Margaret Wetherill (ed.), *Identities, Groups and Social Issues* (Milton Keyes, 1996), 9–63, p. 28.

22 Gerald A. Arbuckle, *Refounding the Church: Dissent for Leadership* (London, 1993), p. 10.

common mind or robust facts. To take a different scenario, persistent complaints that the church building's use for social care is raising costs is a sure-fire intimidation tactic. Foucault's law, however, still often applies. What comes out of the mix of tactics is sometimes not the utopia intended or the outright victory expected. Hence a strong charismatic group gains control of the leadership and at last shakes up the worship style only to be left with the docile and inactive half of the congregation. On the other hand, the rigid type of uncompromising minority campaign seems to win what it wants in some cases, mainly where the minority and majority have considerable common ground.[23] Here a minority wanting resources, say, for helping the local disabled can easily badger or bully a church which already has a strong social conscience. Contrastingly, where there is a greater distance between minority and majority, flexibility and negotiation have proved more influential.[24] Hence for example, in a less socially conscious church, a longer game for the same cause as that above is played out leaving time to offer the case for radical sea-change. Some argue that in such cases the minority might well be the creative and trend-setting group, bringing green shoots to the larger group,[25] though surely many exceptions to this must exist.

In addition, another of Foucault's claims seems validated, namely that in micro-settings of power there is interaction between wider prevailing, cultural expectations and ground-up, local tactics. Foucault's insight is validated in the discipline of group dynamics. Margaret Wetherill concludes accordingly that wider social identities can also influence the mix. This is where small-scale, face to face relations encounter wider unavoidable impact, say large-scale events or the encompassing power of cultural norms.[26] More tellingly, this can result in two competing groups further embedding each other in their norms, identities and claims.[27] In a local church perhaps, contesting parties might both claim to be the ones loyal to their community's shared local tradition and can appeal to it against the other. Mike, a social worker, thinks that because the Leddington Community Church was established as a mission centre in the nineteenth century to help the poor in the locality it should now convert the main sanctuary to a sports hall for the disadvantaged local youth. Leah, a chaplain, however, reminds him that early on the building became a spiritual resource for Christians working in the nearby city centre and strengthening their moral influence there. She claims that a distinctive chapel ambience was still needed for this service. In this example, it is not just different vocations but wider cultural norms that polarize the two parties in this way and the strategy of each only serves to embed the other deeper into their

---

[23] G. Mugny, cited by Brown, p. 28.

[24] G. Mugny, cited by Brown, pp. 28–9.

[25] Moscovici, though challenged by Latané, both cited in Hedy Brown, p. 30.

[26] Margaret Wetherill, 'Life histories/social histories', in Margaret Wetherill (ed.), *Identities, Groups and Social Issues*, 299–361, p. 314.

[27] G. Mugny, cited by Hedy Brown, p. 29.

own preferred world of norms. Undoubtedly in some such situations differing temperaments aggravate everything and power strategies spin into action.

When it comes to wider interactions in groups, there seems not to be one simple sociological formula to explain the interplay between a micro-community and the larger cultural setting. One critical tool of importance to emerge for church here is the group/grid model developed by Mary Douglas and deployed by Gerald Arbuckle with regard to Christian community.[28] The relation between encompassing power and grassroots is different in every situation and depends on the relationship of 'grid' to 'group'. The '*grid*' is about internal regulation of a group. It can vary from very strong (as in a strict regime concerned with safety, say a flight crew or surgical team protocol) to a very weak one, say, highly informal, unregulated, flat communities with a strong dependence on consensus. A '*group*' is strong when it has a very sharp sense of identity over against the prevailing culture and social setting (say in the case of a cult), and weak when held together only by a short-life familiar task (as in the flight crew who will not meet again).[29]

Arbuckle, one of Catholicism's own internal critics holds traditional, pre-Vatican II, hierarchical Catholicism, to be a 'strong grid/strong group' body.[30] However, the same point on the line is occupied by highly autonomous local churches or communities too.[31] For instance strict heirs to the Protestant Reformation can cherish a deep sense of being minority stewards of truth and ethics. Sometimes leaders in strong grid/strong group settings, possessed of a legalist or 'judging' tendency, fall into controlling habits towards the community.[32] This behaviour could for instance, range from close theological surveillance through to the more subtle line of hurdles or grades that pushes someone along a journey possibly involving more and more surrender of a questioning spirit or liberty of conscience. Such a 'strong grid/strong group' scenario ensures top-down static power relations, a simple set menu of relationships between members and leaders. A church of this genre may, according to power theory still manage to contain some interaction of views and transgressive voices, but it may also tip into fostering a centre of control and the constant threat of domination.

By way of contrast, the 'weak grid/weak group' type[33] stresses personal rather than structured group identity and is neither orientated to internal rules nor intimidated by wider society. Relationships in this group are more likely to be reciprocal and democratic. Arbuckle suggests that 'intentional church' would furnish typical examples, for instance unstructured groups such as home churches

---

[28] Developed by Douglas, as expounded in Arbuckle, pp. 80–99.

[29] Arbuckle, p. 80.

[30] Arbuckle, pp. 81–4.

[31] Arbuckle is actually primarily interested in vocational religious 'communities' in particular.

[32] Arbuckle, pp. 83–4.

[33] Arbuckle, pp. 90–93.

and base ecclesial communities in Latin America.[34] And we should probably add in here many groups known as 'fresh expressions' or 'emerging church' where church is playing with new forms of networking and unity, often in small units of the like-minded. *Referent* power would not be strong here. The interplay emerging from power relations would be very different in this group to the strong grid/strong group example above.

In the worst collisions of power moves we naturally expect the consequences to be serious. And where all major types of power tactics, strategies and struggles examined so far accumulate in the hands of one power holder, catastrophe threatens. It is most likely to lead to collapse into a 'Jones'-state. Power relations theory would deem this actually the end of any (even unequal) power relations. Power has petrified, hardened into a condition of domination. In the majority of even these cases, however, the range of imponderables may still be quite high, as we have already suggested. Certainly members of a faith community like church are often ill-prepared to accept this kind of seeming irrationality and messiness together with the sacrifices and compromises carried in its wake.

The work of social dynamics has also detected more subterranean effects of the interplay of power strategies in a social group, what Forsyth calls metamorphic effects. Varying forms of power bring about specific changes in both the main powerholder and in other players. In other words, both may be changed.[35] Participants can turn more submissive or alternatively more defiant and angry.[36] Sometimes they can slump into compliance for a while, changing their strategies only superficially, usually in the face of coercion. Or they can refuse dialogue out of exaggerated loyalty to one position or person.[37] For Arbuckle these strategies, forced by the dominant, lose an opportunity for safely changed behaviour that stems from developing personal agreement or convergence of aims. And this is most likely to emerge where coercion is actually avoided and influence stems from such things as information, clarification, illumination and negotiation. These stand apart from either the force of coercion or the encompassing effects of normalization and subjectivization.[38]

These later activities of clarification and improved communication approximate best to what we have learnt of the desired principles in *koinonia* as strategies countering power moves through respectful attitudes of care and respect with at least a chance that such power moves are offset peaceably. If this aim is viable then it works even with 'referent power'. But that may mean that ideals flow from not just from one privileged party but also from a commonly shared set of values or texts. Informed discussion and negotiation are the corresponding strategies. They might form the focus of a unity that transcends Foucauldian,

[34] Arbuckle, p. 91.

[35] Many authorities cited by Forsyth, pp. 190–99.

[36] Forsyth, p. 191.

[37] Forsyth, p. 191.

[38] Forsyth, p. 191.

unpredictable interplay of power strategies. These do not rest on the 'gaze' or on surveillance or legalistic forms of self-surveillance. Hedy Brown reminds us that strategies of mutual communication differ sharply from thought management techniques, those so-called 'thought-reform' methods adopted by communist states through coercion, re-education, harshness and manipulation.[39] Rather, equality in relationships, mutual respect and attentive listening tend to neutralize drift towards coercive power patterns. This is especially so of relationships in the life of *koinonia* community.[40]

Taken together the practices of respectful communication may provide non-confrontational strategies against meltdown from power patterns in a micro-group, including church. Here, unequal power relations have rightly been seen as a possible powder keg, requiring only a well-positioned leader to strike the match and spark disaster.[41] The danger only increases where Christian teaching naively ignores the insights of such searchers as Foucault, feminism and others, perhaps by denying the sociological reality of church. Then it might fall into overvaluing submission as a spiritual quality. It might esteem coerced selflessness above free decision and over the wealth of all the contributions.[42] When, in addition, exclusiveness and élitism proclaim the exclusive importance of this or that church community, the psychological stakes are raised dangerously high for those thinking of leaving.[43] The exclusiveness then fosters abusive power patterns.

The above analysis founded on group dynamics suggests that commitment to a circle of friendship such as that of the Jesus way, is really a kind of mutual sharing in each other's destinies. That sharing, we would guess, is the most beneficial where participants on the way of Jesus have self-consciously adopted social strategies beyond the more natural power patterns. For instance, they seek a spirituality that takes them out of themselves to foster communication sensitively given and sympathetically received. The effects should be expected to cascade beyond the faith community.[44] A comprehensive, applicable account of group behaviour and dynamics in a religious community like the Christian community intentionally on the way of Jesus is still awaited. However, the evidence of some useful forays in this area tends to confirm the judgement with which we began. Christian church as a sociological entity is as vulnerable to the cross winds of power as any other group. What is plain also is that power relations theory can play a useful diagnostic and prognostic role in reflection on such processes.

---

39 Set out by Brown, p. 52.

40 Compare Watts, Nye and Savage, p. 67.

41 Watts, Nye and Savage, p. 67.

42 Watts, Nye and Savage, p. 67.

43 Watts, Nye and Savage, pp. 68–9.

44 Austin Smith, *Journeying with God: Paradigms of Power and Powerlessness* (London, 1990), p. 91.

Human Psychology and Dynamics

Nikolas Rose writes as a psychology specialist acknowledging the new vantage points opened up by Foucault.[45] A number of 'middle' Foucault's warnings seem to have fallen on fertile soil here. For instance his thought about state production of knowledge and citizens makes an appearance, linked with the ideas of the 'soul of the citizen' and political nurture of individuals.[46] Similarly, we hear that power works through subjects, producing and shaping individuality not denying and repressing it.[47] We cannot enter here into the vexed question in social psychology of the precise input of language into the making of persons and the role in particular of language in social relations. Suffice to say, Rose's contribution emphasizes that the environment in its fullest sense helps people to think and act as individuals. That at least includes the language, aspirations and deeds set in their most valued experiences of community.[48] As a result, people come to master others or master themselves.[49] This echoes Foucault. Therapeutic technologies linked to political shaping of persons are just a newer variety of religion, doing the same job – namely seeking to make us more and more into ethical individuals.[50]

However, it seems that too much in this view is too easily associated with the privileged Western individual as the mighty consumer and the centre of the universe. So the 'other' person comes to be considered only in their value 'to me'. True, it is claimed that the 'making up of people' through robust therapies is not in itself necessarily anti-social. Professional therapies do value and encourage social relations. But it still looks as if social values in some of Rose's work are important only or mainly in the service of the all-important 'individual', hopefully, 'healed'.[51] The results of Rose's reflections are useful and not to be decried. But some views of the relation of individual to social experience will need to go deeper.

---

[45] Nikolas Rose, *Inventing Ourselves: Psychology, Power and Personhood* (Cambridge, 1996). Significantly, Rose founded an international association of researchers whose work was influenced by Foucault and he has edited a volume of Foucault's *Essential Works* along with renowned Foucauldian specialist, Paul Rabinow.

[46] Rose, pp. 77–80.

[47] Rose, p. 151. Foucault is cited in support as asserting that power is not a negation of the person but the creation and employment of him/herself.

[48] See Rose, pp. 174–8, on the earlier exaggeration in Foucault, as Rose sees it, of the person-shaping role of language as a system of evocative signs.

[49] Rose, p. 152.

[50] Rose, p. 156.

[51] Rose, p. 159.

Identity and Strategies in a Christian Community

We have encountered varied perspectives on the nature of interacting behaviours and patterns in grassroots groups. They have suggested that power patterns are not the only possible features in dynamics. Other strategies are present such as caring, mutual communication and openness to being shaped into an ethical subject. This all links in well with the strategies brought into the mix by an internalized commitment to the unity of the Christian *koinonia* as a journey together on the way of Jesus. This is the vision that balances the tendencies of colliding and colluding power strategies. That vision is not mainly focused on the socialization of a person through therapy (though it often proves a major remedy for social isolation). Instead, its demanding ethic, drawn from Christian Scriptures, first values the person for their own sake and worth. It does not commodify an unrealistic bliss in varied relationships though such relationships do become ever more valued. In the Bible social relations do not feature as a handy brand of self-help for the hapless. Therapeutic personal growth is rather a by-product of self-forgetfulness in the Jesus way. Social relations in church express commitment to being followers of Jesus in life and service together. The central (uncomfortable and challenging) fact of a local Christian community regarding its social function is the hope it offers to those outside its community, especially the voiceless and the powerless. At least in principle (for every *koinonia* is a work in progress) this life together, local and global, enshrines the gold standard of a 'transgressive' voice on behalf of others, such as those lacking food, shelter and security as well as hope and meaning. Hence the worthwhileness of life together in service does not concentrate on personal development as a commodity, an end in itself.

The metaphor of a body for church (Ephesians 4.11–16) envisages a shared project where life is exchanged between every part actually *working together* and mutually contributing vital growth to the other. It is this creational, health-bringing aspect of the *koinonia* that could provide the needed intersection between faith resources for social strategies and the sociological reality of church. From this viewpoint, power-relations and their ensuing patterns are real but worked out under a higher law or purpose – of unity in common service and aspiration.

Partakers of local church's common life do expect to form genuine bonds within such group discipleship and out of the values that mark it. Philosopher Maria Morales recognizes the possibility of high standards in such bonds within groups, highlighting for example, honesty, trust, forms of sympathy, openness and freedom.[52] She also identifies the possible negative traits that could scar community in such ways as deceit, envy and even exaggerated, illusory expectations of another person.[53] All this said, in the actual lattice of power relations many unintended

[52] Maria Morales, 'The Corrupting Influence of Power', in Laura Duhan Kaplan and Laurence F. Bove (eds), *Philosophical Perspectives on Power and Domination: Theories and Practices* (Amsterdam, 1997), p. 41.

[53] Morales, p. 41.

permutations of events and results emerge just as Foucault said. Of course, this does not mean that no unintentional outcome at all can be predicted. For instance some social theory expects that when a whole group loyally clusters around one individual over a sensitive issue, conflict will more easily flare. Arbuckle remarks that some of the finest dissenting voices in his tradition, marginalized for the message they brought, have by the discipline of silence avoided the danger of turning into agitators.[54] Such social realities warn every Christian *koinonia* that it ignores typical power patterns and cross-currents at its peril. It is not automatically shielded merely by virtue of being a community on the way of Jesus. One or two case studies will shortly illustrate the point.

Dangers to the *Koinonia* from Dynamics and Power Relations

A detour is tempting here into transformational and non-transformational forms of mediation and of the work for instance of 'Bridge-Builders', the Mennonite mediation service for churches. But focus is required on exploring how an allegedly altruistic culture in Christian community might cope with problematical power patterns and cross-currents.[55] By way of illustration let's take just one of many models and examples used to diagnose church. It is a clinical borrowing termed 'system thinking' which Peter Steinke has adopted as a model for analyzing group behaviour in Christian community.[56] He addresses the key concern of 'healthy' church, and uses the notion of 'viruses'. This approach helps to explain the triggering of power strategies which then clunk into action, fully in line with Foucault's rule. But Steinke's emphasis falls on clearly negative process and results. The key point is that viruses only become effective as they find a hospitable host within the human body, even getting cooperation from a host cell through deception.[57] We may take our pick of the four most deadly viruses that enter the faith community, the sociological body, generating symptoms in the field of relations. The four are: secretiveness, faultfinding, deceiving and triangulation (shifting burdens on to a third party).[58] The key here seems to be secrecy. We state Steinke's idea through an imaginary scenario. Sam complains secretly to Jack about Bea's treatment of him.

[54] Arbuckle, p. 110, naming for instance, Yves Congar, Dorothy Day, Henri Lubac and others. No doubt this is not meant as a charter for the immunity of bullying and other forms of abuse from challenge.

[55] The use of 'allegedly' here, to acknowledge the existence of approaches inspired especially by Nietzsche which reduce altruism to a mere sub-heading of the pursuit of self or power. This was a bold and highly sceptical reductionism which by no means convinces everyone.

[56] Developed persuasively by Peter Steinke, in *Healthy Congregations – a Systems Approach* (Herndon, VA, 1996).

[57] Steinke, p. 56.

[58] Steinke, p. 57.

This is the beginning of host activity for the virus to replicate. The introduction of a third person to the secret of Sam's resentment triggers the replication of a negativity virus capable of spreading resentment through the whole body – which it proceeds to do. Let's take another case study, this time more elaborate. It is pure fiction but based on various actual experiences of Christians in community.

This is the story of the perplexing paint. Bede Street New Church was doing well. It had just built a new youth centre and was at the decoration stage. Priscilla from the leadership team had bought plenty of litres of paint under strict orders from the community service team on precisely the colours desired. It turned out that only this cheap brand could deliver those tones. Then a crisis erupted – triggered by an innocent passing church member. Claire, a doctoral graduate now working in industrial chemistry, spotted an ingredient which she knew was becoming discouraged in the industry because suspected as toxic. It would particularly prove a danger to younger children and hence was no longer used in pre-school centres. And Claire was soon to start helping in the crèche in this very room. She alerted the maintenance manager. She was so concerned that she even offered to buy another consignment of paint and to give professional advice on all paint ingredients whenever needed. Leaders met in a huddle. Was it really true? The money had been spent. This was embarrassing. Priscilla was pure gold in the church and was sensitive just now to a suspected lack of trust in her from some in the leadership. But the information had to be shared with her and with some members of the leadership team. It was decided to write to the Institute of Chemical Safety and to the Industrial Health Society to ask if this ingredient had actually been ruled against. Both organizations gave disappointingly cautious answers because banning legislation had not appeared yet. They offered answers such as 'We cannot comment on this ingredient. But it is always best to choose known safe constituents'. This broad hint was not enough. Copies of the replies went to Claire, giving the impression she was fully included. As a professional, she knew anyway what the answers would be, for unambiguous negative pronouncements could trigger litigation against ICS or IHS by the paint company.

All this time, Claire did not know who it was that bought the paint and whose life she had upset. Nor was she invited to take part in ongoing leadership discussions of the matter. But Priscilla as a leader knew all about Claire and was in a privileged position to pre-empt all moves or queries. At last a well-liked local builder in the church seemed to have rescued the leaders. He assured them that he had never had any trouble with the paint. But Claire was now trapped by circumstances. She knew from her expert knowledge that this paint had been quietly dropped for regulated public buildings. She now could not with a clear conscience take part in the crèche because of being bound by her strict professional standards of safety. She had to withdraw and explain this to the leader in charge of crèche.

However, some credit emerges for both sides in the outcome of the above story. Eventually the leadership team became sensitive to the quandary imposed on Claire and eventually decided that the full inclusion of a member of the church 'family' was more important than paint colour and expenditure or even than a moment of embarrassment to a valued worker. For her part Claire did not create a triangle of intrigue, even though she had enough friends to do so and knew other specialists in the church who would have been equally concerned. Unlike Priscilla she had no partner with whom she could speak safely and openly. But thanks to her, no person C (an influential ally) was drawn into the problem between A and B (Claire and the leadership). She may have suspected a lowered respect for her contribution by some leaders just because she was female and relatively young. But she said not a word to anyone. The offence stopped with her.

However, Claire never found out exactly whom in the community she had embarrassed and so could not mend any fences. It remained a fact that if something similar happened again at Bede Street, the church leader caught up in it would still be a privileged party to all deliberations in a secretive process of discussion. And maybe next time a triangle *would* indeed appear. And the virus of secrecy and distrust would indeed replicate itself right up into the world of power relations.[59] What is more, in the event of a more serious event such as bullying or other forms of abuse in church, it may well become the duty of a Claire, however distasteful the prospect, to create just such a triangle. Power strategies will have forced this upon a whistleblower and the results would be deservedly serious. The lack of transparency in power patterns would then become of a critical, possibly catastrophic order.

This story draws on sociological theory about power patterns and behaviours. There are many other possible variants to it, but there are probably stories like this in the history of hundreds of micro-contexts including churches. The main point for us is that the values drawn from the life of Jesus and the Christian Scriptures can engage and neutralize predictable sociological dangers. In the example given, disaster was averted by a willingness drawn from faith, not to engender destructive division and an equal readiness on the other side to value life together on the way of Jesus. Both courses of action defied natural power differentials, were not without cost and went some way towards following the example of Jesus to be servants to one another, to 'take up the cross', to seek first the peaceable rule of God.

However the threat of power interplay breaking out could have been pre-empted in any case if appropriate checking of power streams had already been more closely followed within the fictional sociological entity called Bede Street New Church. A balancing culture of this kind would include equality in community, transparency, mutual respect, humility and honesty in all dealings. These are the traits which *koinonia* principles should engender and hopefully contribute to the mix of power-play, thus lubricating the natural power patterns that Foucault's rule expects to be present out of differential relations. For, as Foucault predicted, there were rational power strategies operating here but not producing the expected result of the leadership's superior strength. Sung Pyo Jun's research on centres of power in church has suggested what are the most significant factors establishing inequality in church communities. And they come down to just two things: a record

[59] Steinke, pp. 95–6.

of voluntary hard work in the church community (the weapon of the activist) and, sometimes, financial contribution.[60] It was just these that earned privileged treatment for someone in the leadership at Bede Street.

Of course, some suspicious minds might wrongly read Claire's moves as a supremely cunning power strategy too, designed to embarrass and show up others. But it fact in this story it was just an unavoidable ethical decision. That it was not badly motivated, simply reminds us of Foucault's caution that the actual action with its results must be distinguished from the personal intentions of the player. In fact, Claire was genuinely 'helpless', finding all courses of action closed down to her except one costly move demanded by professional integrity, that of silence and withdrawal. Yet the taking of that one possible route in vulnerability harboured more power than she realized. Steinke, indeed, would be able to say that if she had opened up a triangle it would have been a classic case of multiplying the 'accusation' and 'anxiety' present in the community.[61] This fact too is in line with Foucault's instinct that power comes from many sources including those that seem marginalized. None of these centres, even the most disempowered, should be underestimated in the dynamic mix of intended and unintended power behaviours. We shall return later to the notion of power through weakness as a distinctively Christian resource for handling power patterns.

There must be many real stories in various voluntary communities similar to this fictional one. The narrative above, however, illustrates that for church community in particular the Jesus-ways expected to pervade social relationships warrant the highest priority. Attention to them may save the group from implosion. This is true of churches ranging from those of low commitment levels or high insularity across to even dynamic ones that are fully switched on to healthy community together and engage with their surroundings. Ruth Reynard, in an accessible internet article on the subject, observes that simplistic appeals to some generalized biblical truth tend to sidestep the pressing sociological realities and human sensitivities in church communities. Genuine attention to group dynamics addresses not just 'spiritual principles' but also the complex interaction of several influences.[62] We maybe should take this to mean that Christian community develops not as an ideal body, pristine and hewn straight from the Bible, but from a complex mix of sociological factors including biblical values. This calls to mind the very interaction of values and power patterns that we have just been talking about. In addition, of course, we are dealing with individual, personal experiences along with the church's own

---

60 Sung Pyo Jun, 'The Bases of Power: An Analysis from a Resource Dependence Perspective' in *Social Science Journal* 34/2 (2002): 105–30.

61 See Steinke, pp. 56–7, 59, 95–6.

62 Ruth Reynard, *A Discussion of Power as it Relates to a Local Church Context* (no date given), p. 1. http://media.premierstudios.com/nazarene/docs/didache_4_1_Reynard.pdf (accessed 22.08.07).

collective culture.[63] Once these factors are summoned up, skills of understanding and sensitivity can perhaps be nurtured.

This exploration of social relations, dynamics and strategies has only underlined the lesson already emerging for church life together. The unity and usefulness implied by *koinonia* principles can check and counterbalance the unremitting power patterns and power streams in the community. However, in a sociological reality this is only likely to happen if pursued self-consciously and with serious interest. Attending to social factors in such a way could move people over from preoccupation with 'power over' to a Jesus-like concern with 'power to'. And here 'power to' is a way of describing the ongoing transformation of all in the family of the *koinonia* and gradually turning them into fellow travellers on the Jesus way of service, hope and respect. This process, whatever else it is, does not rest on imposition or coercion. In fact it follows a theme of freedom for the community, the next topic to engage us.

Community and Freedom

Goodbye Freedom?

Foucault's late writings now force us to return to the theme of freedom dwelt upon in Chapter 4 where we considered Christian views of freedom. We are reminded that we found freedom under *koinonia* to mean becoming 'disposable for God' and available for others, freedom to participate in the self-giving freedom of the Trinity. Hence it meant not liberalism's 'freedom to pursue your own good', but rather freedom for self-giving to others, particularly in the community's own patterns of social life. It was the supreme and most unlikely freedom of all. This counterintuitive understanding of freedom needs to be before us as we look at Foucault's last stand on the subject.

Foucault's central work had committed itself to bio-power's far reaching influence. His final phase suddenly started promoting themes of self-development and self transformation. He was returning to his early, instinctive search of the independent self in a new quest to rescue it … from himself. He had begun with belief in the personal subject, maybe because he saw that very subjectivity repressed in prisons and psychiatry.[64] As we have seen he then doubted the reality of a self or subject that was not really the product of all-encompassing bio-power.[65] Then in considering micro-groups, the parties who seemed to be behind any mini-

63 Reynard, p. 2.

64 Eric Paras, *Foucualt 2.0: Beyond Power and Knowledge* (New York, 2006). See pp. 157–8.

65 Paras, p. 154.

centres of power, were themselves in part products of the system of making up persons.[66] Even their freedom was in doubt.

The resulting reluctance to uncover any genuinely free self within a society was also all of a piece with Foucault's rejection of humanist self-confidence and excessive optimism. For him liberalism's easy definition of the human individual could not be right. This approach, he reckoned, had invented 'the normal human self' and turned that invention into a sword that stereotyped people and divided society up into normal and abnormal individuals. Naturally Foucault had no time for this and consequently ended up questioning the single most important philosophical basis to support such vicious exclusions, namely the existence of a transcendent self. Hence, for most of the 1970s he was still working up his rather sombre diagnosis of bio-power's silent hegemony over human life, freedom, and the human universe. But he finally and unexpectedly circled back to the freedom of the self.

The persistence of a feel for freedom in such an unpromising Foucauldian environment illustrates the robust character of aspirations for freedom. Hence this concern for freedom matters also to a community on the way of Jesus but on the basis of its own internal logic. The principles of personal faith and a common share in the Spirit's life imply a large place for individual freedom. Authentic freedom lies at the heart of church community, whatever forms of accountability also feature. However, the freedom that marks a Christian faith-community tends to be a socio-ethical one, a freedom that only finds full expression of liberty in a community of committed relations. Foucault in his final phase offered some support to this pattern, though uncertainly. Hence it becomes necessary to press a little further into the topic.

The Return of Freedom?

Paradoxically, people have found that joining the Christian community can bring with it a sense of both increased and reduced freedom. Sadly the reduction of freedom sometimes occurs because church invents norms or assumes them as given. It takes over the normalizing role thought by Foucault to be the domain of wider culture and all-encompassing power. But the early 'followers of the way' joined the movement by free response in choosing the way of Jesus (Acts 8.36; 17.32–4; 1 Thess 1.3,6,9). For without an essentially free assent and acknowledgement of Jesus, a community of the way would not exist. The community's very life rests on the idea of free, unconstrained self-giving in service and generosity to others (e.g. Acts 4.32; 5.3,4; 2 Cor 8.1–6, 9.6–7).

Much modern theology has focused on this theme. Its writers have not envisaged church as enforced communitarianism. Rather they have concentrated on the freedom of a self-giving 'community' of the divine Trinity that draws human relations into a divine life of mutual selfless love. Moreover, the notion of

---

66 Paras, pp. 154–5.

transformation of the self in the way of Jesus often carries an unlikely sense. That is, it revises the meaning of freedom as we have noted, by moving people away from modern forms of self-absorption towards a freedom to include others. Hence the freedom that marks life together on the way of Jesus most naturally means freedom to do good to the other. And it flourishes in a community setting of some kind, large or small, bustling or intimate. Foucault in his final phase surprisingly offered glints of support to this counterintuitive pattern, whatever else he meant by 'the care of self', about to be discussed.

Foucault's final version of the freedom of the human self came in his *History of Sexuality. Vol.3 The Care of the Self.*[67] It indicated a U-turn away from former views[68] where the self could do little to affirm its essential independence and significance. Perhaps this renewed interest in freedom would have emerged in more detail but for his untimely death, since he was talking in 1982 of a new book about the human self.[69] True self and real freedom seemed despite everything to be in close relationship. At any rate, the individual, genuine, autonomous self did indeed after all exist,[70] a possibility that Foucault had either ignored or disparaged during the most influential 'middle' phase of his career. After nearly twenty-five years the original starting point had reasserted itself: 'Prediscursive' human selves emerged from their Foucauldian tomb, free to some degree after all, able to push the boundaries of knowledge and experience.[71] Perhaps, as Eric Paras suggests, Foucault had embarked on this homecoming because for him only a firm notion of the self, of the subject, in the end was warm enough to sustain passion for life and belief in human freedom.[72] On the other hand Patten wonders if maybe the human self never really quite faded away in the Foucauldian scheme. Perhaps, a 'thin' conception of the human self always remained,[73] though admittedly only the bare minimum.[74] Patten thinks he mainly settled in the end for a freedom consisting of the individual's sense of powerlessness, the capacity for self-interpretation, and other powers of self-reflection that go with being a human agent.[75]

---

[67] Michel Foucault, *The History of Sexuality Vol 3. The Care of the Self* (London, 1986).

[68] Paras, pp. 155–7.

[69] Evident in seminars on the 'technology of the self'. See L. Martin, 'Introduction' in Luther Martin, Huck Gutman, Patrick H. Hutton (eds), *Technologies of the Self. Seminars with Michel Foucault* (Amherst, 1998), 1–8, p. 3.

[70] Paras, pp. 156–7.

[71] Paras, p. 158. Note the ringing endorsement of Richard Wolin, 'Foucault the Neohumanist?', *The Chronicle Review*, 53/ 2 (2006): 1–5, pp. 4–5 (electronic version).

[72] Paras, p. 158.

[73] Paul Patten, 'Foucault's Subject of Power', in Jeremy Moss (ed.), *The Later Foucault: Politics and Philosophy* (London, 1998), 64–77, p. 65.

[74] Patten, p. 75.

[75] Patten, pp. 75–6.

To take another though related angle, Foucault in this late work once again gave Christian practice of freedom a surprisingly good review although he ultimately found it to fall short.[76] Despite Christian promotion of a morality born of regulations and laws (not a plus point on Foucault's scale of values) it did nevertheless come up with an ethic based on 'the exercise of a personal liberty'.[77] Admittedly Christians managed to be paradoxical even here by surrendering their personal liberty through an asceticism of self-sacrifice, self-renunciation and self-mortification.[78] Foucault's own 'ethics of existence'[79] had no call for this self-denying element and only wanted to sort out the question of recovering a 'subject' so as to reassert some remnant of human freedom.[80] But he valued another kind of self-renunciation – a programme of continuous self-criticism. It is tempting to take this as a new breath of life, a force of resistance which rose up in his mature mind to overcome anything that claimed absolute necessity over people, including philosophical ideals.[81] One view suspected Foucault was just playing to the gallery to please his new American audience?[82] Another concluded that this was a genuine return to that Enlightenment interest in a world of free human subjects.[83] The resulting practice of 'care of the self' has frequently been suspected of really being narcissism and self-absorption, aesthetic more than ethical. Why, it is asked, should anyone want to bestow ethical meaning on a task like caring for oneself?[84]

As if to anticipate this criticism Foucault recognized in *Care of the Self* possible problems implied by an excessive interest in the self. In particular, he hastened to clear classical Greek and early Roman philosophies of individualism (whether in an existentialist or consumerist sense).[85] For individualism was not the same as the personal pursuit of salvation in ascetic practice. Nor was it the same as the classical calling to know yourself for the purpose of transformation and self-

---

76 Paras, p. 155.

77 James Bernauer, *Michel Foucault's Force of Flight: Toward an Ethics for Thought* (London, 1990), p. 180.

78 Bernauer, p. 180.

79 Foucault's phrase in 1983, cited by Patten, pp. 75–6.

80 Foucault cited by Patton, p. 77n.

81 Bernauer, p. 180.

82 Johanna Oksala, *Foucault on Freedom* (Cambridge, 2005), p. 191 following Tuija Pulkkinen. Oksala notes the lack of a prior personal subject to build on, at least in the sense of a stable reality, a starting point. See Jon Simons, *Foucault and the Political* (London, 1996), pp. 60–67, for a further treatment of humanism and freedom in Foucault.

83 So Paras, pp. 153–8, who seeks to validate this new move only recently from Foucault's later unpublished lectures actually given to *French* audiences in French.

84 Oksala, p. 196.

85 Foucault, *The Care of the Self*, p. 41. Compare also his defence in Michel Foucault, 'Technologies of the Self', in Luther Martin, Huck Gutman, Patrick H. Hutton (eds), *Technologies of the Self. Seminars with Michel Foucault* (Amherst, 1998), 16–48, p. 22.

purification.[86] Such early disclaimers, Foucault obviously felt, cleared the way for him to praise the techniques and intentions of the ancient art of caring for the self through demanding disciplines. Care of the self emerged as a new (though ancient), liberating technology of the self. It focused on the whole person, namely on body, conduct and being. And it aimed at ambitious transformation: happiness wisdom and 'immortality'.[87]

Having focused for so long on the domination of self by top-down cultural powers, Foucault now thought in 1982 that the time had come to consider how individuals act upon their own selves.[88] It was none other than Socrates himself who had invented care of the self, and later philosophy had also returned constantly to place it at the heart of 'the art of existence' that philosophy claimed to be.[89] The successful care of the self enjoyed its own rewards in classical Greek thought. If a person turned away from the distractions of the external world, from unworthy ambition and from fear of the future, the processes of one's personal past became a treasure store of self-knowledge. As a result of such disciplines commitment to progress in self-crafting now became sacrosanct.[90] The heights had already been scaled. The self had been accessed. One's limits had been acknowledged. Now no disturbance attacking one's tranquility was beyond the soul's control. Serenity accompanied the experience of oneself. Such a truth, the truth of a person's self, of what that person is and does and might do – this became central to making a subject of ethical thought and action. This was true freedom.

Hence Foucault's 'care of the self' successfully removed the illusion of the self as an inner refuge or place of sanctuary for flight from the real world.[91] And yet in the end the terms to describe Foucault's care of the self still looked too much like self-absorbed attention to autonomy.[92] Even self-mastery reflects the limited liberal view of autonomy as relating to the world through mastery and control.[93] For his part, Foucault suspected that Christian asceticism, unlike his, was not a self-transformation process for freedom through discipline at all but a technology for top-down control of human selves,[94] even though a genuine ethical concern perhaps lay at the heart of the Christian ascetic tradition.[95] That tradition,

---

86 Foucault, *The Care of the Self*, p. 42.

87 Martin, et al, p. 18.

88 Martin, et al, p. 19.

89 Foucault, *The Care of the Self*, p. 44.

90 Foucault, *The Care of the Self*, p. 66.

91 Bernauer, p. 181.

92 Bernauer, p. 180.

93 See Richard Bauckam, *God and the Crisis of Freedom: Biblical and Contemporary Perspectives* (Louisville, 2002), p. 41. The subject of freedom is vast, but for the gist of current Christian responses Bauckham's summary is excellent, especially pp. 26–49.

94 Foucault, *The Care of the Self*, pp. 235–40.

95 Charles Taylor, 'Foucault on Freedom and Truth' in David Couzens Hoy (ed.), *Foucault: A Critical Reader* (Oxford, 1989), 69–102, p. 83.

especially in its monastic form, was trained too much on self-renunciation. It did not appreciate the priority and true value of the individual.[96]

Undoubtedly some monastic practices were guilty as charged. However, this is not the whole story. A Christian 'technology' of the self need not depend on the unholy trinity of legalism, guilt and self-devaluation found in some traditions and practices of self-denial, which though sincere were sometimes extreme. Other traditions are rediscovering today the ideas of simplicity and discipline. But they envisage these practices as healthy ones supporting personal freedom albeit conceived as a freedom to be for others. These include such ways as the simple life, structured spirituality, activism and advocacy for the disadvantaged, forms of sacrifice for others' benefit, reconciliation and negotiation, protest, peaceful response, volunteering and honest, critical self-evaluation. Christian asceticism in antiquity does not constrain and limit the varied possibilities today for transformation of the individual into ways of freedom through exacting activity. Bare asceticism may indeed fall foul of Foucault's accusation that it devalues personal freedom. But 'self-renouncing' that reflects Trinitarian self-giving can indeed imply true Christian freedom.

Power, Community and 'the Care of the Self'

A questioning of Foucault in this final phase is tempting, as his last book based freedom for the self on ancient Greek and Roman practices. But Foucault sometimes seemed to overlook or at least sit lightly to some cold facts, namely that these carriers of noble culture were exclusively rich, male and well-connected.[97] But for the moment we note with gratitude the surprising fact that some aspects of the work contain shrewd advice for micro-groups and especially community and freedom for church.

For one thing, renovating and freeing the person demanded time so was therefore seriously intentional. It allowed the devotee to meditate on oneself, recollect, read and review his life, with the aim of uncovering afresh the grounds of rational conduct.[98] It was a real activity, no mere feeling or attitude. It resembled the farmer tending his field or a king taking care of citizens.[99] If you embarked on this quest you took pains with yourself.[100] It compared with an extended academy course for a practical vocation. It involved demanding physical exercise, practical tasks, varied activities, health regimes, meditation and the study of books.[101] This

96 Foucault, *The Care of the Self*, p. 43.

97 Foucault, *The Care of the Self*, p. 67. Compare Foucault, 'Technologies of the self' in Martin et al, p. 31.

98 Foucault, *The Care of the Self*, p. 51.

99 Foucault, 'Technologies of the self', p. 24.

100 Foucault, 'Technologies of the self', p. 25.

101 Foucault, *The Care of the Self*, p. 51.

attention to effort and application easily applies to church as a family of freedom for others. Freedom is often hard won.

Moreover, like the project of community building, the practice of making the self resembles the pilgrim nature of church. The one embarked on this project of the self did not enjoy a clearly visible future. Life was like a writing project. If you knew how it was going to end you would not write it. The 'game' of self-making was therefore worthwhile inasmuch as the end remained hidden.[102] Groups in general are open to this uncertainty, but especially the community of the *koinonia* on the way together. So the 'not yet' and hidden future marks every venture of church. Notwithstanding the hope that often energizes people on the way of Jesus, a too-fixed certainty of the near future works against maturity, with impatience and in favour of clashes of power. Despite urgings to know the will of God about every move, it is healthy for a community of the way, as for an individual, to know adventure, discovery and what it may take as surprise from the hand of God. Willingness to experience this kind of vulnerability might relativize claims made to know with certainty and detail the right way ahead ('pure truths' we recall) which sometimes turn up in a community's life and mission. That vulnerability shared as part of the *koinonia* can therefore calm ahead the power struggles that often surround rival, unduly unambiguous claims.

Perhaps most significantly, care of the self, despite its overtones of self-absorption was for Foucault not carried out alone. It most often progressed as a genuinely social, rather than solitary practice. What's more, in the project of self-discipline along with others, roles might be interchangeable. Friendship and mutual obligations were all part of the care for self.[103] Hence the project of one's self-development required help from others, a decision that also intensified relationships.[104] At first sight it looks appealing to a view of freedom based on life together in Christian *koinonia*. Especially important is the notion that in Christian concepts of freedom, love is most free for it accepts limitations from other persons and yet transcends them.[105]

All the same, we cannot overlook that some feminists have questioned this final Foucault. Dianna Taylor, despite Foucauldian sympathies, lists many feminist doubters.[106] Social relations, according to Foucault did help to discipline the self

---

[102] See Foucault's perspective on it in Michel Foucault (Interview), 'Truth, Power, Self: An interview with Michel Foucault', in Luther Martin, Huck Gutman, Patrick H. Hutton (eds), *Technologies of the Self. Seminars with Michel Foucault* (Amherst, 1998), 9–15, p. 9.

[103] Foucault, *The Care of the Self*, pp. 52–3.

[104] Foucault, *The Care of the Self*, p. 53.

[105] Bauckham, p. 45.

[106] Including Grimshaw and McNay: Dianna Taylor, 'Foucault's Ethos' in Dianna Taylor and Karen Vintges (eds), *Feminism and the Final Foucault* (Urbana, 2004), 258–74, pp. 266–7.

perhaps and play a part in personal formation.[107] But this was not enough. Relations should be much more central and actually constitute the self as a social being. For Amy Allen mutuality in relations is still lacking in *Care of the Self*.[108] And more complaints seep out, for example that in Foucault's approach one must resolutely maintain the correct order of things in ethics – first the care for self and only after that the care for others. Moreover, the ethical quality of care of the self did not even spring primarily from projected beneficial results for others.[109] In fact 'ethical relationship' had to do merely with nurturing one's own freedom.[110]

This audacious and typical re-casting of ethical thought by Foucault came up against protests like that of Johanna Oksala. For her the ethical individual should always emerge in a relation to 'the other'.[111] This will certainly mean a reversal of the order in *Care of the Self*. Most of all we should see the ethical self as actually constituted by relationship. One was truly a moral being through possibilities for exchange, for receiving from, and giving to the other person. Foucault, by contrast, simply made the other person a stage in one's own individual self-project.[112] A clear echo of Oksala's relational approach sounds right through much current theological literature in such obvious fields as being-as-relation, Trinity and church as communion.

Whatever the truth here, Oksala feels bound instead to follow Barry Smart in praise of Levinas and his view of freedom and ethics. Levinas preferred to ground the subject in a relation to 'the other', a principle allegedly drawn from Hebrew biblical texts.[113] Whereas Foucault's ethical subject was the privileged man of antiquity, Levinas embodied the ideals of a helpless and enslaved people, stressing the ethic of responsibility for one another in enslavement and humility.[114] The note of moral responsibility and accountability for other selves, it is claimed, is missing from Foucault's self-making.[115] Certainly views will differ on what constitutes ethics and the ethical subject.[116] But a Christian view reflecting on the ethical life of church community together is likely to resemble Levinas more than Foucault.

---

107 Oksala, p. 193. See also Dianna Taylor's defence of Foucault on this score, 'Foucault's Ethos', pp. 266–7.

108 Amy Allen, 'Foucault, Feminism and the Self', in Dianna Taylor and Karen Vintges (eds), *Feminism and the Final Foucault*, pp. 248–50.

109 Foucault, cited by Oksala, p. 194.

110 Oksala, p. 193.

111 Oksala, p. 194.

112 Oksala, p. 196.

113 Oksala, pp. 198–207. See also Barry Smart, 'Foucault, Levinas and the Subject of Responsibility' in Jeremy Moss, (ed.), *The Later Foucault. Politics and Philosophy* (London, 1998), 78–92, especially pp. 81–3, 88.

114 Oksala, p. 201.

115 Oksala, pp. 191–2.

116 See useful summary introducing Foucault on ethics in Simons, pp. 34–6.

Christian writings often echo ideas like Okasala's insistence on the presence of the 'other' in one's real freedom. Markus Barth has argued that it is possible, for example to find this in Paul.[117] The early people of the *koinonia* in Paul's view thus emerged as a complex object: a 'body', a new humanity. This early view meant that church was a social reality with diverse elements, capable of harbouring unequal power relations like those which so ruthlessly divided the layered society of ancient Rome. But in fact, says Barth, Christian notions of salvation aspired to overcome such dividers in that same empire.[118] Hence continues Barth, acceptance before God on the basis of faith in Jesus without personal merit did something new. It redefined intersubjectivity for ever and neutralized *nomos* (law) as a threat, as well as the many oppressive *nomoi* (laws) that split society into various strata. The power relations and differentials inherited from the past, together with their symbols, were expected to melt before the gift of free grace and new relations (intersubjectivity) in Christ.[119] We might add that this theme emerged also in Paul's correspondence with the Corinthian church. The call to the way of Jesus also excluded any boasting of relative positions and power relations that marked Corinth as a typical Roman city.[120]

The main point is clear: Oksala's misgivings about Foucault's closing phase would be shared by many Christian authors today. Despite significant and frequent exceptions, many theological writings have now abandoned individualist perceptions of freedom and meaning-making. Instead they anchor the reality of the self to relational existence. To use an old philosophical axiom from Africa: 'Because we are, I am.'[121] The communication of efficacy that Pasewark urges,[122] then, would be the communication of empowerment, self-worth and meaning upon each other in the sharing of some kind of 'common life' and covenant. This would be true freedom. It would mark a radical advance beyond Foucault's care of self, and furnish another lubricant for competing power strategies in a local church community.

---

117 For example, Markus Barth, explained in Lewis S. Mudge, *Rethinking the Beloved Community. Ecclesiology, Hermeneutics, Social Theory* (Lanham, 2001), pp. 56–7.

118 Markus Barth cited by Mudge, p. 56.

119 All as developed from Markus Barth cited by Mudge, p. 56.

120 See Timothy B. Savage, *Power Through Weakness: Paul's Understanding of the Christian Ministry in 2 Corinthians* (Cambridge, 1996), pp. 58–60 and many other passages in that work.

121 Quoted in Kofi Appiah-Kubi, in J. Parratt (ed.), *A Reader in African Christian Theology* (Aldershot, 2001), p. 20.

122 Kenneth A. Pasewark, *A Theology of Power: Being Beyond Domination* (Minneapolis, 1993), p. 5 and throughout.

The Last Strains of the Care of the Self

Apart from the key question of freedom and ethics, the building of a *koinonia* style of community may still have something to learn from Foucault's final calls to attend to the care of the self. For a start we have his claim that the aesthetics of the self really concerned the formation of the self as a thinking and ethical agent. And this maturing could come to expression in 'transgressions' against those normalizing forces that attack both the creation of oneself and the unity of humankind.[123] The assertion falls in line with the view of Simons that genuine transformation must disturb deep cultural assumptions that people have about themselves and the world. And such a disturbing would be prior to the changing in turn of any systems.[124] In the classical world, we learnt earlier, care of the self implied that such transformation of the self implied *labour*.[125] It was not luxurious self grooming and indulgence.

The medical metaphor also played a large part in the mentality of the person embarked on classical self-discipline. It defined the care of self as in the Greek schools of philosophy.[126] Hence, the practice of discipline on the self went beyond treating oneself as merely imperfect and ignorant but also entailed a searching self-critical honesty. In the medical metaphor of course this was the admission of ill-health.[127] Care of the self posed as a kind of permanent medical care. One had become a doctor to oneself.[128] So the practice defined by Foucault entailed self-testing and examination. It might mean going forward to austere physical tests to prove a capacity to face life's disasters. Foucault's disciplined care of the self most certainly included self-examination, or a critical daily review of improvements upon the self. A legalism was possible here admittedly, though not inevitable. For the issue was ongoing quality self-management.[129] Foucault's ideal of self-examination evaluated work in progress now and in the future, so did not aim to stir up guilt for what was in the past.[130] It pragmatically focused on future progress towards wise behaviour rather than ethical demands.[131] In this sense it did not resemble Christian pastoral power disparaged by him, that type which could probe even secret motives and intent.[132]

---

[123] Bernauer, *Flight*, p. 183. See Simons, pp. 68–80 and his extensive consideration of transgression and the art of the self.

[124] So Simons, p. 124.

[125] Foucault, *The Care of the Self*, p. 50.

[126] Foucault, *The Care of the Self*, pp. 54–8.

[127] Foucault, *The Care of the Self*, p. 57.

[128] Foucault, 'Technologies of the Self', p. 31.

[129] Foucault, *The Care of the Self*, pp. 61–2.

[130] Foucault, 'Technologies of the Self', p. 34.

[131] Foucault, 'Technologies of the Self', p. 62. See also p. 33.

[132] Foucault, 'Technologies of the Self', p. 33.

Christian community has more to say than this about discipline, especially on the ethical intention which always comes down to reflecting the image of Jesus as a community of the way. But church still takes from this care of the self that the changing of the world for good may sometimes require attention to self and re-evaluation. Journeying together and fulfilling a mission was dependent on ongoing personal transformation first. Power strategies change in churches as people themselves change. Hence the best guarantee of healthy church in the presence of power must surely be the responsiveness and increasing sensitivity of members. For church this clearly boils down to personal growth within the setting of a living community of the *koinonia*, a common life. The honest and humble reflection on the foundation Christian texts together is a necessary part of transformation. Such a community has through such candid reflection to become ever newly attuned to the crosswinds of power in a local setting. This will improve its ability to be on guard for possible internal conflicts.

Lastly, as mentioned earlier, the goal of all this concentration on the self in Foucault's ideal discipline was not individualist indulgence but an ethics of self-control, being one's own master, answerable only to one's own self.[133] And that flower did not blossom best in isolation. Rather it did so with the help of others, in company with confidants, friends, guides and directors. For this work progressed most effectively as a genuinely social practice. It was not solitary self-discipline. What's more, these roles could be interchangeable. Friendship, mutual help and reciprocal obligations were all part of the care for self.[134] Hence the project carried out on your own self sought help from others and so intensified relationships.[135] Shaping the self in community! This recalls Christian conceptions of the self, shaped, fulfilled and developed only in a community of fellow travellers on the way of Jesus, partners, family and friends. The practices of self-criticism, re-evaluation and review are not necessarily enhanced by hermit spirituality. Partakers of *koinonia* principles learn and grow together in the company of fellow strugglers, pooling their insights and transgressive voices. True, the classical ascetic communities no doubt inflicted power bids upon each other as they learnt and perhaps competed. This happens anyway in every sociological reality and so will occur in church too where it should also help to deflate self-importance. This way of transformation as a social practice, it seems, might even pre-empt power bids and so provide lubrication to power behaviours and strategies. But it is just here that distinctive theological resources now become crucial.

---

[133] Foucault, *The Care of the Self*, p. 65.

[134] Foucault, *The Care of the Self*, pp. 52–3.

[135] Foucault, *The Care of the Self*, p. 53.

Chapter 7
Spirit, Power and Weakness

Our examination of power has brought us to a new stage, one where we must now uncover further theological guidance for handling power. With one eye constantly looking ahead to this stage, the critical discussions have sharpened up many of the issues. Now at least we have a fuller picture of what it means for a church community to be a sociological reality, facing questions of power that any 'micro-group might have to handle. By way of brief review, we take note again that the main challenges for a local church stem in part from differentials of status and influence inescapably present in any modern micro-group along with the resulting power relations. These relations in turn generate ever-changing hidden streams and moving patterns of power together with wide-ranging strategies. Such strategies might be conscious or unconscious, self-seeking or well-seeking. They might range from shameless bids for power to silent forms of avoidance that neutralize such bids. These highly diverse behaviours produce conflict and even concert, collision and collusion, producing an end result that might on occasion strongly favour one party's wish but more likely produces an unplanned and unpredicted conclusion.

However, power patterns did not appear to be the only possible contributions to group behaviour. They primarily stem from the classic conception of power as 'power over', though often performing also as a 'power to'. They can be offset by forms of more convincing 'power to', those to be found in such transforming streams as caring, or transparency or the internalizing of *koinonia* principles of unity and community.

This latter development provides an opportunity to search for some key Christian distinctives that might equally serve as counterweights to power behaviours in a local church. Christian views of 'the Spirit' must surely be prior here.

Spirit of Power

Does the *dunamis* in church community really have to be dynamite, awesome power? Certainly, the idea of awesome power has been very appealing to many Christians wanting to see themselves as privileged in the power (*dunamis*) of the Spirit. Troublingly, such impulses exploit a widely agreed theological principle of the common gift, the *koinonia* central to Christian community. What is the meaning of *koinonia* if not to participate in the Spirit, to have a common share as signalled by Paul's famous words: 'You have all been baptized in one Spirit and have drunk one Spirit' (1 Cor 12.13). Moreover this urge to link *koinonia* and

Spirit has ecumenical consensus behind it, despite variations over just how the Spirit is connected with word, sacrament or organization.[1] Whatever else it may be, the *koinonia* is a common participation in one Spirit of power.[2]

All this said however, one is bound to probe whether the association of power in particular with this selfsame Spirit inevitably poses serious dangers to the very principle of a common participation in the Spirit. Might the so far benign idea of a common life and sharing in the Spirit also acquire a rather more power-laden and perhaps even unhealthy dimension? We already know that sometimes it does. Enlisting the Spirit in human aspirations for 'power over' has, for many, sometimes left a bad taste, a stain or lifelong scars. People have been known to seek the 'power of the Spirit' in pursuit of impressive 'spiritual' exploits or types of personal charisma that enhance authority or give an edge in group power relations. Leaders in many kinds of traditions have at times claimed the backing of the Spirit to manipulate or pre-empt decisions about expenditure, mission strategy or innovative doctrine. Similarly, it is not unknown for authoritative groups to claim the Spirit's power in their theology, skilled or otherwise, so acquiring their own privileged 'power over' other voices. Anyone interested in the *koinonia* of the Spirit, then, cannot ignore the meaning of the phrase, 'the power of the Spirit'. This term inherited from very early church has to bear a sense that fits with the major theme of common participation in the Spirit.

What follows now takes up this question, but for the sake of clarity is restricted to engagement with three typical writers rooted in today's power context, who between them offer very different angles on a Christian way of viewing the Spirit's power.

Power and Grace: Kyle Pasewark

The first writer is Kyle Pasewark in his *Theology of Power* which appeared in 1993 and has attracted much attention.[3] Michel Foucault had by then long been making waves in cultural criticism, not least throughout the United States. As a scholar in that country, Pasewark took Foucault seriously enough to devote around 50 pages of his book to him. In consequence, the chief insights he drew from

---

[1] World Council of Churches, *The Nature and Purpose of the Church: A Stage on the Way to a Common Statement: Faith and Order Paper No. 181* (Geneva, 1998), p. 11.

[2] For Reformed-Catholic agreement and a wider ecumenical basis see Antii Saarelma, 'Church and "Sacrament" in Bilateral Dialogues', in Tamara Grdzelidze (ed.), *One, Holy, Catholic and Apostolic: Ecumenical Reflections on the Church. Faith and Order Paper No. 197* (Geneva, 2005), 51–61, pp. 54–6. For a strong strain in Irenaeus in the second century see Douglas Farrow, *Ascension and Ecclesia: On the Significance of the Doctrine of the Ascension for Ecclesiology and Christian Cosmology* (Edinburgh, 1999), p. 68.

[3] Kyle A. Pasewark, *A Theology of Power: Being Beyond Domination* (Minneapolis, 1993).

Foucault were to reject the zero-sum view of power, and to endorse Foucault's radical exposé of 'power over' in the social world today. For Pasewark too, 'power over', rather than being an occasionally activated solemn sanction, was pervasive and all-encompassing, just as Foucault had said of bio-power. But for Pasewark the theological response should be to redefine power by concentrating on it as 'power to', and for him that meant the 'communication of efficacy',[4] a notion soon to be explained. However, Pasewark did not attempt to integrate his understanding of Foucault into his ensuing analyses of Luther and Tillich. So we should perhaps think of him writing about power, domination and efficacy while looking over his shoulder at Foucault. Nevertheless, even with that duly noted, there were two outcomes for Spirit and *koinonia* in his work that throw light on this chapter's concerns.

In the first place, Pasewark takes note of a particular presumptuous tendency emerging in the religious tumult of Luther's day. Some Christians felt powerful enough to evaluate the spiritual authenticity of another person's faith-claims. This was usually on the basis of observed behaviour. Denial of someone else's participation in the power of the Spirit proved a temptation to many an agitator in that sixteenth-century world of changing loyalties, mutual anathemas, and wild claims to be certain in doctrine. But, Pasewark tells us, Luther was more alert to the dangers than most. He sought to undermine such moves by stressing the unavoidable moral imperfection of Christians.[5] Christians routinely did and said things not consistent with the presence of the Spirit and the Spirit's fruits in a *koinonia* community (especially the fruit of selfless love). But such failures did not endow other members of the *koinonia* with a special power to read off from this an absence of the Spirit from another person. Of course, those 'spirituals' of Luther's day, were not skilled to discern in their views a theory of unequal power relations at the very heart of a common share in the Spirit.[6] Pasewark uncovers an important conclusion here, namely that shifting power imbalances tended to multiply as a result of narrow claims to the Spirit's power.

In the second place, Pasewark offers his own definition of power. He starts with Luther's rule that the power of God is such because it is always *for us*.[7] Pasewark calls such power 'transactive'.[8] His reading of Luther here points to a divine life or power flowing to the believer who is consequently empowered to benefit others too. This is what Pasewark means by that 'communication of efficacy'. Foucault had slid from 'power over' into 'power to' because for him bio-power produced and transformed persons for a healthy role in society. Unlike Foucault though, for Pasewark 'power to' was productive not so much in conditioning and normalizing

---

[4] Pasewark, p. 198, pp. 206–7.

[5] Pasewark, p. 185. Elsewhere he still holds to inward grace normally making its way out in external appearance in the worship of God and care for other selves (pp. 189–95).

[6] Pasewark, pp. 185–6.

[7] Pasewark, p. 197.

[8] Pasewark, p. 197.

individuals but in dispersing life and benefits to people. What is more, if power is such, then the word cannot be made to describe domination, just as paradoxically Foucault protested right to the end. For Pasewark, Luther's approach shatters the identification of power with domination.[9] Luther wrote that it is the special role of the Holy Spirit to bring life.[10]

We find ourselves now edging closer to Moltmann's definition of the Spirit's power as life-giving and the wellspring of life, to be elaborated shortly. So Luther's use of the term 'power' applied to the Holy Spirit, did not coincide with Foucault's sovereign power, the power to destroy nor with disciplinary power, the power to exclude. Rather, the Spirit was about 'efficacy', the communication of life (and the Hebrew *ruach* of Genesis 1 was his starting point). This was the 'power' in which the Spirit specialized. Thinking of the power of God should evoke this sense of divine efficacy more than divine sovereignty (although the latter has its place).[11]

If this approach of Luther's is true to the biblical *koinonia*, then searching questions confront that over-hastiness with which some value the Spirit's power as for instance a tool of compulsion through miraculous phenomena, or a spiritual 'power over' others autonomously held by a charismatic figure in a congregation. For in Luther's mind the Spirit's power concerned the conveying of life.[12] However, Pasewark also sees in Luther an opposition to the idea that either 'power over' or even 'power to' might be held as a personal possession by anyone.[13] Legalism, the most intentional form of excluding people, is usually self-serving – designed to make the Spirit something more awesomely possessed by one over another.[14] Divine power cannot be an inward possession but only exists in relationship, flowing out from one to the other. It is tempting to develop this theme in the light of a widespread theology of the self-giving 'communication' of life within the Trinity itself. But this cannot be pursued now.

Power and Secular Powers: Lee Snook

'Spirit' of Power and 'spirit' of Power

The second writer of interest offering a rethink concerning church and the Spirit's power is Lee Snook.[15] The use of Foucault is not strong here but the author is aware of the zero-sum approach to power and naturally rejects it. However, he

[9] Pasewark, p. 201.

[10] Martin Luther in Pasewark, p. 201.

[11] Pasewark, p. 202.

[12] Pasewark, p. 187.

[13] Pasewark, pp. 206–7.

[14] Pasewark, pp. 206–7.

[15] Lee E. Snook, *What in the World is God Doing? Re-Imagining Spirit and Power* (Minneapolis, 1999).

also senses the need to challenge any notion of a *koinonia* enjoying a definite 'power-edge' over the rest of the world. In the order of experience, he claims, the experience of the Spirit is first.[16] Power, he insists, takes not one but many forms. The Spirit is more to do with real powers in the secular realm than narrow interests of church.

From here Snook moves to his main idea: the 'Spirit of God' is nothing other than the secular form of God's power in the world.[17] Or again, the Spirit, according to the Bible, is the power of God pervading all forms of secular power.[18] All this arose for the author because he was forced to consider the 'omnipresence' of power while working in Africa and to learn from his experience of religious world views there. He also acknowledges the other influence on his work, namely process theology. Out of such interactions he has taken much more seriously than before the possibility that the Spirit underlying the many powers in the world is the same as the Spirit of Jesus. He does not want to say that everything *is* the divine Spirit/power but only that the Spirit/power is pervasive of all creatures and that all creatures are alive and present in that Spirit/power.[19]

The view that the Spirit is connected with the secular realm has of course been frequently heard during the last few decades in theologies of the Spirit as *ruach* (Hebrew) or 'life'. These would only mark a radical departure from classic Christian belief if they saw the Jesus-centred experience of the Spirit as nothing more than a particular form of a general secular experience of the Spirit.[20] So Snook does nothing unorthodox in querying whether the Spirit is found *only* where there is the appropriate bishop, or where preaching is correct or charismatic gifts are found. In itself this approach does not amount to a disconcerting claim – rather it could be seen as a timely questioning. Snook's service to community in *koinonia* here is to warn against demands for unquestioning compliance on the basis of 'Spirit-anointed' or 'called' leadership, or docility before serious abuse of privilege in preaching, or attempts to stifle discussion through alleged displays of 'charismatic power'. At this point he issues a reminder of the principle that truly the Spirit is not held at the disposal of anyone in the common life of the Christian community.

In addition, a significant extension to Snook's discussion of Spirit as power is his account of the divine 'comedy' of salvation. He speaks of a 'comedy' in the classic sense that the salvation story contains retrospective reversals which reveal the truth, the real situation. The Christian Scriptures disclose such a reversal specifically through the resurrection. This surprise in the narrative overturns the triumph of human powers and the ambitions of the great and powerful. The Spirit's

---

16 Snook, pp. 3, 6.

17 Snook, p. 6.

18 Snook, p. 6.

19 Snook, p. 21.

20 Compare the conception earlier, in Chapter 2, of the *koinonia* community as no more than a specific form of community in general.

power here comes down to the power to reconcile the conflicts in the narrative. In this way people may 'get the point' that God's power is not like that of exalted human icons.[21] It is a mere extension to salvation narrative, then to imagine the completion of the story in a final reconciliation of 'all to all',[22] of divine order to human order.[23] For Snook the power in the story of Jesus contrasts with that exercised by human seekers of power. Snook does not elaborate but we might suggest here that it is the power of divine love and self-emptying that turns out to lend real meaning to the notion of freedom for women and men in his suggested divine comedy.[24]

In this way Snook poses the question of how well self-denying love in a church community might provide an alternative ending that turns tragedy into comedy through unlikely strategies. What is found in this or that story of power patterns and their interplay with behaviours other than power ones? Does a local church narrative turn out to be an uplifting comedy of reversals? Might we recognize the 'Spirit's power' in a crucial internalizing of strategies of the Spirit?

In Snook's view, to repeat, the power in the Spirit of Jesus is neither powerlessness on the one hand nor domination on the other. Rather that power is the spoken witness of Jesus to the truth.[25] For power is one thing, and truth another. Obviously, Foucault would object to a clear-cut separation of them but all the same Snook sustains the duality for several pages. And yet, though they are opposed, he controversially roots both of them in the same divine Spirit-power of Jesus. And the truth is that which 'limits and relativizes' without actually destroying.[26] In fact this same sacred pact with the truth that balances power passes to all those who are disciples of Jesus. All this is possible because the Spirit/Power of truth belongs to no-one and eludes human control.

There is an implicit challenge here, whether intentional or not, to Foucault's Copernican revolution on knowledge and power. Foucualt would challenge Snook's simple, straight and sustained contrast between power and pure truth, as we have seen. We recall that Foucault's view has, rightly, been questioned for being too sceptical altogether about truth and for ironically undermining his own confident statements. Snook, therefore, is not necessarily wrong to privilege 'truth' in such a way. Previous chapters have already set 'transparency' over against power behaviours.

Snook's notion of truth's significance is supported in the Christian narrative but goes beyond only words and reaches to behaviour. For example, the disciples

21 Snook, p. 41.

22 Snook, p. 43.

23 Snook, p. 41.

24 Snook specifically rejects the notion that the Spirit's power in Jesus is the 'power of powerlessness' though equally it is not the power of domination (p. 49). In fact it turns out to be the power of 'truth' (p. 50). See on this below.

25 Snook, pp. 50–51.

26 Snook, p. 51.

of Jesus were to recognize the futility of Roman jockeying for privilege and power. But in the full narrative Jesus did more than speak trenchant words of truth. Rather he also stood out boldly as the very *being* and *living* of truth and so presented an outrageous transgression going across coerciveness and the rule of naked, self-serving power. Moreover, according to the Jesus narrative such lived-out 'truth' stemmed from the 'power of the Spirit'. It can be taken therefore to point us to the original meaning of the 'power of the Spirit'.

So then, we suggest that two points arise from Snook's account in helping us with power streams, patterns and strategies in church community. First, according to Snook's divine comedy, no 'truth' can consist only of intellectual or spoken statements. In a Christian community only this transgressive truth of self-denying love as a 'strategy' additional to power patterns may be expected to offset unhealthy power moves. 'Regard the other as better than yourself', urged Paul (Rom 12.10). This one life-principle of the Spirit's *koinonia* as following the way of Jesus, counterbalances and 'transgresses' (as Foucault would say) natural power patterns and discourse. It is a resource for handling power strategies.

Secondly, Snook's approach is controversial in seeing the Spirit's power in Christian contexts as a sub-division of generic worldly power. Christian thought more naturally sees the Spirit in the Christian community as precisely the element that transcends church as typical sociological reality, the power of the coming age. Church as community needs to see the Spirit's power as fully one with its particular commitment to the Jesus way as energized through, and internalized by, the Spirit. Snook's approach, however, is more problematical in the way it risks implying that the same Spirit indifferently produces redeeming, life-giving power on one side and negative, destructive power on the other, all because Spirit is simply the same as power. And thus, however unintentionally, the scheme is likely to lend some degree of legitimization to negative forms of power. Indeed he seems to be resigned to this result. For he appears willing to draw a parallel between the early Christian theme of unity in the Spirit and the unities of ordered life that occur in the world generally. Hence he can even call forms of imposed order 'intimations' of the Spirit.[27] At the very least this claim appears not to satisfy wide differences between external, imposed order and a more genuine, individually internalized unity of the human spirit.

True, the 'unity of the Spirit in the bonds of peace' compares in some ways with positive parallels outside of Christian communities, especially groups manifesting camaraderie, loyalties and shared struggles.[28] Nevertheless Snook clearly means more than this, insisting that the Spirit permeates *all* powers in the world, including practices of leaders '*with the power to dominate*' (italics mine).[29] In case we think we did not hear right, it is repeated. The source of all power and

---

27 Snook, p. 53.

28 Snook, p. 53.

29 Snook, p. 54.

order is the Spirit, so accordingly good, and hence *the power to dominate cannot be inherently bad.*[30]

It will already be obvious why some words are given here in emphasis. Snook is surely treading on dangerous ground to be so accommodating to domination in the human world, even allowing for the fact that he concedes domination's pragmatic limits for achieving goals. The power of the Spirit, he argues, through a series of alternative 'imaginings', takes different (actually diverse, even contradictory) forms. In fact this Spirit lies behind anything deserving of the description 'power'.[31] Hence domination may trace its noble origins back to the divine Spirit. Snook's lack of embarrassment about this is plain from the standard-bearers he has chosen to illustrate domination's usefulness, such as Pontius Pilate, the former President Mobutu in Congo (then Zaire) and the masters of the former Soviet Union. Hence he can only fend off the worst implications of these choices by qualifiers. One such qualifier is therefore meant to cushion the impact. He makes the important concession that the Spirit's power is not *primarily* coercion, or domination.[32] But most Christian theology would want to go much further and deny that in the setting of the Bible the Spirit of Jesus is in any way at all associated with coercion or domination.

There are obvious problems to Snook's approach in a world still harbouring much injustice through coercion and domination, though admittedly chaos has its victims too. Suffice to say that it is in order to stress the Spirit as behind social cohesion that he appears driven to handle the nature of the Spirit in this way. The Spirit, it seems, assumes the work of sovereign power and bio-power rolled into one! Not many authors of political theology interested in justice and liberation for the oppressed will feel completely secure with Snook's qualifiers. He rightly condemns those who use the God-given power of the Spirit against the particular goals of the one who gave it.[33] But this censure may not be enough to dispel suspicion that he lends too much assistance to negative forms of power in the world, indeed the worst forms of 'power over'.

Interest in universal spirit is also an emphasis of much feminist writings. But feminists tend not to take Snook's route. Anne E. Carr, for instance, though favourable towards process theology writes that the work of the Spirit in people's lives is 'necessarily relational'.[34] We should therefore think of the Spirit's power as a 'persuasive' one. The Spirit's power emerges from the ground up and in a

---

30 Snook, p. 54. It is a possibility because the Spirit who sources the power does not have control over how the power is used.

31 Snook, p. 10.

32 Especially Snook p. 43: The former Mobutu's Congo where the results of violence and the obscenity of child-warriors endured for a long period. Find other references around Snook, pp. 10, 20, 52ff.

33 Snook, p. 54.

34 Anne E. Carr, 'Providence, Power and the Holy Spirit', *Horizons*, 29/1 (2002): 80–93, p. 91.

relational environment not a controlling top-down one. The power of the Spirit concerns *empowerment* and an *enabling*, which emphasizes '*relatedness*'.[35] And that relational, persuasive empowerment of the Spirit aims at spreading about a 'power to', that is, the believer's participation in the continuing work of Jesus in the world, a 'this-worldly' action, embodiment and responsible expression of the Spirit's power.[36]

Snook's approach seems very strange because he himself has already referred negatively to those who wish to be in high in the pyramid of a theocratic rule and who wish to exact obedience from others. But here that very forbidden fruit seems to enjoy immunity on the basis of the Spirit as sourcing undifferentiated power. Snook's approach, perhaps undeservedly, seems therefore to have a libertarian, free-wheeling feel to it of the sort that has invited criticism not needing elaboration here.[37] The one point apparently agreed among most modern theologians is that domination now has no place in a Christian understanding of power and the Spirit in the *koinonia* or elsewhere.

Might Snook's apparent inconsistency be resolved? Perhaps an unusual sense of 'dominate' is in the author's mind. Maybe for him it means no more than 'strong and competent government' though this would be a generous rehabilitation for the word 'domination'.[38] And such a move surely leads into slippery ground if we have in mind the many totalitarian states where domination's fruit is ever more atrocities. More relevantly to our purpose here, domination cannot be recognized as an appropriate expression of power in local church community. Even Paul, whose practice we consider later down the line, only rarely falls back on personal authority and seems to assume throughout that it is not desirable for anyone, including himself, actually to dominate fledgling churches. His strategy for realizing genuine unity, at least in church life, lies in the challenging life of the way of Jesus who did not grasp after reputation but chose the way of humility (Phil 2.1–16). The ideal 'power of the Spirit' for him was selfless love to bring about unity in the wealth of gifts and voices (1 Cor 12–14). This is the Spirit's way for unity in the church community in his writing. Any disciplinary action, rare even in Paul, points back to that one way and even so can still be resisted.

---

[35] Carr, pp. 80–90.

[36] Carr, p. 92.

[37] See especially Walter Wink's trilogy exposing with grace the evils of the 'domination-system': Walter Wink, *Engaging the Powers: Discernment and Resistance in a World of Domination* (Philadelphia, 1992), *Naming the Powers: The Language of Power in the New Testament* (Philadelphia, 1984), *Unmasking the Powers: The Invisible Forces that Determine Human Existence* (Philadelphia, 1986).

[38] See a more typical theological analysis of power by the Catholic feminist theologian Anne E. Carr, resulting from considering the question of divine power as a form of coercion. She strongly contrasts this approach with the working of the Holy Spirit: 'Providence, Power and the Holy Spirit' in *Horizons*, 29/1 (2002): 80–93.

So perhaps the root cause of the perils risked by Snook is simply that he stays provocatively true to his chief idea: *everything is power* (= Spirit) even if power is not everything.[39] The problem with any such view which generalizes divine power or divine Spirit/spirit, is that we are left with undifferentiated, autonomous power as a brute fact in the universe. The concept of Spirit/spirit turns into a mere cipher for anything that can lay claim to observable effects. It means everything (including the utterly intolerable) and, then again, nothing. Or indeed it denotes too much diluting of the 'spirit' until it is the same as every influence in the universe, or perhaps even every*thing*. Despite the highest of intentions, Snook's version of this generalization of the Spirit, partly driven by process thought and African naturalism, could only with difficulty avoid implicating the very Spirit of Jesus in the worst features of human life.

However, one statement must soften any criticism here. It is that the problem Snook encounters also faces just about every Christian theology in a different way, namely the reconciling of divine presence with the worst of human ugliness. Few can claim completely to have cracked the problem. There can be no quarrel with Snook's claim that there can be no ultimate and unambiguous way of imagining the Spirit's activity in the world of bad deeds.[40] Nevertheless, we must head off any assertion that so much as *seems* determined to legitimate oppression or offer it a bolthole.

Moreover, Snook does eventually turn to a more positive expression of the Spirit's power, if somewhat fleetingly and perhaps at the risk of neutralizing his other stance described above. He moves from considering power as theocracy to weighing up power as freedom, and then as justice.[41] No longer do monarchs and dictators take the foreground, but now rather prophets and the prophetic tradition.[42] The call for justice in prophetic voices, it turns out, does not overturn order. On the contrary it stands for new social order against disorder. The prophets promote interplay between unity and justice.[43] Nevertheless we are looking at freedom as the keynote of the Spirit's power.[44] Rulers and generals no longer symbolize power in the discussion but instead the imagination turns to explorer and entrepreneur to understand power as freedom. The power of this freedom comes from the Spirit, though the Spirit does not determine the specific use of such empowerment.[45] Alongside this there must be held the imagining of justice whose standard-bearers are the peacemakers.

---

[39] Snook, p. 20.

[40] Snook, p. 79.

[41] Snook, p. 64.

[42] Snook, p. 10.

[43] Snook, p. 10.

[44] Snook, p. 64.

[45] Snook, p. 64.

Power, Spirit and Pentecost

What, then, is the main insight on power and Christian community in particular to be gleaned from Snook's approach? More than we might expect in the light of the discussion so far, for he effectively highlights a dilemma facing all ecclesiology. How does one distinguish between power at work in the world generally and power in the life of Christian community and do so without unduly playing down the sociological nature of church? And what part does the Spirit play in such an account?

Traditionally, these questions in doctrinal writings on church have just been ignored, or more charitably, not yet addressed. But the desirable objectives are probably clearer in our time than ever before. First, it is important to recognize, as Snook does, forms of power which inhabit church in much the same way as they do elsewhere in the world in general. Here Foucault helps us. Before him we thought power was only a niche activity of dominating personalities, and all about scrambling and competing for slices of the limited power-pie. He has shown us that sociological differentials exist in every social group and scatter power-relations right through any group's entire complex of relationships. *Everyone* in a community is involved in power-relations because such relations are just an inevitable angle of social existence. Hence the local church community shares this feature with every other social grouping, perhaps aggravated by the forces of conviction and activism. In this sense, power inhabits it in roughly the same way as other groups

Secondly one would want to identify a working of the power of Spirit of Christ in the community of the *koinonia* community, which is distinctively tied to Jesus and yet not in any way implying such power as a unique privilege of church. Here we find ourselves gazing at an ancient and venerable dispute, for many related issues have raged around the so-called *filioque* controversy for centuries. Most importantly, how does it make a difference to our understanding of the Spirit (and therefore of the Spirit's power) to associate the Spirit in a specific way with Jesus' activity and not primarily, or just generally, with activity in the creation? Normally, the more we generalize the Spirit, the more diversity we encounter in settling on a meaningful answer to this question. But in fact Snook latches on to an insight that could prove very fruitful. He concludes that there was a purpose to the early believers' wait for the power of the Spirit (Acts 1.8). They had to receive the courage to venture beyond Jerusalem as witnesses to the way of Jesus, his resurrection and his 'kingdom'.[46] It was a willingness to cross borders, into the wide world of unfamiliar cultures, and, if necessary to die for the sake of the Good News about Jesus. It was the power to venture out with what was already 'known' by the disciples but not yet borne into the wide world by them.

If we were to take this single insight and utter it again in Foucauldian tones, we should find ourselves describing the power of Pentecost in the following radical

[46] Snook, pp. 68–9.

way. The power of the Spirit of Pentecost enables members of a community on the way of Jesus to break the mould of the prevailing culture and instead to live out the way of Jesus in word and actions. That way in Jesus' day was a challenge to the accepted patterns of power generally accepted in their Roman environment. We encounter here the 'transgression', or trangressive 'truth' once more, but not restricted to *spoken* truth. Now the transgressive statement surfaced in relationships, mutual service and life-giving renunciations of self. Its distinctiveness turned on resistance to the top-down culture and the endlessly layering ways of power in the Roman world. In the power of the Spirit of Jesus, a decision to live out transgression against prevailing power patterns in society, would stand out vulnerably in the way that Jesus stood out.

Therefore to take the meaning of Pentecost and the power of the Spirit of Jesus in this way, points away from quite traditional understandings of power and Spirit usually dominant in ecclesiology. Many hardly move beyond some preoccupation with 'spiritual authority'. The less positive versions of this include situations such as those where authority consists in a highly directive, non-accountable group leadership in a local church, or a personal teaching authority too conscious of its own knowledge and instruction, or an authority claiming privileged miraculous experiences or deeds. None of these, surely, have yet captured the sense of power at very heart of Pentecost. That rather appears to concern the Spirit's power present in the whole church community. Such power turns the *koinonia* community outwards so that its interest in power takes a different colour altogether. In the Spirit of Jesus it seeks to know power in the shape of the *martyria* or witnesses. So its internal relations and handling of power patterns testify to the way of Jesus Christ. Then notions in the Jesus narrative such as setting the oppressed free, releasing the poor, healing the sightless, bringing peace, spring to mind as the chief forms of Pentecostal power. Such traits arise from what Jesus said the power of the Spirit would do through his work as the Servant of the Lord. Yet as long as the common life of a church community is dominated by an unaccountable authority figure or a self-serving spirituality, this outworking of the Spirit's power will not germinate and spread life. Accordingly, when the real, central meaning of Pentecost hits the *koinonia* community, the Spirit is surely already bringing unity in heart and mind. But then it would not be a unity imposed or engineered from above, or consist of a bureaucratic uniformity or depend on a naturally powerful personality. Rather, such a view of the Spirit's power surely suggests that the Spirit of the Christian tradition fosters a unity of uncomfortable but empowered diversity. Church community becomes a place of courageous, mutual truth-speaking with matching actions, transgressive truths which can counterbalance negative power moves especially dominating ones. It will indeed have leadership, but one tempered by the transgressive equality of individuals implied by the *koinonia*.

Christian theologies tend to assume that no generalized power in the world will make possible this venture of the Jesus community let alone actualize it. This journey of *koinonia* community across boundaries, stepping out behind Jesus, speaking and living out Good News, is taken to need more specific empowerment than that which general energies usually supply. On this account empowerment in church community only springs from the distinctive power of the Spirit of Jesus, based on the distinctive Jesus way. According to the Christian Scriptures, this Jesus is at the same time fully human and the centre of the cosmos (Eph 1.21–2; Col 1.16,17 for just two examples). Hence the power of the Spirit of Jesus is certainly not imprisoned in the Jesus-community. But then again that power is not present to church in quite the same way as everywhere else. As Ralph Del Colle has it, personal transformation and the building of community disclose the public power of the Spirit.[47] The result is a sharing of the Spirit in diversity in local church and a carrying of that experience outwards in joint service for the empowering of others.[48] Hence in traditional theology the power of the Spirit in a community of the Jesus way may be distinctive but should not be exclusive or introverted.

Power and Life: Jűrgen Moltmann

Attention in recent times to the subject of Spirit and power can hardly ignore the influential work of Jűrgen Moltmann.[49] Moltmann has for many years toiled to find a reconciliation between Eastern and Western traditions on the Spirit. He has remained faithful to the Western emphasis on the Trinitarian Spirit of *Christ* while responsive to Eastern Orthodoxy's wider vision of the Spirit's activity in the whole world. His proposals on the *filioque* controversy[50] possibly deserved more ecumenical fruit than they have so far yielded. Granted, his own doctrine of the Spirit first received sustained attention by him precisely as the Spirit of the church,[51] but even here the green shoots of his fresh thinking pushed above the surface. For instance he treated the sacraments of the Spirit as events made porous to the whole non-churched world. So for example he wrote of a communion table of hospitality, an open invitation to any who would come,[52] and described baptism as a stage of initiation into openness to the world.[53] He also stretched the 'notes of the church' to touch politics and social action.[54] But above all he stressed the

---

47 Ralph Del Colle, 'The Holy Spirit: Presence, Power, Person', *Theological Studies*, 62/2 (2001): 322–34, p. 327.

48 Del Colle, p. 327.

49 Muller Fahrenholz, pp. 58–61 and the continuing significance of Moltmann even for today despite postmodernism and relativism.

50 Jűrgen Moltmann, *Spirit of Life: A Universal Affirmation* (London, 1992), pp. 71–3, 292–5, 306–9.

51 Second edition: Jűrgen Moltmann, *The Church in the Power of the Spirit: A Contribution to Messianic Ecclesiology* (London, 1998), The first edition in English was 1977. In fact it was more about church than about Spirit.

52 Moltmann, *The Church in the Power of the Spirit*, pp. 244–6.

53 Moltmann, *The Church in the Power of the Spirit*, pp. 226–41.

54 Moltmann, *The Church in the Power of the Spirit*, pp. 337–61.

Spirit's life-giving activity and so selected decisively the controlling theme of his later handling of pneumatology.[55]

Then came translations of Moltmann's *God in Creation* (1985),[56] followed by *The Spirit of Life* (1992),[57] *The Source of Life* (1997)[58] and *The Coming of God*,[59] all deeply pneumatological. It became abundantly clear in these works that for Moltmann the Spirit's empowering in no way gave the green light for forms of 'power over', either within or by the *koinonia*. Usually an emphasis on 'power over' regarding the Spirit arises from such things as an interest in a miraculous vindication of church mission, or political clout for church, or in 'power over' for some select group. Instead, in Moltmann's approach the idea of a Spirit of power paradoxically spelt only too clearly the very opposite – the vulnerability in and of the Christian community. For him the presence of the power of the Spirit always implies openness, vulnerability and humble commitments in the *koinonia* community. Moreover, the Spirit of God was on the side of life everywhere not just in churches. So in the *Spirit of Life* and *The Source of Life* the main thrust of Moltmann's approach was to start even more emphatically with the Spirit as vital and vitalizing. Hence Spirit-power equated with Spirit-life, the Hebrew *ruach* or breath, that which impregnated the whole world with its life.[60] This could never be restricted to some kind of special life found only in church, even the church of Messiah, even in church in the power of the Spirit. Rather this same Spirit of God is encountered wherever there is overflowing, luxuriant and precious life in the wealth of the world's natural and creative domains.

To this degree, Moltmann's notion of spirit as underlying all life, might seem to resemble other theologies of the Spirit and nature. But he enjoyed one special advantage in describing the Spirit as *life*, and not merely as *power*. Life is a positive quality, contrasting of course with the negative of death. Had Moltmann presented the Spirit primarily as equal to the underlying power in the world, he would have found himself deifying, and so dignifying, the many destructive powers intrinsic to our human and non-human creation. As we have seen, this is the kind of problem that dogs such pneumatologies as that of Lee Snook's. Hence Moltmann was emphatic in rejecting pantheism in any form. And the Spirit of life always stood out in distinction from powers of death and negativity. In fact the Spirit drove out death in its many guises as 'power over', such as oppression, injustice or merely simple, cynical discouragement.[61] But God could all the

---

55 A major theme of Moltmann in both *The Spirit of Life* and *The Source of Life*.

56 Jűrgen Moltmann, *God in Creation : an Ecological Doctrine of Creation* (London, 1985).

57 *The Spirit of Life, A Universal Affirmation* (London,1992).

58 *The Source of Life, The Holy Spirit and the Theology of Life* (London 1997).

59 Jűrgen Moltmann, *The Coming of God : Christian Eschatology* (London, 1996).

60 Moltmann, *Church in the Power of the Spirit*, p. 191, but also throughout *The Spirit of Life*.

61 Moltmann, *Spirit of Life*, p. 128.

same be experienced 'in and under' everything in the world simply because of the presence of the Spirit of life in places of death. God was holy power in the world as opposed to unholy powers. The Spirit was power, but strictly the power only of life, the eternal wellspring.[62] The experiences of the world thus retained their varied character, often containing elements of death and negativity. However that underlying positive of life, the Spirit, may often be discovered through and in death-like experiences.[63] For God is to be found not indiscriminately in the presence of power but in the creative power of life.[64]

It seems fair to read Moltmann's talk about the Spirit at this point as focused not on God as 'power over' but on a divine 'power of', more explicitly the power of life or 'vitality'. The significance of this for *koinonia* became clear too. This energy, vitality, life was concentrated in a 'charismatic' community of diversity in unity. Church lived in the sheer variety of its charismata, which included roles and contributions of all kinds, and was united in a fellowship of the single energy of the Spirit.[65] Moltmann's work on church as a whole implies that no role or contribution aims at layering or privileging in that power, that one energy.

He also went on to clarify what he hoped for in his plea for the mutual reciprocity of Son and Spirit in connection with the power of 'the Spirit of Christ'. What came to the front of the discussion now was this: the Son was the one who suffered for the creation and the Spirit was the intimate Spirit of that suffering Son. Jesus perceived his mission from what we see in the baptism narrative. He knew himself as Messiah, and loved of the Father, through the Spirit. This Spirit 'led' Jesus 'into the mutual history between himself and the Father.'[66] So this energizing Spirit enabled humble service to sinners, the sick and the poor. The Spirit's power was upon the Son *not for the sake of the Son himself but for others*.[67] More startling still, Moltmann suggested that the descent of the Spirit in the baptism of Jesus not only indicated the divine *Shekinah*, that is, God's presence. It also signalled a 'self-restriction' and 'self-humiliation' on the part of the Spirit. For through being in close association with the Son in reciprocity, the Spirit identified with the suffering of the Son's life and mission. The Spirit was the companion of Jesus in his sufferings, drawn into them and providing strength to Messiah in them.[68] The power of exorcism in the Spirit pointed to the withering away of everything that could not endure in the presence of the cross. So what shrivelled in its sight was violence, greed and arrogance, so often the marks of 'power over'.[69] By this companionship of suffering solidarity, the Spirit made possible the final sacrifice

---

62 Moltmann, *Spirit of Life*, p. 35.

63 Moltmann, *Spirit of Life*, p. 35.

64 Moltmann, *Spirit of Life*, p. 42.

65 Moltmann, *Spirit of Life*, p. 274.

66 Moltmann, *Spirit of Life*, p. 61.

67 Moltmann, *Spirit of Life*, p. 61.

68 Moltmann, *Spirit of Life*, pp. 51, 62, 191 and *Source of Life*, pp. 16–18.

69 Moltmann, *Spirit of* Life, p. 18.

of the Son. And out of that same unity the Spirit became the energizing Spirit of the resurrection. Christ was raised through God's *ruach*.[70] The Spirit therefore is now that divine energy of life, life-giving in the raising of Jesus and onward into his continuing presence through the ages. Moreover, the Spirit as the fountain of life would in the end transform this passing world.[71] The end of the mission of Jesus on earth marked a resurrection newness for all disciples of Jesus.[72] The community of faith emerging from this embryonic life would hence grow in the realm of the Spirit into a charismatic community, with newly vitalized gifts and capabilities.[73] By this Spirit of humble power and mutual self-giving as companions of the way of Jesus, the community of believers should replicate Christ in the world. But disciples go there only as tied closely through the Spirit with the suffering and selflessness of Messiah. This is the natural and preeminent domain of the Spirit's power.

Moltmann, Spirit and Power in Church

It is now possible to turn back to the question of what Moltmann's recasting of the *filioque* controversy in such terms would mean for power in a community on the way of Jesus. It would surely shift the key meaning of the Spirit's role in church dramatically. Hence when theology speaks of a church in the power of the Spirit of *Christ*, it does not primarily intend a local church community identified by authorities and structures, or signs and wonders that compel submission,[74] or powerful speakers of words, even true words, or endowments of worldly power. Moltmann's work can be restated this way: the power of the Spirit is the power for church in some measure *to be to the world as Jesus living in the Spirit was*. The Spirit of the resurrection empowers a community of the Spirit precisely for this. Any remarkable gifting, leading or speaking then becomes purely a subset of the selfsame 'pneumatic calling' of a church community to the mission of the self-giving Jesus through the power of the Spirit.

It may indeed be correct also to draw a secondary meaning from Moltmann's work. This is that 'being to the world as Jesus was' promises ever increasing transformation in that same world.[75] Hence we are firmly in the domain of 'power to' and moving away from that popular political sense of 'power over'. Such a community, we might then argue, cannot avoid brushing against those questions

---

70 On Moltmann's use of *ruach* see Geiko Muller-Farhenholtz on Moltmann in *The Kingdom and the Power: The Theology of Jurgen Moltmann* (London, 2000), pp. 184–7.

71 Moltmann, *Spirit of Life*, p. 66.

72 Moltmann, *Spirit of Life*, p. 68, *Source of Life*, p.19.

73 Moltmann, *Spirit of Life*, p. 69.

74 See Moltmann, *Source of Life*, p. 65, where the healing power of Jesus came not from his Lordship but from his sufferings.

75 Muller-Farhenholtz, p. 187.

of freedom and power raised by Foucault. A church in the Spirit's power might reasonably be expected to envisage freedom under a specifically Christian form, that of the community of *koinonia*.

Such a form of power in community particularly seems to offer a more radical type of freedom, one that both resembles and differs from Foucault's late quest to free the self from top-down suppressive forces of culture. Therefore, despite common fears, this Jesus-inspired freedom from the Spirit should not be taken to oppress and normalize the self through crushingly impossible ideals. But instead we should see here the authentic power of the Spirit of Jesus setting free people who are on the way of Jesus. However, for Moltmann as for other writers considered, Christian freedom is not primarily freedom *from* but freedom *for*. It is a freedom to be, freedom to do, freedom to become what Jesus was and did for the world. Those who open themselves to such freedom are not captured and oppressed by it but released and energized. The Spirit of Christ stands for them as a freedom power of life not death.[76] The Spirit's power is in whatever drives out death, welcomes the marginalized and comforts the sad, displaying the true 'powers and energies' of the Spirit of life.[77] Or to put it more simply, the power of the Spirit is the power of God's life-giving love.[78] So for Moltmann, freedom is a new empowerment in the social domain. Its future there springs from commitments to a shared project,[79] for church community, that of living, speaking and embodying the Good News of the way of Jesus in human lives.

The irony here is that it was Foucault who set Christian communities an example of just such a freedom in his unremitting advocacy for the mentally ill and imprisoned. Paradoxically, he did not need to conjure the 'aesthetics of the self' in order to install the best form of freedom or transgressive power against bio-power. Nor did he need the reassuring fluidity of an ever-changing self of which he sometimes spoke. Freedom *for* and power *to* (and the 'power *of*' life too Moltmann would insist) were already present in his activism, testifying to the fact that bio-power did not after all extinguish resistance and freedom in him. For Moltmann this is also the calling of church community, though church must take its lead, and draw its strength, from the distinctive life of Jesus through the Spirit's power.

Power, Spirit and Freedom

It is now possible to detect where Christian theology as represented in these three writers differs from Foucault's approach to freedom. For Foucault freedom is the shifting, listless capacity to be different from one moment to another, in

---

76 Muller-Farhenholtz p. 190, on Moltmann.

77 Moltmann, *Source of Life*, pp. 19–20.

78 Moltmann, *Source of Life*, p. 55.

79 Moltmann *Spirit of Life* in several places, but see especially pp. 117–20.

order to resist the determining force of disciplinary and bio-power. In his later work, as we saw, Foucault reached for this kind of freedom through aesthetics, or creative shaping, of the self. We saw that some feminist writing supposed here an inadequate conception of the self as constituted in relationship.[80] In addition Julio De Santa Ana speaking from a background in Catholic liberation theology roots freedom not merely in being set free but in a capacity to multiply the gift of freedom.[81] This freedom means that those living in the power of the Spirit are freed from 'legalism', a word unusually indicating here that the order of the world cannot exercise an oppressive control over those set free.[82] Equally important, this gift of freedom in the Spirit's power founds a new community, one that multiplies freedom by pursuing justice and inclusion for marginalized peoples.[83] This is the nature of real freedom where the word and values of Jesus fill the consciousness. They are like powers or energies that enter the mind and enable action against the diverse threats posed by oppressive human power. Strangely this is a power and freedom emanating precisely from a state of powerlessness.[84]

It would be too much of a digression to pause and turn aside into lengthy discussions of the *filioque* debate, the personality of the Spirit or the Spirit and the secular world. Suffice to say however that one should ask in passing, what connections stand out concerning the relation of church to world in the domain of the Spirit. For Lewis Mudge 'community' signifies the 'whole communal reality' in the world whether that stems consciously or not from Jesus and the Spirit's power.[85] Mudge leaves the revision in no doubt. Christian congregations are not so much primary sites of 'the Spirit's people-gathering work' but a way of discerning every kind of Spirit-formed social reality in the world (a view which was questioned in Chapter 2). For Mudge, Christian congregations decipher and make visible the universal power of the Spirit in the broad universal making of 'people of God'. So what if something of such human community does appear outside of church? This feature beyond church can be recognized as the Spirit's doing and be welcomed. It is not surprising that Mudge is attracted to the work of Peter Hodgson which looks to Hegel's prioritization of the movement of history and to Michael Welker's wish to generalize the Spirit.[86] But can that response

80 See discussion of *Freedom and Self* below.

81 Julio De Santa Ana, 'Spirit of Truth – Set us Free!', in William Barr (ed.), *Constructive Christian Theology in the Worldwide Church* (Grand Rapids, 1993), 429–38, pp. 433, 434.

82 De Santa Ana, p. 433.

83 De Santa Ana, p. 433.

84 De Santa Ana, p. 433.

85 Lewis S. Mudge, *The Sense of a People: Towards a Church for the Human Future* (Philadelphia, 1992), p. 30.

86 Mudge, pp. 143–8.

stem exclusively from Mudge's notion that the term 'people of God' signifies the 'whole communal reality' in the world?[87]

It is already fairly conventional for theology to suggest that the Spirit reveals to the world the presence of the rule of Jesus in creation. This position tacitly agrees that the action of the Spirit is not limited to the community of Christians.[88] But surely one need not submerse the *koinonia* common life in a reductive general community building project in order to be open in spirit to this idea of community in the wider world. A community of faith usually attributes the special character of its community life to knowledge of the way of Jesus and to the Spirit's creation of that life among its members. Members see that their participation springs from the recognition not of a universal self-reliance and power now appearing in them. Rather they attribute everything to the power of the Spirit in making the life of Jesus theirs.[89] They sense the Spirit of freedom specifically in a shared dependence on the Spirit, on a sharing of goods and gifts, joys and sacrifices – all providing a 'window' on the final transformation of everything.[90]

The WCC statement on the nature and purpose of the church, then, summarizes this angle of view perfectly. On account of the eschatological Spirit and also of the Word of God, church as a product of Word and Spirit finds itself already to be the eschatological community.[91] Similarly a traditional approach finds the Spirit to be the chief mode of God's presence in world and *koinonia*, linking church to the absent Jesus of the ascension.[92]

The later companion WCC statement, *The Nature and Mission of the Church*, specifies what the period of absence and anticipation entails.[93] A *koinonia* community is not only called but also 'empowered', an implicit reference to the Spirit. And that empowerment follows from the *maturia* (martyr, witness) character of church, enabling it to share in the suffering of all peoples and the chief means of this quality is to care for poor, needy and marginalized people and

---

87 Mudge, pp. 90–91.

88 Donna Geernaert, 'Church as Koinonia/Church as Sacrament', in Tamara Grdzelidze (ed.), *One, Holy, Catholic and Apostolic: Ecumenical Reflections on the Church. Faith and Order Paper No. 197* (Geneva, 2005), 62–77, p. 74.

89 See for example James K. A. Smith, *Who's afraid of Postmodernism: Taking Derrida, Lyotard and Foucault to Church* (Grand Rapids, 2006), p. 107.

90 Douglas Farrow, *Ascension and Ecclesia: On the Significance of the Doctrine of the Ascension for Ecclesiology and Christian Cosmology* (Edinburgh, 1999), p. 71.

91 World Council of Churches, *The Nature and Purpose of the Church: A Stage on the Way to a Common Statement: Faith and Order Paper No. 181* (Geneva, 1998), p. 18. See Farrow for a heady statement of this, p. 28. It is a perfectly classic statement and valid if set against the balancing data of sociological reality, which Farrow himself handles, p. 11. See also p. 125.

92 Farrow, p. 270.

93 World Council of Churches, *The Nature and Mission of the Church: A Stage on the Way to a Common Statement. Faith & Order Paper 198* (Geneva, 2005), p. 26.

to shoulder the burden of advocacy for them.[94] Equally this quality also entails a following of the Jesus way, bearing marks of the cross.[95] In a rich and incisive passage the statement makes clear that true *koinonia* community involves being empowered. That same empowerment was for the exposing of unjust structures with an eye to transforming them. The community is empowered, that is, to bring words of hope and to engage in acts of compassion, the task of reconciliation, care of creation and commitment to the healing of broken relationships.[96] Every one of these concerns, of course, are known to activate all people of goodwill whether in church or outside of it. But what marks the Christian community as partakers of the *koinonia* of the last times, is its freely admitted dependence in these actions on the power of the Spirit and its desire specifically to walk the way of Jesus in conformity to him, making known and 'living the love of God'.[97]

Despite the theory on power, and the power in the theory, an inflated self-importance on the part of churches still occurs too often. Its prophets have therefore still had plenty to talk to them about, and often. In these circumstances, an appeal like that of Lewis Mudge's to a universal people-shaping Spirit, looks especially attractive. It is even more so for also avoiding indistinct generalizations of the Spirit, say, as power in every conceivable guise. Despite the attractiveness of Mudge's approach, however, the detail might be judged to let it down. For to be true to its founder a Christian *koinonia* community needs to discern itself as a distinctive site of the way of Jesus and of the Spirit's power. Otherwise it is unlikely to have the passion or the insight to decipher Jesus-like community for a wider population. It must itself be more than a sign. It must also *be* that which it discerns and in a fairly special form too. And that special form will have something to do with its intentional and conscious attachment to Jesus as 'Lord' and to the Spirit of Jesus similarly. Mudge admits that in practice, outside the community of faith the Spirit's community-shaping work may be potential, partial and fragmentary.[98] But if we take our lead anyway from the Christian Scriptures and the early Christian community we find something beyond general, vague references to 'spirit' power in the world.

The communities of disciples springing up around Jesus differed dramatically from any emasculated or randomized view of the Spirit's power. While painfully imperfect in many ways, even in the first blush of the way of Jesus, the community of his Spirit nevertheless stood out clearly as a distinct, identifiable site of the Spirit's power. For them, the Spirit re-shaped people in the example, words and life of Jesus, in order to resist person-shaping forces pressing down to 'squeeze them into its mould' (Rom 12.2). It was an understatement to designate such communities merely as a sign of the Spirit's universal activity. They sensed a

[94] WCC, *The Nature and Mission of the Church*, p. 26.

[95] WCC, *The Nature and Mission of the Church*, p. 16.

[96] WCC, *The Nature and Mission of the Church*, p. 26.

[97] WCC, *The Nature and Mission of the Church*, p. 26.

[98] Mudge, p. 39.

demand on them to become a radical anticipation of the universal kingdom.[99] The church community in the Spirit understood itself as the intended radical vanguard of such spiritual transformation – a community gathered around the Jesus way and consciously committed to it. In the second century this understanding made possible a natural recognition of kindred movements when the new faith came to engage its surrounding intellectual culture. Nor was the community of the way naively unaware of its own counter-cultural character in the slavedom called Rome. The Spirit then is taken in the early Christian account to be forming distinctive communities around the way of Jesus. And an equally distinctive, disruptive, transgressive character attaches to the same 'power' associated with this Spirit. However, this is the Spirit of Jesus the vulnerable one. This fact alone leads us at last to wrestle with one more slippery notion.

Power, Spirit and Weakness

We saw earlier that Lee Snook was uneasy with the idea that Jesus was powerless. There is some justification for this caution when looking at power in the founding documents. It would perhaps be better to say that power is indeed attributed to Jesus, but power of a radically different and startling kind from that normally under view in ancient times. His was the illogical, counterintuitive power which operates after a person has laid aside every possible bid for domination. We recall that domination denoted 'power over' stripped bare of any possible flux or reversals. With power renunciation we are admittedly in a tricky area and feminist theology illustrates the conundrum well. On the one hand, as we have seen, it shuns 'power over' in social relations and promotes instead a 'power to', energized by interactive relationships that draw on vulnerability and corporateness. On the other hand its analysis of present realities cannot always find comfort in Foucault's reassurances of power as now diffused and neutral, even possibly being a mere construct. Some feminism wants to declare an only too real and identifiable 'power over' today, not just affecting the oppressed women of the world but all who are pressed down to underclass levels. The appropriate response, for these feminist viewpoints, is a continuing struggle for liberation, an uncovering of the domain of 'power over' as an act of realism and in order to engage within it. This awkward balancing act, however, dogs attempts by theological writers to define the power that attaches to Jesus and that challenges the disciples of his way.

---

99 This is the famous theme, of course, of Jűrgen Moltmann, *Theology of Hope on the Ground and the Implications of a Christian Eschatology* (London, 1967), and echoes throughout his subsequent works. Charles West reads the Pentecost event as the *koinonia* of Messiah, inheriting and universalizing the *oikomune* of Israel and the dispersion: Charles C. West, *Power, Truth and Community in Modern Culture* (Harrisburg, 1999), pp. 60–62.

Pasewark, Weakness and Power

However, first we must pay attention to feminist reticence on talking up 'weakness' as a Christian virtue attached to power. This reluctance finds support from an unexpected quarter in the shape of Kyle Pasewark's landmark Lutheran study on power. We recall that Pasewark adopted a view of power as strictly 'power to', and traced it in ripples of effectiveness or efficacy flowing out from one domain to another. Given this understanding, by definition power can never be described as weakness. Efficacy can never be ineffectiveness. Hence he further argues that any such 'transvaluation' of power into weakness cannot work. His approach reflects reluctance for adopting a seemingly strange word usage where weakness at the same time goes under the description of power. That usage would also by remorseless logical process, transvalue God's own sovereignty and power into divine weakness (and the reverse!) which is an inversion too far.

Moreover, according to Pasewark, using the word weakness here overlooks the stubborn fact that sovereignty, even God's, must include an element of domination and compulsion.[100] But few feminist writers, let alone process theologians, would subscribe to all these assumptions. So what Pasewark really shows is that in places where the word 'power' should be restricted to the sense 'power to' (for him 'efficacy') it would run into problems if found describing power also as weakness.

This brief excursion is helpful in highlighting how categories have to be clear in any discussion of the slippery concept of power. It is possible, misguidedly, to dismiss weakness or vulnerability from the theatre of critical debate on power. Actually weakness is not quite deployed in the way Pasewark suggests. For in this exchange it denotes self-renunciation/vulnerability which proves in the end to trigger 'powerful' results. This conclusion could be inferred from Pasewark's own notion of power as efficacy. In renouncing or letting go of 'power over' (weakness) one may still look to be effective (or efficacious) in the sense of 'power to' and 'power with', particularly, say, for the benefit of others. Hence, the approach only *looks like* the transformation of power into its opposite, namely weakness, for the formula turns out to be not 'power *instead of* weakness', but 'power *through* weakness'. In Pauline language it is still power, only it is the 'power to', the efficacious, empowering-of-others kind of power. This recognition does not transvalue power into weakness at all. Instead we are looking at a power, an effectiveness or efficacy, making its entrance only *through weakness* (so for example, 2 Cor. 4.7; 12.9,10; 13.4,9). And here the 'power to', springing from weakness, takes a very specific connotation. It is simply the ability to give up the privileges of 'power over' in order to bring to someone else the benefits of 'power to'.[101]

---

[100] Pasewark, p. 321.

[101] See Graham Tomlin, *The Power of the Cross: Theology and the Death of Christ in Paul, Luther and Pascal* (Carlisle, 1999), p. 4. After all, this is the only meaning of

Power Through Weakness

So provisionally, with this clarification in mind, we have to turn to the fountainhead of the 'power through weakness' thinking on power. The stream runs, of course, straight back to Jesus and to Paul. This fact should surely not surprise us since the shape of history owes so much to an obscure, politically powerless carpenter in a despised country dying the death of a helpless criminal. If this is not 'power to' out of no-'power over', or 'power through weakness', it is hard to imagine what is. The sayings of Jesus about service and humility thus have as their background the enslaving, sticky web of patronage and overlapping obligations and hierarchies that marked the dawn of the Imperial Augustan age.[102] Such a stifling, stratified society gave rise to numerous struggles to trample down the person below on the slippery pole while striving for a new position higher up. Especially in the higher reaches, vicious power-games and ruthless treatment of those considered inferior scarred human relationships. Jesus has thus been seen as a 'disturbance' at the lowest point of the pyramid (of power).[103] The cross of Jesus, then, it could be claimed, represented an ethic which was subversive of these prevailing top-down dominations.[104] It seems accordingly that the disempowered status of Jesus, a carpenter from no-hope Galilee, uniquely illustrates an effectiveness through weakness that ran transgressively against the prevailing perception of power as 'power over' or not power at all.

Still, the formulation of weakness as releasing power came to its sharpest expression in the theology of the apostle Paul. 'Power through weakness' could have been his epitaph … and in a way it did in the end become just that.[105] Some of the problems raised over Paul and power, particularly by feminists, will be taken up later. For many attempts have been made to penetrate the spirit of Paul and his understanding of church. However what we find in the Corinthian correspondence squares fairly well with our analysis so far. Paul shunned 'power over', a human achievement through superiority of speech or wisdom. In contrast to the Corinthian city's power patterns, he turned away from speechifying that was self-serving and which stemmed from arrogance.[106]

It was at this point, that Paul claimed to have been among the Corinthians frankly in 'weakness and fear' (1 Cor 2.1), most likely recalling his feeling of inadequacy and his humbling by a sense of the one real power and majesty –

---

weakness and 'power to' in the narrative of Jesus.

[102] Joel Green and Mark D. Baker, *Recovering the Scandal of the Cross: Atonement in New Testament and Contemporary Contexts* (Carlisle, 2003), p. 39.

[103] Austin Smith, *Journeying with God: Paradigms of Power and Powerlessness* (London, 1990), p. 65.

[104] Green and Baker, pp. 40–41.

[105] Hence the title choice by Timothy Savage: *Power Through Weakness: Paul's Understanding of the Christian Ministry in 2 Corinthians* (Cambridge, 1996), p. 174.

[106] Savage, p. 72.

God's.[107] The contrast between Paul's own lack of power or 'weakness' and God's power seems to resurface in 2 Cor 4.7 ('when I am weak then I am strong').[108] In Paul's account the powerful (efficacious) Good News was carried about exactly by the weak. The weak brought about life for others (2 Cor 4.12).[109] In fact the power of life seemed to depend on the weakness of the bearer. It was only weakness (which included humility) that could carry forward the 'power to', the effectiveness of divine power.[110] Moreover this was a weakness modelled from the constraints upon the very life-experience of Jesus himself. 2 Corinthians 13.4 sums this up: 'He (Christ) was crucified because of weakness … we're also weak in him.'[111] Surely the words here imply that to be weak in Christ did not mean weak *character* or even powerlessness. They pointed rather to sharing in the self-renouncing, servant-like faith centred on God and on drawing down God's power.[112] In fact suffering could be a dying like Christ's, metaphorically speaking, so that the perfect power of Christ could burst out (2 Cor 12.9).[113] *Koinonia* itself sometimes appears as *sunkoinonia*, participation with Christ in his life and his suffering (2 Cor 1.7).[114]

Timothy Savage, however, for all his emphasis on weakness in Paul wants to qualify a reading of Paul's celebrated self-deprecation. He concludes that Paul's determination to foster humility and avoid the celebrity status sought by others was wrongly taken as a sign of personality weakness. And to make matters worse Paul allowed himself to strengthen the caricature by his own tongue in cheek language.[115] In that case, Paul was not really weak. It has all been a mistake in exegesis, compounded by his own mocking rhetoric. It indeed has to be admitted that Paul was not exactly ineffectual, despite his disclaimers. He inspired church action, planted churches and did not blink when they looked to him for leadership. Moreover, he was recognized as the apostle to the Gentiles. He caused a stir wherever he went and powerful political figures listened to him. Yet we know he genuinely felt inadequate for the task. It was not mock-humility or irony when he reported that he felt in low spirits, even in despair and inescapable stress. The Corinthian correspondence, as we have seen, showed this clearly. So the claim to be weak might well be ironic or misleading only to the extent that despite

107 Savage, p. 168.

108 Savage, p. 72.

109 Savage, p. 178.

110 Savage, pp. 166–7.

111 The choice of critical text and the translation of Timothy Savage, p. 174 .

112 Savage, pp. 174–5.

113 Savage, p. 177.

114 As pointed out along with many other examples of a similar vocabulary by L. F. Fuchs, '*Koinonia*: Text and Context for the Church', *Ecumenical Trends*, 22/Fall (1993): 1–15, p. 2.

115 Savage, p. 185.

genuine human frailties Paul still turned out to be a channel of power, only one that depended upon those weaknesses.

Hence Savage too holds that Paul saw his powerlessness as an advantage, so that the divine efficacy ('power to') may also spring from that same spot. Paul's true power here was a far cry from powerful status in the great Roman social hierarchy. Ian Bradley suggests this power is best seen in the light of the Greek *dunamis* rather than the Latin *potestas*, a way of communicating an energy,[116] not unlike Pasewark's 'communication of efficacy'. Hence Christian sacrifice, it is suggested, accomplishes such ends by yielding and giving up rather than by forcing and imposing – the love that endures and suffers, also saves and heals. It has 'power to' achieve these precisely through self-emptying and self-giving.[117] In passing it is worth suggesting that a handling of the subject in this way could therefore by-pass Nietzsche's oft-cited antagonism to Christian 'unmanly' weakness. His grumpy irritation with what he saw as Christianity's emasculation of humanity through wimpering weakness somewhat missed the point. He failed to see the sophistication of a constructive and productive sense to power in the robust early Christian narrative. Jesus-logic called for a self-renouncing and tough adventure, but one that deliberately stood apart from political power. Nietzsche no doubt would have found the resulting effective power ('power to') only the more irritating.[118]

Such an argument all fits with ecumenical agreement over the purpose of churches. According to this, the *koinonia* community is empowered to identify with human suffering through advocacy and by caring for the poor, needy and marginalized.[119]

One more viewpoint demands attention here. Writers reflecting the women's movement have generated perhaps the most pressing of questions today. In summary, they challenge us to ask whether traditional valorizing of the crucifixion event may too easily impose further unwarranted self-sacrifice upon those already marginalized and oppressed. Katherine Keller, a widely published representative

---

116 Ian Bradley, *The Power of Sacrifice* (London, 1993), p. 36. He was specifically interested in this principle as an answer, even ten years ago, to the crisis of non-sustainability in the environment.

117 Bradley, p. 36.

118 See Tomlin, pp. 303–4: Nietzsche was particularly incensed against the God of the Cross found in Luther and Pascal. He judges this God, as Tomlin notes, to be one that seduces, intoxicates, anaesthetizes and corrupts (p. 304 sourced on p. 56). Equally, the notion that the theology of the cross is a denial of life has been countered by seeing it as an honest acknowledgement of powerlessness before God and the power to give up special privileges for the other. So Tomlin, pp. 304–5 who finds it strange for Nietzsche to see this as feebleness of nature.

119 WCC, *Nature and Purpose of the Church*, p. 16.

of this view will be enough to capture the main points.[120] Although there are great differences between the sufferings of Jesus in the biblical narrative and the suffering, say, of the oppressed women and men of the world, both undergo unjust and violent domination.[121] The main issue arising then from feminist analysis concerns the commendation of further disempowerment for those already disempowered quite enough. Equally, it questions whether the overcoming of injustice should depend on a divine 'powerlessness'.[122] Rather, for Keller, the issue is that of spirit let loose by the power of love to overcome and prevail through all adversity. If loyalty to the struggle for justice results in a body's crushing, nevertheless the spirit bent to the struggle will still emerge to inspire others.[123] This is felt to be a better understanding of, say, the resurrection of Jesus than using it as a 'bizarre' proof of God's omnipotence, as seen in classical theism.[124] The Christian tradition's view of the resurrection is, of course, much richer than that, as the biblical texts themselves show (for instance 1 Cor 15.35–58; Phil 3.10–14). Even so, it is being argued here, belief in the successful struggle of Jesus against oppressive powers cannot rest on a theory of a divine almighty power. Ultimately we must therefore reject recourse to a Messiah riding in on a white horse, leading armies of angels.[125] But this reinterpretation by means of a triumphant love itself supposes the very notion being criticized by Keller: that 'weakness' may have its own triumphs and enjoy efficacy, the 'power to'. Can we bring differing viewpoints together then?

Reconciling Opposites on 'Weakness'

What might join the two viewpoints, namely those that play down the weakness of the cross and those that emphasize power through weakness? Maybe there is one thing that they do have in common. Neither of them glorify suffering or weakness for its own sake. Most of the contributors to the discussion accept that renunciation of 'power over' for its own sake might entail a necessary embrace of the costs of the struggle described so well. And it is a Christian struggle, the struggle of Jesus and of many of his followers down the ages. It is a true and worthy exertion, so that the 'weakness' involved in it bears fruit, perhaps only after many seasons and centuries have passed. Equally the term 'disempowerment' indicates something different altogether. It is imposed and inescapable. It does not involve a choice, a thoughtful renunciation for a good end though pain does indeed often mature humanness.

120 Catherine Keller, 'Power Lines', *Theology Today* 55/2 (1995): 188–203, p. 202. See also the summary of Darby Ray by Green and Baker, pp. 175–86.

121 Bradley, p. 255.

122 Keller, p. 202.

123 Keller, p. 202.

124 Keller, p. 202.

125 Keller, pp. 202–3.

At a human level, the mere notion that weakness ultimately may have efficacy gains some illustration from observable, though disturbing instances. These are moments in history where the absence of any 'power over' leads, sometimes grotesquely, to 'power to'. This can happen dramatically in strange moments and as simply emotive facts in the dramas of everyday life. They are certainly not meant here to illustrate some principle of divine working or intention – only to illustrate that it does, bizarrely happen. The brutal manner of the execution of Iraq's president, Sadam Hussein, captured on a mobile phone, is an example. When made public the event transformed him in a few moments from the perpetrator of crimes against humanity into a hero in death, from villain also to victim, leaving a final impression that clouded the more accurate one of him as a brutal dictator. For he gained a notorious dignity in the face of indignities and won himself a disturbingly effective last statement.

All the same, feminist writers have alerted us to real and present dangers, and an honest qualification must therefore be added. Vulnerability, including moments where suffering of the innocent is present, frequently yields no such reversals or effective results and from a Christian point of view such moments remain a problematic mystery to human view.[126] However, the point being made here is a very modest one. It only points to facts. These merely illustrate that it is not incoherent to perceive vulnerability as sometimes containing a capacity to lead power. From here it might have that capacity also, even for good, in a local church community. Absence of 'power over' may indeed on occasion be 'productive' and lead to positive (as well as negative) effects: a 'power to', as distinct from a 'power over'.

The possibility of paradoxical power out of weakness does not prove some universal Christian imperative to seek out suffering. It was to male, free, if non-privileged, Jews that Jesus spoke the values of the cross, not to women and slaves. The founding documents of Christian faith do not prescribe an obligation to defend injustices and sufferings as having some kind of value in themselves. Nor do they commend weakness as a subtle and clever political strategy for the struggle towards final good, like a policy of so-called passive resistance at protests. Nor again does the power in weakness require the renunciation by every Christian of all use of natural influence in the world so that greater good may come. Foucault has shown us that this is impossible anyway. To be related in human society is to belong in a nexus of power whether consciously or not. Similarly, to be a society in the world involves power in the sense of effects on others, perhaps occasionally in contractual situations, even 'power over'. Rather, power in weakness demonstrates the great vitality and range of 'power to' even when stripped of political strength in the backrooms of power-grabbing. So it questions the hegemony of 'power over' as the chief source of 'power to'. And in the light of such revisions it interrogates very deeply all *desire and motivation* focusing on 'power over'.

---

[126] For a sensitive and thoughtful probe into such mystery see Bradley, pp. 249–54.

Foucault's analysis of local power-relations helps us in this matter by reminding us that powerlessness does not have to be an intentional power strategy in order to influence outcomes. These outcomes flow from the unpredictable interplay of different events, dynamics, policies and truth-conceptions. For Christians, though, there is no better example of this than the early Christian narratives where the persecution of Christians contributed to the rapid spread of the Jesus-faith.

So here Foucault is a better guide than Nietzsche. 'Power over', even in its murky depths as domination, does not always get its way. The results of actions by those with 'power over' may not be what is intended. The complexity of interplay in human social relationships can sometimes actually favour those holding no 'power over', turning just such people unexpectedly into the way of 'power to'. There is a Christian line on this. In the way of Jesus and his followers, the turn-over for the disempowered often crops up when in and for the name of Jesus, they speak and act transgressively. Then it really is a case of 'power to' through weakness, that is through no 'power over'.

But what does this discussion mean for a *koinonia* community? Not, surely, an internal, doubly scheming strategy and subversiveness waged from an appearance of weakness. Surely it means rather, a willingness in many situations not to resort to forbidden channels of power even if this seems to leave one genuinely in an exposed position of weakness. Hence no Christian way out exists in an authentic *koinonia* for most forms of 'power over', especially mental or spiritual bullying, the politically intentional building and misuse of power-bases, manipulativeness, intellectual or official pulling of rank, or threats. These all belong, one way or another, to domination, the worst form of 'power over'. This does not exclude proper, legitimated channels of difference and protest conducted in transparent and, so far as possible, equitable ways. Political ethics will offer different interpretations here of what fits which category. This is not our subject. But we are now in a position to return to the question asked earlier: what, more precisely, is the power that attaches to Jesus and also to the *koinonia* of the Spirit of Jesus?

Koinonia of the Cross

The beginnings of an answer to this question lie more open to view before us now than when the enquiry began. We have come across the claims to identify the 'power of the Spirit' not primarily in organizational authority in a local church, or spoken teaching or 'signs and wonders', but in the Spirit's effectiveness in replicating the way of Jesus in the life of the community. And of course, it is a life bearing the burdens of the poor and oppressed, tackling problems by *marturia*, vulnerability and pain-sharing. As Barbara Schwahn reminds us, Ernst Käsemann argued that the cross is *the* true sign of the church and that church is only Christ-like when it takes seriously that sign of the cross. It has been argued that a 'theology of the cross' provides the key criticism of power. It can especially root out unequal power-relations operating in a church.[127] Paul used the death of Jesus to expose a selfish power exercised by the wealthy and influential in the 'Lord's Supper'.[128] Today, in line with Foucault's dissection of micro-power strategies, the cross of Jesus also asks how far church life really does display fluid relations that offer a counterweight to typical power strategies. The death of Jesus then probes commitment to mutual submission, serious pursuit of another person's good, and concrete demonstrations of genuine love.[129]

Of course such things were written before women theologians so competently drew out clarifications about a religion of the cross.[130] Douglas Farrow argues that even an ex-Donatist censured a church which could not criticize itself in the light of Jesus' death, and which failed to see its own 'post ascension precariousness'.[131] Here Farrow relentlessly pursues a theme he deems of critical importance for ecclesiology, namely the need for church to embrace its vulnerability and dependence on the Spirit of Jesus, more specifically in the period of Christ's absence. Irenaeus, he argued, saw this priority even in the second century. No triumphalism was found in Irenaeus. Farrow suggests that instead, the Word and Spirit now in the final age pushed the church back to the cross as the ground and pattern of its engagement.[132] It is well-known that Irenaeus's scheme turned on the expected renewal and transformation of all things through the Spirit's renewing power (grace 'perfecting nature' as is often said). And yet he also stressed the church of the martyrs.[133] Christ's lowly status, ambiguity, and scandalous suffering is the only form his glory may now assume in a fallen world.[134] Moltmann does not surprise us by weighing in here with the blunt assertion that even the healing work of Jesus stems not from divine power as usually understood but from the vulnerability of the cross.[135]

Christian Community in the Ways of 'Weakness'

What we learn from a small selection of viewpoints in theology is that the association of the Spirit with power does not after all hinder the conception of

---

[127] Tomlin, p. 296.

[128] Tomlin, p. 296.

[129] Tomlin, p. 296.

[130] Barbara Schwahn, 'The Sacramentality of the Church: Points of Convergence and Issues to be Addressed', in Tamara Grdzelidze (ed.), *One, Holy, Catholic and Apostolic: Ecumenical Reflections on the Church. Faith and Order Paper No. 197* (Geneva, 2005), 40–50, p. 44.

[131] Farrow, p. 128.

[132] Farrow, pp. 72–3.

[133] Irenaeus cited by Farrow, p. 73.

[134] Farrow p. 223. See also pp. 226–7.

[135] Moltmann, *Spirit of Life*, p. 62.

koinonia as a common share in that Spirit. At a *koinonia* level 'the power of the Spirit' or 'from the Spirit' does not speak of power relations through an unequal possession of Spirit-endowed powers or knowledge. Rather it promises a common capacity for mutual life-giving activity and concern. And far from belonging to power advantages, the power of the Spirit marks power to empower through weakness. The humble sharing of life together on the way of Jesus only enhances the *koinonia* in what it is supposed to be. And with these insights we have discovered a further phrase in the interplay of the prepositions: '*power through*'. That is, 'power through' what is called weakness. Moreover, this may include vulnerability, non-privilege and even suffering. Far from dismantling the unity of the community the commonly shared power of the Spirit is precisely the glue that holds it together. Or to improve the metaphor, in the common life of the way of Jesus, power through weakness functions as the lubrication that flows between power relations and strategies, so turning danger into creative group synergy, or 'power with'. We have again reached the very heart of those distinctive Christian resources that might provide the cantilever to the play of power strategies in the micro-group called church. The evidence for this should lie in the turning outwards of all forms of 'power to' in service of the suffering and oppressed. And so power patterns are after all refocused in the life and example of Jesus himself where power is seen in the forms of vulnerable service and energy.

Chapter 8
Power, Authority and Community

It could be argued that in churches the word 'authority' is at the same time less suspicious and more contentious than 'power'. Traditionally inclined Christians may have a natural instinct to move to the defence of authority even while still disparaging power. This is perhaps because the bare word 'power' summons up thoughts of abuse, danger or threat whereas 'authority' has usually suggested recognizable religious, social and moral order. In fact it also often stands for mission but this association is frequently missed. Moreover the Scriptures do indeed back up such comparisons. 'Power' as 'power over' gets short shrift from Jesus but authority is associated with legitimacy, personal qualification and the *exousia* (authority) given to early church at Pentecost and to apostles. Most traditions, therefore, can locate their precise site of authority. These range from the papal and conciliar forms in Roman Catholicism to the local church meeting in Baptist ecclesiology. We can only acknowledge the variations here but cannot address them in any detail.

Accordingly, this chapter does not move too deeply into the contentious field of authority and ecclesiological order. The subject is one of the more sensitive areas of ecumenism and not to be tackled lightly. Instead we keep our focus and concentrate on authority as a legitimated form of power within a local church community. In other words it is going to be considered as simply continuing the question about power relations, power moves and those factors that offset these. As throughout the book we are not primarily concerned with wider church structures but local church dynamics. And once again it is assumed that the local setting will indeed touch, and be touched by, wider structures of which it is a part. The mechanisms of such connections vary widely, but rightly or wrongly the argument assumes a strong degree of comparability between local church experiences when it comes to strategies and crosswinds. For different traditions recognize only too easily their own dynamics repeated in the experiences of others. Offices and processes may be different but the dynamics between human beings underlying them not so.

But what could this mean for Foucault who never wrote a book about ecclesiology? True he did write about some aspects of church practice. Much of the material concerning us comes from the latest phase of his writing, but a background is already in place from the 1970s, particular from *History of Sexuality, Volume 1.* Perhaps former Catholic Foucault's appearance was overdue anyway.

Foucault, Words and Authority in Church Practice

By the time of 'final' Foucault church belief and practice had got off lightly at his hands. But now at last attention must turn to his most powerful challenge to what he labelled the microscopic practice of authority in churches. His message on pervasive power to church arrived like a biblical prophecy suddenly turned on a pious self-satisfied listener. He had already felled the classic forms of power and exposed them to critical view: sovereign powers, modern state, captains of mental health and national security, framers of law and weavers of culture. These had all been summoned to face the music. Who had escaped so far? Church!

True the odd rumble of thunder, an omen for church, may have been heard earlier in Foucault's treatment of power's multiple reincarnations throughout the ages, but he really turned up the heat on church with the publication of the first volume of his *History of Sexuality*. The book, as we have seen, alleged that control of citizens advanced through subtle ways of creating human identities, rather than through laws and regulations such as oppressed in the days of sovereign power. But most important for us just now is the evidence Foucault cited to support the place of sexuality in the normalizing or conditioning of society. It was designed to cause sharp division in French culture. For the finger of suspicion pointed straight at the Catholic confessional.[1]

'Confession' and 'Pastoral Power'

Confession

We need to keep in mind that Foucault's critique of 'pastoral power' and the 'sacrament of penance' was not trained on all church confessional practice ever but only on the practice's high point in late, seventeenth-century French Catholicism. By then it had developed and refined itself following the challenges of the Protestant Reformation. It had a new self-confidence and hence newly meticulous rules of self-examination sprang up.[2] The rites of confession and penance now took more and more interest in sexual sins and hunted them right down to their details and consequences.[3] In this practice 'everything had to be told'. True, only a small minority of people, even then, went to confession and did the job properly. But even so a technique for surveillance and normalizing had been established for the formation of a true self and a self of truth. It involved processing desire into discourse at the priest's prompting. Everything about sex had to pass between

---

1 For an extended and lucid account of Foucault on this, J. Bernauer, *Michel Foucault's Force of Flight: Toward an Ethics for Thought* (London, 1990), pp. 158–65.

2 Michel Foucault, *The History of Sexuality, Vol 1: An Introduction* (London, 1979), p. 19.

3 Foucault, *History of Sexuality*, p. 19.

relentless 'millstones' of speech.[4] For Foucault all this confessional apparatus and technique then lay to hand for bio-power to pick up and adapt in the allegedly scientific normalizing of such things as sexual behaviour when political and economic forces came along.[5] It is a matter for historians to determine whether this historical connection is sound, but Foucault certainly believed he could identify in his experience the use of confessional techniques under the cover of 'science' within such institutions as mental hospitals, prisons, schools and military establishments in an effort to establish 'normality'.

It was as early as the mid 1970s that Foucault first aired such connections. Seventeeth-century Catholic practice resembled, for him, techniques appearing in the industrialized era. For Foucault, in this way government, disciplinary power and bio-power continued to pick up religious, negative sex-chatter and now applied its technique to social control along with other norms of identity. And that meant not only the control or stimulation of populations. The 'incitement' by scientific discourse to talk endlessly also enhanced further the power of new secular authorities to whom 'confession' was made. Foucault resented for example many physicians, psychiatrists and social scientists whom he had already taken to task for their less than neutral 'science'.[6]

So his bold theory was simple. What might have remained as a niche technique of Catholic formation of a minority had now passed over into a secular 'confession', visited first upon the more vulnerable in society but then rippling out to an entire population in popular normalization. A new effect of state economics had been born, one to promote an efficient demographical process including a 'policing' of the person's identity, especially through the vulnerability of their sexuality. The modern era's apparent liberating of sex turned out in Foucault's theory in 1976 to be much more an invisible net tightening firmly round society.

In 1977 and beyond, the main theme did not change but one clarification emerged. Foucault conceded that the term 'confession' could understandably irritate many people and he admitted that there were of course differences between the experience of Catholic confessional and that of encountering Freud.

Yet the shared ground was still the more significant.[7] For all that Foucault meant by confession was the process that forced a person to give a discourse, or truth about themselves, especially their own sexuality, one that could have

---

[4] Foucault, *History of Sexuality*, p. 21.

[5] Foucault, *History of Sexuality*, p. 23.

[6] Hubert L. Dreyfus and Paul Rabinow, *Michel Foucault: Beyond Structuralism and Hermeneutics* (Brighton, 1982), p. 176.

[7] Foucault in 'The Confession of the Flesh' in Colin Gordon (ed.), *Power/Knowledge: Selected Interviews and Other Writings 1972–1977: Michel Foucault* (Brighton 1980), pp. 194–228, pp. 216–17

profound consequences on that person.[8] This was a fundamental issue.[9] More on this was still to come.

Pastoral Power

The Foucault of his final years came to identify 'pastoral power' as much more significant in the history of control than just a contribution to Christian moral rigour. There were also roots in Christian practice of the early centuries. Pastoral power in its vocational form was a specific intrusion of authority into the personal domain. This power's real importance lay with its depth of incursion into the human interior life, as he argued in some late reflections on the subject.[10] In the Greek use of the metaphor, shepherding was primarily political but in the Hebrew version, 'pastoral' concern for individuals went beyond merely their prosperity and had a long history.[11]

However, the Christian form of Hebrew shepherding as it appeared in monasticism took a novel turn by focusing more on the shepherd's self-giving.[12] Monastic rule also worked for the individual's obedience to a 'shepherd' (personal director), compliance that went beyond a general Christian ethic and even the monastic community's own distinctive code. The practice was at its most acute in submission to the abbot.[13] In this practice the 'shepherd' drew on a searching exposure of the needs and motives of the one who was shepherded. Self-examination emerged as crucial to this 'pastoral' leading.[14] Moreover, Christian pastorship had now created a 'game' with high stakes such as a person's very life, identity and connection to 'truth'.

So Foucault concluded at least three key points and they include some comments which bear on the idea of authority in local church community.[15] First, the second-century Christian faith had emerged distinctively as a salvation religion, leading from life to death through rules of behaviour for a transformation of the self. For

---

8 Foucault, 'The Confession of the Flesh', p. 211.

9 Foucault 'The Confession of the Flesh', p. 216.

10 Michel Foucault, '"Omnes et Singulatem": Towards a Critique of Political Reason', in James D. Faubion (ed), *Power* (London, 1994), pp. 298–325 (previously known from 1979 as 'The Tanner Lectures'). In this work Foucault contrasted Greek and Hebrew versions of the shepherd-king.

11 Foucault, '"Omnes et Singulatem"', pp. 301–3.

12 Foucault, '"Omnes et Singulatem"', p. 308.

13 Foucault, '"Omnes et Singulatem"', p. 308.

14 Foucault, '"Omnes et Singulatem"', pp. 309–10.

15 The spirit of these breathes through his very late work: Michel Foucault, 'Technologies of the Self' in Luther Martin, Huck Gutman, Patrick H. Hutton (eds), *Technologies of the Self: Seminars with Michel Foucault* (Massachusetts, 1998), pp. 16–49. The ideas belong to the period towards the end of his life, after the series of seminars in the United States on 'technologies of the self'.

many, probably most, theologians of course this description would seem a mix of truth and near-misses, but we must leave this fact aside. Secondly, Christianity was a faith more concerned with truth statements than most religions of the time, as it is even now. Thirdly, linked to such truth-statements were deeper statements, namely those about *the self*. Each believer had an obligation to know their own identity, locate desires, know failures and acknowledge faults. Without this it was impossible to attain purity of the soul. And in due course a key element of this process was, of course, self-disclosure of the heart's intimate secrets.

From this history we are urged by Foucault particularly to appreciate a word made famous by the second-century Christian thinker, Tertullian: *exomologēsis*.[16] For Tertullian this word denoted a loud 'confession' or calling out to God. It pointed to a ritual of identifying oneself as sinner. In second-century Christian community, it made for a hard life to commit serious moral or religious offences and then acknowledge them. Processes of humbling came into play. *Exomologēsis* dramatically picked out the penitent.[17] As we have noticed already, the monastic practices of self-examination eventually became even more intensely inward and rigorous, supervised by a spiritual director or some other leader invested with greater 'pastoral' power beyond simply the regular confessional. The self-searching was directed by another self to whom absolute obedience was due. The principles were the same: self-disclosure, self-blame, obedience to truths, self-renunciation and especially verbalization. We recall the central place of words in the theory of 'confession' mentioned already. In the modern bio-power version, self-examination, freed from self-renunciation, *could positively constitute a new self.*[18]

Foucault did not indulge in polemic against Christianity for its part in the story of such practices. The real target was more secular, namely that universalized pastoral power freed up from religious rules for wider non-religious use. He was decrying the hijacking and recycling of these practices for social imposition on a general population.[19] Moreover, the probings in due course of disciplinary power

---

16 Foucault, 'The Confession of the Flesh', p. 211.

17 Foucault, 'Technologies of the Self', pp. 40–41. Ultimately such penitence involved a kind of 'ritual martyrdom'. Expression of regret and willingness to pay the price spoke a complete break with the past, and a breaking away from self. The actual techniques of self-examination paralleled similar practices in Stoicism, although of course the 'rules' sprang distinctively from Christian teachings. For Tertullian's balancing notion of the power of the spirit and forgiveness, see Roy Kearsley, *Tertullian's Theology of Divine Power* (Carlisle, 1998), pp. 86–7, and for a critical summary: Roy Kearsley, 'Baptism then and now. Does Moltmann bury Tertullian or praise him?' in S.E Porter and A. Cross (eds), *Dimensions of Baptism* (Sheffield 2002), pp. 236–252..

18 'Technologies of the Self', pp. 48–9.

19 This had only prompted modes of resistance: Michel Foucault, 'The Subject and Power', in James D. Faubion (ed.), *Michel Foucault: Power* (London, 2002), p. 326.

into the soul life of individuals through allied modern techniques revived the political form of the shepherd-king … with deadly, even 'demonic' results.[20]

It is important here in passing to determine whether we are looking at essential aspects of Christianity in the practices Foucault traces, since the implications for all Christian community life together are huge. Clearly some expressions of Christian faith did indeed develop extensive practices of pastoral power in post-biblical developments. So it has to be agreed with Foucault that Christian thought eventually introduced not only an elaborate code of ethics, but also a new form of face to face power relations into the religious life of the ancient world.[21] However, some balancing factors deserve special attention.

For one thing, the powerful pastor was at this ancient turn in history as much a novelty to the Christian community as to other ancients. For instance, Christian faith was well into the process of organization before 'pastoral power' can be detected in early Christian writings. The confessional pattern of spirituality, impregnated with power, was an innovation that only began to stir two hundred years after the community of the Jesus way came into existence, with a full flowering arriving even later. It was a strategy of its time and context, particularly the pervasive authority culture, the brutal class-layered nature of society, the fear of ethical lapses in a pagan environment and the ever-present threat of torture and persecution. Leaders in the second century onwards were caught in a double jeopardy, namely both the temptation to a worldly life and the fear of persecution. Leaders naturally feared the demise of the faith for ever and sought to supply some steel in the face of fiery tests. It would be just too easy for us now, especially with the handy gift of hindsight, to criticize a desperate measure devised for desperate times. What following Jesus meant in its essence could so easily be obscured by such a struggle.

So it has to be granted that at the time of Tertullian in the second century, catechesis, or preparation for baptism, was indeed already a serious affair. But it was really only the rudimentary basis for the later confessional practice that Foucault criticized. Moreover, rigorous pastoral power depended not just on Christian elements but also on Greek thought's own contribution to traditions for formation of the self. Here, as we have seen, a body-renouncing ethic usually held sway. So the deep examination of someone's 'self' through pastoral technique can variously be explained without counting it to be of the essence of Christian pastoral practice. It is surely not a coincidence that various streams of reformation in the sixteenth century declined to take on board oppressive and intrusive forms of confessional and pastoral scrutiny. However, a new class of persons had indeed entered society in the ancient world, a group called 'pastors', where the term included a special form of *power*. Moreover, though not linked with imperial sovereignty, it did entail the production of 'truth' about the individual's own

---

20 Foucault, '"Omnes et Singulatem"', p. 311.

21 Foucault, 'The Subject and Power', p. 333.

self.[22] So whatever selfless good was intended (for in persecution the pastors were prime targets), this pastoral power only became effective through knowledge of people's inner life and of their innermost secrets. Certainly this aspect is relevant to authority in the life of a local church community.

However, despite implied criticism of Christian practice, Foucault was really only concerned with the ultimate, wider, social application that resulted from this fateful course of events.[23] While pastoral power slowly waned within church organization it multiplied outside of that framework, now shorn of the humanizing emphasis on salvation and the shepherd's sacrifice. An alliance of pastoral technique and worldly aims took hold in the 'modern matrix' of the modern state.[24] The transfer of pastorship into the wider social domain, according to Foucault, came to mark out individuals more forcibly as if enforcing a 'law of truth'. Various interests had muscled in on the act, including police, family and hospitals. But the same tactic of individualizing and shaping people's real selves bound these centres together.[25] So Foucault's ultimate interest was really in issuing a political alert to people about economic force, state violence and the way power adapted public knowledge to shape us as indviduals.[26]

With these later claims Foucault's life had succeeded in annoying almost everyone, a habit which prophets tend to have. He brought bad news for various camps in France across a spectrum from the conservative Catholic faithful to the liberal establishment. Of course, the picture he painted was just too simple and, moreover, involved sweeping speculation, albeit often astute. It contained near and clear misses in its understanding of Christian essence and history. Moreover it perhaps stretched credulity by looking too much like an overstated conspiracy theory. But maybe it was close enough to the truth for inescapable problematics to fly out at any micro-community with convictions, especially one like a Christian community.

Christian Community and Confessional Power

The conduct of church community today now comes under the spotlight once again. In particular is there any degree to which power theory about confession and pastoral power contains significance for the present? The specific matter of sexuality itself aside, any Christian community would have to give attention to at least three angles in particular. First, it would need to approach with care the general project of the 'formation' of Christian disciples through 'truth' (a kind of 'transformation' of human beings), whether in church or training of leaders. The

22 Foucault, 'The Subject and Power', p. 333.

23 Foucault, 'The Subject and Power', p. 333.

24 Foucault, 'The Subject and Power', pp. 333–5.

25 Foucault, 'The Subject and Power', p. 335.

26 Foucault, cited in Bernauer, *Michel Foucault's Force of Flight*, p. 166.

notion of 'spiritual authority' in local church life is often not far away in such settings. Here it would be essential to have sufficient depth of thought, as well as sensitivity to human behaviour to honour freedom. Equally, responsible practices would want to avoid a form of 'discipling' that included elements resembling either crude control or more subtle bio-power.

Secondly, it would want to avoid inappropriate authority amounting to control through eliciting from the inner self an account of secret pain and struggle that should only see the light of day through the person's own free choice, in the most healthy setting and at the right time. The creation of excessive self-surveillance is one bad thing and serious enough, but the desire to see into souls is yet another. This kind of deep searching and access works through enquiry to the drawing out of response, admission and confession. It is therefore only too capable of power abuse. Christian leaders responsible for confessions (even for the benign purpose of reassurance or absolution) no doubt know the possible explosive potential and fall-out possible in the process. They hopefully only proceed with fear and trembling. Other, less formal, more spontaneous practices of spiritual authority and interrogation might not be so careful. The same caution applies to soft or hard versions of Christian counselling, especially those informal ones where professional confidentiality is taken too lightly. Soft versions usually amount only to sympathetic listening and sharing of insights. But even that can be carried out with overconfident, shallow and over-authoritative responses to the counselee.

Thirdly, the growth of 'magic' words within a church's life together could easily multiply also the forms of 'power over' and increasing pretensions to spiritual authority. Insider clichés with special meanings wield the power of exclusion that carries dangers enough. But securing docile consent to a powerful vocabulary of expectations or fears may easily do even more damage. The hearers then fall into easy, trigger use of the terminology and this aids the production of further unspoken norms and unreflective consent to leadership. The practice of authority in this way is probably doomed to manufacture shallow followers of the Jesus way with an equally superficial view of discipleship, church and mission. It reflects the power of the mantra. We need only take phrases like 'respect my office', or 'start moving in the Spirit', or 'allow me to speak a word into your situation'. Such jargonized, lazy speech tends to reinforce claims to authority. It also easily evokes efforts at self-surveillance that are not obviously connected with following the way of Jesus. Such talk can eliminate, in advance, the liberty to query any norm for Christian living, that has evolved locally and been handed down in a church community. This kind of language can eliminate genuine choices of integrity by members. Hence varied power formulae block the Christian freedom which is essential for an authentic following of the person and values of Jesus.

Moreover, the specialized discourse of a leader becomes the most subtle of power moves, well suited for producing a docile, unquestioning following. This would surely endanger true community and move people away from genuine 'life together'. Such a downturn could shift a church community towards the dangerous ground of manipulation and a sub-culture of local bio-power, just as

Foucault expected. An obvious candidate for this judgement is so-called 'heavy shepherding', the modern practice in some extreme churches of a supervising authority directing a member's most personal choices such as those regarding job, spouse or home. But we do well to remember that similar traits appear in slightly less-heavy versions, and are all the more dangerous for appearing lightweight at first. These traits could be such requirements as directing all voluntary financial contributions exclusively to the local cause, or normalizing daily life by disapprovals of hobbies and interests, or producing rigid expectations on church attendance. And this variety of surveillance and purifying can simply be a senior partner to receptive, compulsive legalism natural to some people.

Foucault's verdict on early Christian pastoral power may not matter in the end so far as judgement on churches in ancient history are concerned since stringent confession was at that time an outcome of a peculiar set of circumstances. Moreover, what Foucault really wanted to do was underline his belief that techniques to probe the inner life remain all the more deadly for having been honed through centuries. Undoubtedly, these techniques really do exist and they have the 'productive' (person-shaping) power that he attributed to them. He was perhaps right to see these techniques in their modern, secular form as, among other things, a struggle to find a new ground for personal individuality.[27] Whatever the case, he has generated serious points of which to take account when appealing to authority in community.

Authority in Modern Ecumenics

The subject of authority in a local church context is caught up in distinctions such as those we have outlined between 'power over', 'power to', and 'power through', etc. It makes no difference whether a claim staked in 'power over' emerges in a defensive pronouncement from a cleric or one from a volunteer leader. Either way the words, 'I always tell my people ...', reveal the pleasure in imagining that the congregation is hers/his. At any rate, the focus of attention for authority remains the micro-setting of local Christian community. Complaints are in order that the discussion in this chapter has now cleverly evaded a brush with such topics as episcopacy, hierarchical leaderships, the place of synods and various further problems of para-church authority. However those skilled in these topics are already writing on them vigorously and the literature is extensive. However, connections to wider settings of authority are going to lie in the immediate foreground even in this chapter. The specific narrowing to power dynamics is therefore in no way meant to play down the very serious issues worthy of attention in ecumenical contexts,[28] nor to ignore that they make a difference to specific processes and

27 Foucault, 'The Subject and Power', p. 332.

28 See Gert Jansen, 'An Overview of Some Faith and Order Papers on Authority' in Tamara Grdzelidze (ed.), *One, Holy, Catholic and Apostolic: Ecumenical Reflections on*

practices, at the very least. There is no absolute purity to local church autonomy in such a connected and communicating society as ours.

But what is 'authority' and how does it differ from simply 'power'? It is commonly argued that authority is a subdivision of power but one which enjoys some form of legitimation, and often qualified by built-in limits to its reach.[29] Versions of power as authority include such familiar domains as the bureaucratic, legal, charismatic, personal and cultural. On Foucauldian analysis, some of these spheres of authority flow through society quietly and painlessly normalizing and 'making up' people. They shape individuals into subjects or selves, and lock horns with micro-communities in the far reaches of the social body. And they may each be styled as an 'authority' because they are legitimized. This happens in some cases partly through being internalized by people's voluntary, perhaps unconscious, recognition of norms. This often emerges from ongoing self-surveillance. However, the scene has changed since Foucault first wrote. Now an increasing independence of spheres and multiplying centres of authority, especially the charismatic, personal and cultural, guarantee that there are no absolutely dominant centres of power in modern egalitarian societies, just as the later Foucault realized.

For church today the character of authority as legitimized by those affected is the reality that such authority must face and indeed often does. Authority can make rules and provide penalties but it may in this way be undermining its very claim to recognition as authoritative. It can of course appeal to God as the higher authority and therefore the last stop in accountability. But actual appeals to this ground are carefully rationed today. In any case this theological appeal does not free authority from the concrete sociological reality that in practice it needs internal affirmation from the faithful. In mind here, more than traditional structures, is the unconstrained bids for power in some local churches, especially highly autonomous ones. Further questions might also haunt the ultimate appeal to God or the Holy Spirit. Who confirms that this rather unusual direct line is at this point warranted and real? How is it to be convincing to those who choose to come under its directions? Who legitimates the authenticity of the appeal? How do we detect if the whole process is passing over from a legitimate and internally recognized authority to a form of power technically termed domination?[30]

Naturally it is widely recognized that the word 'authority' can easily be used carelessly, misused systematically, and even used abusively.[31] This can apply

---

the Church. Faith and Order Paper No. 197 (Geneva, 2005), 97–103, p. 99, particularly concerned with agreement about who teaches authoritatively.

29 Paul Avis, *Authority, Leadership and Conflict in the Church* (London, 1992), pp. 20–22. For useful clarifications see especially pp.19–25 as typically opening up key issues.

30 For domination as the abuse of authority, see Avis, *Authority, Leadership and Conflict*, pp. 20, 22–3.

31 Hannah Arendt, 'Communicative Power' in Steven Lukes (ed.), *Power* (Oxford, 1986), 59–74, p. 65.

within a micro-community such as the *koinonia* just as much as through imposing historic hierarchical structures. An independent local church can harbour non-legitimated power as much as a huge structure. In addition, of course misuse does not in itself invalidate right use, though it might be a practical litmus test for it.

All the same, because of the shabby reputation of authority as 'power over', a new, refined sense of the concept has emerged, that of competence, or perhaps reputation.[32] But then again the complaint immediately follows that authority as know-how almost lacks the element of power at all even though those possessing it might take advantage of another.[33] Foucault, of course, could not possibly separate know-how and power in this way. Power is the chief participant in orders of knowledge. Know-how is suffused with power and may be the most potent form of it, even though open to testing.[34]

The cautious conclusion then, from admittedly a selective range of authors, is that authority as a common word stands for a specific type of power, one where acquiescence is not coerced or enforced.[35] We take an illustration from another field, that of modern party politics. The higher authority of government is publicly and visibly accountable at the ballot box. It is in this way that such a political authority, by and large, tends to avoid absolutism and coercion.[36] Moreover, government's own decisions are binding upon itself and enforced by other appropriate bodies with legitimized power (= authority). In this way a truly well ordered 'organization' may operate with appropriate balances and checks.[37] Perhaps it is desirable to have a clear centre where collective authority rests but this need not be at the top of the chain of control.[38]

Technically, then, neither coercion nor persuasion are a necessary feature of authority.[39] However, for that very reason, top-down, dominating forms of power may find 'authority' a convenient, squeaky-clean camouflage to shelter behind since the appearance of being a legitimized power is more likely to secure compliance.[40] This is often a prize striven for in local church communities, including independent churches. However, in practice, in a local community of those on the way of Jesus, the presence of a firm authority may only be the beginning of further questions: How is authority in this local church legitimized and by whom? Under which

---

32 Avis, *Authority, Leadership and Conflict*, p. 23.

33 Avis, *Authority, Leadership and Conflict*, p. 23.

34 Not denying of course Moltmann's rhetorical dig that knowledge (of atrocities) today spells a sense of powerlessness, of human helplessness: J. Moltmann, *The Source of Life, The Holy Spirit and the Theology of Life* (London, 1997), p. 21.

35 Avis, *Authority, Leadership and Conflict*, p. 25.

36 Talcott Parsons, 'Power and the Social System', in Steven Lukes (ed.), *Power* (Oxford, 1986), 94–143, p. 113.

37 Parsons, pp. 114–15.

38 Parsons, p. 116.

39 Arendt, p. 65.

40 Arendt, p. 65.

agreed conditions? To what extent? For how long-before change of authority holders or review of practice? In such micro-settings all or some of these enquiries often cannot be answered. The legitimate nature of the power again falls under question. Then again, we recall that according to Foucault authority has often been buttressed through 'pastoral power'. The formidable strength of unquestioning obedience sits uneasily in the context of local church. Caution about authority, it seems, is in order given the difficulties in regarding it as power legitimized by the community's specific consent or by a claim for its position on the chain directly below God.

Feminist Insights on Church Authority

Feminist writings have been particularly exercised over the place of authority in the world today. Their works can take the form of thoughtful critique of the concept, or of criticism and rejection of it. Kathleen B. Jones is one of those who are critical.[41] Institutional forms of authority, she complains, often need to establish detached rules and such a way of working is especially appealing to male leadership. The instincts involved, she concludes, sprang originally from the gender division of duties. That is, the women were restricted to private activities especially the 'compassionate' nurture of children, while the men on the other hand were distanced by the demands of public duties where rules took precedence over unreliable 'feelings', specifically 'compassion'.[42] The genderized division of duties has become less sharply defined over the twenty years since Jones wrote, but the contrast still resonates for many. Authority in society still tends to quickly fall into detached rules. These are governed by a vertical command and obedience pattern of handling problems without recourse to 'feeling', rather than by horizontal mutuality.

However, it is admitted by Jones that the integration of compassion into formal political process could indeed humanize political types of authority, especially where they incorporate critical voices and public interests.[43] Accordingly perhaps we could say that in the case of local church community, those continuing to uphold a command-obedience type of authority could still introduce the notion of a compassionate structure. This would enhance what has already emerged in previous chapters about the caring, transparency, mutuality and so on, those factors which can offset power patterns in the group.

It seems then that the notion of authority in top-down political structures can be tempered by the presence of compassion and that the same can happen

---

[41] Kathleen B. Jones, 'On Authority: Or, Why Women Are Not Entitled to Speak', in Irene Diamond and Lee Quinby (eds), *Feminism & Foucault: Reflections on Resistance* (Boston, 1988), pp. 119–33.

[42] Jones, pp. 124–5. See also pp. 119–34, especially p. 120.

[43] Jones, pp. 130–31.

in the life of churches. In addition, as Foucault suggests, many other strategies and patterns will most likely be present. Realism in legitimate authority has to take account of such things as the voluntary character of members' faith, and *koinonia* principles of equality. Leaders usually need too to take account of how they are perceived in their behaviour patterns and strategies. Official authority can simply be compromised by lapses in unofficial, personal authority. Hence Steven Croft makes clear his commitment within the Anglican tradition to what is sometimes called 'servant-leadership'.[44] He avoids all sentimentality and fiction in his description. But the over-riding and guiding quality of leadership in a local church is still that of service.[45] At the very least, authority on these terms is paradoxical. It is increasingly enhanced by vulnerability, by preference for the other and an attitude of privileged serving. The least effect of this would be to focus on authority as 'power to' whatever occasional episodes of 'power over' might be involved. The counterweight of service is no less significant in churches where authority in leadership is not so officially taught but one would not know it. Adopting counterweights to authority as a pattern of power might serve to help modernize and recycle its meaning for church in the twenty-first century. Equally, however, there is also always the possibility that such strong new wine might burst the old wineskins, leading to a more radical recasting of authority in leadership in local church life.

A more revolutionary feminist viewpoint appears in Carter Heywood. She has summed up authority less reflectively and much more radically. She trains her criticism neither on conservative nor liberationist followers of Jesus, but at all who assume an 'authoritarian spirituality'.[46] She is not at this point attacking that favourite target of feminists, namely hierarchy, but only 'authoritarian power'. However the similarities are painfully close. In an approach reminiscent of Foucault's work on domination, she defines authoritarian power as a dominant party enjoying power over another, even in the domain of the 'spiritual'. This power is understandably seen by her as very much 'possessed' as a kind of personal property because the relationship between weak and strong remains unchanging and undisturbed. The stronger player too is unchanged, because unchallenged and hence untouched as a result. However, the dominated sadly are indeed changed, crafted by the judgement and will of the dominators.

Some would say extreme claims are attached to Heywood's insights, and she seems willing to re-write the Jesus narrative. These should not become a distraction from her main point about authority. Her viewpoint concerns a top-down structure to authority, whether in a large organization or small social unit like a local church. The ascendant source of authority is not subject to change or adjustment. No U-

---

44 Steven Croft, *Ministry in Three Dimensions: Ordination and Leadership in the Local Church* (London, 1999), pp. 67–82, especially pp. 76–7.

45 Croft, p. 77.

46 Carter Heywood, *Saving Jesus From Those Who Are Right: Rethinking What it Means to be Christian* (Minneapolis, 1999), pp. 58–9.

turns are possible. Appearance of weakness must not surface. Inner doubt about one's expressed public view is impossible. Heywood argues instead for mutuality and common decision-making and roots this in a mutuality of all things. Moral and spiritual building of the world is therefore more fitting to a world from the hand of God, one in which mutuality, not structure, neither top-down power nor hierarchy, is the basis of our lives.[47] This is a determined attempt to concentrate on mutual 'power to', a listening to one another, rather than 'power over' as a basis for relationships.[48] In fact authority itself (though not authoritarianism) can in theory survive this emphasis, for authority listens as well as speaks.

Reception and Authority

Is there anything in the wider, ecumenical debate about authority that might throw just a little further light on authority, power patterns and local church? The notion of 'reception' perhaps could serve the purpose. It possibly offers a clue from the larger scale down to what is at stake on the smaller scale of the micro-group. Even the careful, even-handed WCC document, *The Nature and Mission of the Church*, insists that the topic of reception draws attention to the relationship between authority and life together.[49] Talk of 'reception' has in fact been around for a long time but reception's most spectacular role came in the aftermath of the Lima Faith and Order Conference in 1982, which produced the discussion statement *Baptism, Eucharist and Ministry*. As a result of that short document, responses to the invitation for comment poured in from around the world, generating six thick volumes.[50] This was a 'reception' process on a global scale, and unequalled since. The responses were inevitably mixed but are still an impressive example of how broad and informed assembly came to be endowed with further, if often qualified, authority through a humble process of reception. For Gillian Evans 'reception' is integral to true authority in church, and she supports her view from an impressive review of key pronouncements, ranging from Aristotle through the Catholic Thomas More to post reformation Anglican luminaries.[51] What goes for broad, impressive processes is surely true at the micro-level too, even if concerned with situations and decisions rather than sweeping doctrinal formulation. Active authority on the

---

47 See Carter Heywood, pp. 62–3. To accept this observation does not oblige one to follow Heywood in excluding God, or Jesus, from a status of appropriate top-down authority.

48 Heywood, p. 59.

49 World Council of Churches, *The Nature and Mission of the Church: A Stage on the Way to a Common Statement. Faith and Order Paper No. 198* (Geneva, 2005), p. 21.

50 Max Thurian (ed.), *Churches respond to BEM Vols 1–6, Faith and Order Papers Nos. 129–144* (Geneva, 1986–1988).

51 G. R. Evans, *Problems of Authority in the Reformation Debates* (Cambridge, 1992), pp. 256–8.

ground might be said really to achieve its ends when it is contributed to by all and internalized in the life together on the way of Jesus. This process enhances authority as truly legitimized and effective as a 'power to'.

Meantime on the ecumenical front Catholic voices also vigorously affirm the fact of reception.[52] If a body with so clear a view of authority can be affirmative then the possibilities for processes of mutuality have a future. True, for Mary O'Driscoll, authority in the Catholic tradition remains very much intact. She stands strongly by the notion of the 'light of faith' as pointing to the authority of God.[53] William Henn also sees authority as a gift of God and reminds us that Catholic theology would welcome a more positive attitude towards it.[54] In addition he suggests that a human structure of authority is necessary to sustained mission, worship and service.[55] However these factors should all be seen in the light of a positive view of consensus as seen in reception, though too vast a grassroots contribution should not be read into that.

Theoretically, then, an authority could be envisaged which is focused through the united mind and passion of a whole community inspired, say, by visionary, light-touch, enabling and empowering leadership. This could be particularly appropriate at the level of local church. The approach may indeed present more of a challenge to newer forms of authority than to traditional ones. For instance one could cite instances of the authority of powerful individuals in local independent churches who blatantly ignore consensus. Authority here is sometimes shored up by theologically coercive warnings about submission to God.

'Power over' came to clarity in Foucault's analysis as docility, passive assent or acquiescence. For Gillian Evans often this can be the unintended but actual response to claims of personal divine authority[56] rather than a genuine shared understanding and willing acceptance. Authority, she suggests, belongs to God and should appears in the community, making itself felt in the consent (or consensus) of the faithful.[57] Here it is God being heard in the flow of communication, the vitalized interplay, the constant checking of each other and personal and corporate growth in understanding.[58] This is a description which sounds in tune with Foucault's account

[52] Mary O'Driscoll, 'Response to "An overview of Some Faith and Order Papers on Authority"', in Tamara Grdzelidze (ed.), *One, Holy, Catholic and Apostolic: Ecumenical Reflections on the Church. Faith and Order Paper No. 197* (Geneva, 2005), 104–8, p. 105. See also William Henn, 'Reflections on Authority and Authoritative Teaching in the Light of ARCIC II' in Tamara Grdzelidze (ed.), *One, Holy, Catholic and Apostolic: Ecumenical Reflections on the Church. Faith and Order Paper No. 197* (Geneva, 2005), 124–32, p. 127.

[53] O'Driscoll, p. 105.

[54] Both as argued by William Henn, 'Reflections on Authority', pp. 124–5.

[55] Henn, 'Reflections on Authority' p. 125.

[56] Compare Evans, pp. 258–9. Traditional views also criticize a passive understanding of 'reception': O'Driscoll, p. 105.

[57] Evans, p. 257.

[58] Evans, p. 257.

of the endless interplay of strategies and contributions which constitutes a social micro-context as it interacts with its environment. Transformation of situations springs from the very fluidity and openness to change and from susceptibility to the actions (including, we might say, effective or 'performative' speech or opinions).

Authority and consensus in the local church community, in the light of these reflections, might mainly question an authority which achieves only a bare act of obedience. Accordingly, the *koinonia* principle of a common share in the Spirit points to a truly Christian compliance not routinely compelled but rather internalized as a sincere response to the Spirit of God. Against such authority there is no law! Transparency and humility would naturally mark an authority of this order and the response most in line with the *koinonia* is that willingly offered on the basis of rightness and inner conviction rather than mere external pressure. We have realized, thanks to Foucault's penetrating critique, that the most effective strategies of resistance in power relations are sometimes those of avoidance, simply sliding past external pressure or command. The power of complacency and passive non-compliance has proven its effectiveness in face to face relations, and even formal, official authority cannot always overcome it. With regard to the local community on the way of Jesus, a personal and wholehearted 'reception' is what completes authority. We venture to suggest that the essential factor in a Christian form of authority is an intention of positive, transforming 'power to', rather than distraction by 'power over'. If 'power to' fills authority, then it may make less difference to the outcome what the exact centre of authority is, whether a single figure over a great body of the faith or a local self-directing community of believers humbly working out their deliberations together in mutual listening. This fact in no way relativizes the range of wider differences on authority, a diversity which addresses many other issues besides relations and strategies at grassroots, truly a work in progress. [59]

Authority, Trinity and Participation

The latest ecumenical discussions have produced bold proposals for opening out the meaning of authority.[60] One approach, for instance, is the claim that the infinite mutual loyalty of the Trinity supplies the clue to authority in church.[61] 'Authority'

[59] For a well-reasoned plea for the inclusion of theologians in the process of authoritative doctrinal formulation, see W. A. Visser't Hooft, *Teachers and the Teaching Authorities* (Geneva, 2000).

[60] See contributions to Grdzelidze, *One, Holy Catholic and Apostolic*.

[61] Donna Geernaert, 'Church as Koinonia', p. 72. See also Orthodox agreement here in Daniel Ciobotea, 'Holiness as Content and Purpose of Ecclesial Authority' in Tamara Grdzelidze (ed.), *One, Holy, Catholic and Apostolic: Ecumenical Reflections on the Church. Faith and Order Paper No. 197* (Geneva, 2005), 91–6, p. 92. See also the similar contribution from Orthodoxy below.

remains but only exercised through mutuality, namely the common life of the *koinonia* community.[62] The grace that brought authority into being is expressed in a leadership freed from worldly forms of power. Authority is made known through the power of healing and reconciliation in the Good News.[63] Moreover, the authority of Jesus in the church community, in its common life, springs most of all from empowerment for unflinching service. It draws principally on values found in the actual life of Jesus as Lord: sharing of the good news, the dignity of persons, the value of communities, witness against unjust structures, callings to repentance and intercession. Of such things does real authority consist for church.[64] However, danger is detected in some theology from the later layering of powers in Christian history. For symbols of empowerment in the history of church obscured the radical transformation of power relations implicit in the Gospel.[65] And so fingers sometimes point today at modern Christian success culture and continued political privileging. These, many feel, belong to settings long gone and the use of symbols from them today can only disempower members of modern *koinonia* communities. Today, it is argued, we need a new network of symbols that re-empower through a deep sharing along the lines of covenant and community.

Daniel Ciobotea's contribution from within Eastern Orthodoxy surpisingly echoes such views, namely in his point that the purpose of authority is the display and communication of divine love in the Trinity to the world.[66] Authority is associated with the new beginning, human participation in life of the Trinity.[67] Before the life of authority seen in Jesus shows that within the very divine being authority is about sharing. That is, it points to shared responsibility and the co-operation that goes with that.[68] The result is that the ordained clerical office, in its different forms, exercises authority by sharing in duty and love for human beings.[69] Plainly we have here no concession to modernity and postmodernity, for it is an Orthodox view deeply rooted in consideration of biblical texts. The same is true with Gert Jansen from a Reformed background, who distinguishes between official, institutional teaching authority ('deontic') and moral forms of authority ('epistemic' and 'existential'). The latter rests on moral example, solidarity or authentic, self-denying forms of

---

62 Geernaert, p. 72.

63 Geernaert, p. 72.

64 Geernaert, p. 72.

65 Lewis S. Mudge, *Rethinking the Beloved Community: Ecclesiology, Hermeneutics, Social Theory* (Lanham, 2001), pp. 64–75.

66 Daniel Ciobotea, 'Holiness as Content and Purpose of Ecclesial Authority', in Tamara Grdzelidze (ed.), *One, Holy, Catholic and Apostolic: Ecumenical Reflections on the Church. Faith and Order Paper No. 197* (Geneva, 2005), 91–6, p. 92.

67 Ciobotea, p. 92.

68 Ciobotea, p. 92.

69 Ciobotea, p. 93.

life.[70] This view does not seek to abolish teaching authorities but appeals to them for space for, and recognition of, these other moral forms of authority. But for Jansen, new structures are needed for involving mutual accountability, decision-making done together and ministries that are 'relational'.[71]

The final report from this debate, as in so many ecumenical papers, is quite open-ended. The statement that authority is a gift (to be shared with others in the life of the Trinity) and a duty (to be carried out in the way of communion)[72] could equally be interpreted as praise for authority residing in a common life or as a recognition of traditional hierarchical authority. All the same, signs of new, softening notes in the vocabulary of authority appear: 'freedom', 'mutual accountability', 'relational', 'interdependent', 'dialogue' under the canopy of shared confidence in the teaching of the Christian Scriptures and the doctrinal 'tradition'. Once again, along with an emphasis on authority as gift, character, service and holiness, there are many possibilities for application to the smaller scale of local church.

Varied levels of power are also part of the picture of authority. Pyramidal power is neither restricted to traditional hierarchies nor a feature only of big organization. It could just as easily be developed from autocratic leadership of an independent congregation as preserved in an ancient tradition. Much rests on the perception of authority figures near the top of the pyramid.[73] The social experimenter, S. Milgram concluded that obedience to an authority figure in groups often involved the abdication of responsibility.[74] Empirical evidence has been offered to suggest that democratic leadership in various groups generate a higher quality of work in the workplace than either laissez-faire approaches or authoritarianism. Equally, authoritarian strains in pyramidal power are especially blamed for dismantling a sense of community and common purpose by generating aggression or apathy.[75]

---

[70] Gert Jansen, 'An Overview of Some Faith and Order Papers on Authority', in Tamara Grdzelidze (ed.), *One, Holy, Catholic and Apostolic: Ecumenical Reflections on the Church. Faith and Order Paper No. 197* (Geneva, 2005), 97–103, p. 102.

[71] Jansen, p. 100. His position is, after all, nearer to Gaenert than to O'Driscoll.

[72] Report: 'Authority and Authoritative Teaching in the Church' in Tamara Grdzelidze (ed.), *One, Holy, Catholic and Apostolic: Ecumenical Reflections on the Church. Faith and Order Paper No. 197* (Geneva, 2005), 162–5, p. 163.

[73] Some studies in the workplace suggest that also the style of authority and leadership at various levels is able to destroy or create morale and a sense of common purpose. Nikolas Rose, *Inventing Ourselves: Psychology, Power and Personhood* (Cambridge, 1996), p. 145.

[74] Cited by Hedy Brown, 'Themes in experimental research on groups from the 1930s to the 1990s', in Margaret Wetherill (ed.), *Identities, Groups and Social Issues* (Milton Keynes, 1996), 9–63, p. 20. Milgram's simulated experiments, published in 1974, are still famous for showing the shocking way reverence to authority overwhelms the individual's moral sensibility. See S. Milgram, *Obedience to Authority* (London, 1974).

[75] Rose, p. 145.

Equally the language used about service and obedience can render unseen the fact of human traits of leadership and the exercise of 'power over' that it entails.[76]

In the light of these sober statements, the claim earlier by William Henn that authority must be seen as biblical and a gift depends in some measure on what you think authority is in the first place. This lends significance to Martyn Percy's warning that humanly structured authority can only truly be a gift if it is gladly received, and has passed over to those on the receiving end in a genuine culture of exchange.[77] Paul Avis too is insistent therefore that authority is not *naked* power.[78] Even God's authority is vulnerable to decision from a free human acknowledgement and voluntary obedience.[79] Even the authority of Jesus did not preclude his being taken and crucified.[80] We should want to add that the power that some church bodies possess, even in our era, the power to make people happy or very miserable frequently does not equate with true biblical authority. That is something altogether different. That would be genuine authority – a moral authority, as Avis points out, able to deal honestly with members of the *koinonia* community and citizens of the wider world.[81]

Some of the contributors mentioned above anticipate at least one defence on behalf of authority in top-down leadership. That is, it is often pleaded that without established authorities everything will go wrong, that people have a felt need for allegiance to such authorities. Two points, however, warrant consideration. First, the authority concerned need not be any particular prescribed figure or select group. Authority could in theory at least belong to the collective loyalty of the community. It would have to do with their loyalty to Jesus – his person, his values, his example and his commands as all perceived together in Scripture and the memory of Christian communities. This is often the case in most traditions, as for example in councils, conferences and synods. Secondly, authority need not necessarily be found at the top of a power-chain stretching downwards. Parsons does not quite say so,[82] but by implication his view of political power allows that a legitimized power in an organization (= authority) could, by this maxim, theoretically be invested in the whole community (say, meeting together in self-critical reflection). Equally a plenary consultation could delegate such authority to any chosen group or person in its midst, or even repeatedly reinvest it, say, in a series of short-life groups. It is

---

[76] Lydia Harder, 'Power and Authority in Mennonite Theological Development', in Benjamin W. Redekop and Calvin W. Redekop (eds), *Power, Authority and the Anabaptist Tradition* (Baltimore, 2001), 73–94, p. 92.

[77] Martyn Percy, 'Authority in Contemporary Theology' in Tamara Grdzelidze (ed.), *One, Holy, Catholic and Apostolic: Ecumenical Reflections on the Church. Faith and Order Paper No. 197* (Geneva, 2005), 141–7, p. 143.

[78] Avis, p. 19.

[79] Avis, p. 20.

[80] Avis, p. 20.

[81] Avis, p. 20.

[82] See his discussion above.

becoming clear that an open-ended authority model, whether within micro-groups or wider bodies, can accommodate a wide range of possibilities.

This being so, it is hardly a surprise to find Lewis Mudge appealing for the end of what he regards as history-bound, dated conceptions of authority. Neither Catholic nor Reformed and Independency systems escape his scrutiny. The main issue in human communities for him is whether power in its midst is for empowerment or enslavement of the people.[83] Hence since symbols and meanings have in the past related closely to empowering and disempowering processes in the West, the Bible's symbols are still critical. Therefore, empowering of people can follow only when the Bible is really used as a condemnation of history and of its enslavements, not when the biblical message does not properly engage people in their actual historical circumstances.[84] This is the task of church authority. Persistent unequal power relations would then need to be recognized and engaged under a critique of power, the true work of authority. Moreover, for Mudge, much defence of traditional patterns of authority in church fail to take account of the late twentieth-century's discovery that power is not as simple as even Marxist views maintained but is on the contrary highly complex. Stubborn patterns of authority ecclesiology can fail to see that new social symbolism may need to come into play to preserve the underlying truths to which old ones pointed.[85] Lydia Harder similarly worries about an idealism with regard to church authority that can discourage local church from facing up to and addressing the actual and real power relations present in every community.[86] On this view, authority now is not so much concerned any longer with internal discipline. Authority in the local church, as for a wider constituency, is rather concerned with biblical mission committed to justice and empowerment through good news and true solidarity.

Authority Past and Present

The moderating and adapting of power has a long history. The sixteenth-century reformers saw the centrality of priestly dispensation of the sacraments as necessarily qualifying, at the very least, the authority and power of God.[87] The well-known fact that Luther, displayed ambiguity on reform of the episcopate,[88] does not neutralize the Reformers' new way at the time of looking at priestly and episcopal authority. Those were stormy days, when public anarchy always

---

[83] Mudge, *Rethinking the Beloved Community*, p. 67.

[84] Mudge, *Rethinking the Beloved Community*, p. 67.

[85] Mudge, *Rethinking the Beloved Community*, p. 69.

[86] Harder, p. 92.

[87] Evans, pp. 202–3. However, Catholic theology is less vulnerable to this concern when it views priestly power at the altar as representing what is really the power of Christ as high priest.

[88] Evans, p. 228.

threatened and radical political and spiritual ideas could both contain truth and encourage mayhem. They were dangerous times for thinking of changing time-honoured structures and the legacy of authority. For similar reasons, Calvin's allegedly authoritarian impact on Geneva is only fairly understood in the light of a watching Catholic world looking for the least evidence of public moral decline which it can blame on the Reformation.[89] Authority stood firm. Even the doctrine of the priesthood of all believers did not usher in a new habit of mind asserting democracy, equality and a new social vision.[90]

In our own time, the recent WCC document *The Nature and Purpose of the Church* includes some additional strong statements offered by some contributors on structured authority.[91] Forms of authority, it is held by some, can sometimes run counter to the equal exercise of the whole range of Spirit-given gifts (charismata). Equally, patterns of domination, subordination and abuse are, it is claimed, bound up with the very nature of hierarchy.[92] The implication, it seems, is that given the nature of human handling of power, even legitimized power in the form of authority will too easily lend itself to abuse in the church. And in this it will be helped along by any extreme confidence in idealist views of church, especially its leadership, and by any denial of the sociological realities of church in its character as a social group. It is interesting that the sister document *Nature and Mission of the Church* is relaxed about the continuation of the Episcopal, or supervisory, office in church if that office handles the idea of authority with a light touch. The authority of Jesus was located in the service of others, as shown in the washing of the disciples' feet.[93] Authority is not therefore formal and impersonal, but comes on a relational basis and in the form of interdependence.[94]

The themes outlined on authority in these official documents take yet sharper form in the discussion trail found in the follow-up publication.[95] The papers come together as a critical moment in the discussion of authority in the church. They point to the crossing of a bridge, a shift, from authority as a mere subdivision of power ('legitimized power over') to the multiple ways in which authority may be a form of 'power to'. The categories thus defined in the foregoing chapters come back into prominence. Authority as 'power to', reaches to forms of service, works of enabling and liberating action. Moreover, ultimate and final authority is in a person. The person of Jesus as incarnating God's own self, then, delivers not a legal formula or structure for authority but, according to Paul Fiddes, describes

89 See Roy Kearsley, 'Calvin and the power of the elder. A case of the rogue hermeneutic?', in A. N. S. Lane (ed.), *Interpreting the Bible* (Leicester, 1997), 113–29.

90 Evans, p. 228.

91 *Nature and Purpose of the Church*, p. 49.

92 *Nature and Purpose of the Church*, p. 49.

93 WCC, *The Nature and Mission of the Church*, pp. 21, 60.

94 WCC, *The Nature and Mission of the Church*, pp. 21, 60.

95 Tamara Grdzelidze (ed.), *One, Holy, Catholic and Apostolic.*

the drawing of human beings into divine fellowship and a cluster of relationships marked by freedom.[96]

The Nature and Purpose of the Church carefully and faithfully reproduces this side of the debate, noting its dependence on the Christian doctrine of divine Trinity. This, it held, exhibits order without inferiority of being or nature.[97] Other forms of layered authority can exist and some modern charismatic congregations have fallen under sharp theological scrutiny for instance.[98] In some cases top-down authority in such independent charismatic congregations appears even more oppressive than any conservative or traditional version, tending to control people's lives as social beings and detailing such pyramidal arrangements as gender inequality. Such views seem to enjoy only a superficial similarity to Paul's account of the purpose of spiritual gifts in 1 Corinthians despite confident claims to be primitive church exercising spiritual power. Paul Fiddes judges the inspiration for such organizational micro-authority to be entirely secular, drawn from current patterns of management and government and generally indebted to modern thought, though still pyramid-like, developments.[99]

Baptist churches also, while avoiding a strict account of highly structured authority, can tacitly consent to its assumptions in over-deference to the spiritual authority of the church leadership.[100] The unproven assumption in all these approaches is the idea that authority from above comes straight down from God, delegated downwards to a person or group who are the conduits further downwards. However, for Baptists, the authority of Christ speaks not through a delegated figure but in the whole fellowship of the local committed community of the *koinonia*.[101] There is always a discussion to be had on the conditions and means by which this authority actually works but it is meant to resemble what we tracked in our discussion above of consensus and 'reception'. On the scenario thus set out, vitalizing and energizing authority is what emerges when leadership and wider community each play their part in a consciousness of the authority of Christ.[102] Such an authority even then does not consist of mere command-obedience, let alone coercion. Rather it embodies the full identification and participation of a whole community in the heart and aspirations of the mission-making God in Jesus Christ. The appointment of someone to manage these processes of common life and authority in a local *koinonia* community introduces no further formal line of authority. It merely brings the perspective of theological resources and the wider

---

96 Paul S. Fiddes, *Tracks and Traces: Baptist Identity in Church and Theology* (Carlisle, 2003), pp. 50–51.

97 WCC, *The Nature and Purpose of the Church: A Stage on the Way to a Common Statement: Faith and Order Paper No. 181* (Geneva, 1998), p. 49.

98 Fiddes, p. 84. See also Percy, pp. 141–7.

99 Fiddes, pp. 84–5.

100 Fiddes, p. 85.

101 Fiddes, p. 85.

102 Fiddes, p. 86.

family of churches to the local Christian community in this shared-out authority rooted in a common *koinonia*.[103]

Foucault can only describe a micro-community by reference to power strategies, born of power inequalities, with an unpredictable emergence of power that 'transforms' in some way or other. But a Christian view of authority pushes *koinonia* towards the conversion of the transforming strategies themselves. Catalysts for this are the example of service in Jesus, the breath of the Spirit of Jesus and the mutual upbuilding of an authority of the common life and quest. The sociological reality does not go away here, but for Christian faith it encounters other, balancing processes governed by the radical new strategy of the one leader, namely Jesus.

Power, Church and Sacraments

Any reader hoping at this point for a major examination of the well-known persistent differences over sacramental theology faces a disappointment. The focus is still resolutely upon issues of power. And the line of argument will follow threads already in place in previous chapters. By way of consolation, however, familiar concerns and terms must occasionally surface even in this specialized treatment.

The *Nature and Purpose of the Church*, begins with the now familiar idea of church as sacrament.[104] The idea most prominently emerges in the canon *Lumen Gentium* of the Second Vatican Council. It claims that the church is both sign and instrument for effecting union with God and within humanity.[105] Even this claim, however, is not without qualifying language. In this calling the church is dependent upon God and only the Holy Spirit makes possible any cosmic union.[106] Not all churches like this terminology, because such language in their view threatens to cloud both the unique sustaining work of Christ and the flawed character of church on the earth.[107] However, church can be a 'sign and instrument' nevertheless.[108] But it is interesting that even this comes not in the garb of an authority from the Spirit or authorized access to divine grace. See for instance the subtle restating of church

---

103 Fiddes, pp. 87–90.

104 WCC, *The Nature and Purpose of the Church*, pp. 21–2. Reproduced in WCC, *The Nature and Mission of the Church*, pp. 27–8 following through its discussion of church and mission.

105 *Lumen Gentium* as developed by Emmanuel Clapsis, 'Does the Church Have a Sacramental Nature? An Orthodox Perspective', in Tamara Grdzelidze (ed.), *One, Holy, Catholic and Apostolic: Ecumenical Reflections on the Church. Faith and Order Paper No. 197* (Geneva, 2005), 17–26, pp. 18–19.

106 Clapsis, p. 18.

107 WCC, *The Nature and Purpose of the Church*, p. 23.

108 WCC, *The Nature and Purpose of the Church*, p. 23.

sacramentality in Eastern Orthodoxy to exclude the dispensing of salvation.[109] For many the meaning more nearly approaches to Moltmann's portrayal of the Spirit (see the previous chapter).[110] It points to a church sent out in discipleship and service. To paraphrase the argument, church is seemingly a sign not through sacramental power but through the power of its service in humble participation in God's reconciling, healing and transforming work upon creation. The only power in 'sacramentality' or 'instrumentality' in this final summary is the power of service in mission.[111]

How, then, does the question of power play out in church thinking about sacraments and power? With the variety of approaches historically, it would be optimistic to expect too much convergence here.[112] Chiefly it is agreed that church as a sign either to itself or to the world, begins with Christ, whether as primal sacrament or high priest or the real celebrant. Sacrament, then, would be a sign not of triumph and power but of the humble way of Jesus made alive in the *koinonia* by the Spirit of power as we have seen. The lubricant of the Spirit's power of vulnerability is what most makes church 'sacramental' in the dynamics and power relations of its life. And in this regard it underlines every conclusion from previous chapters that has led up to this point. Theologically power is transformed in truly Christian sources from purely 'power over' to 'power to' (healthily transform), 'power with' (the community of the *koinonia*), 'power from' (the Spirit of humility and solidarity in Jesus), 'power through' (vulnerability and perhaps weakness). To be Christian, authority whatever its structural form surely has to reflect these forms of power too.

---

[109] WCC, *The Nature and Purpose of the Church*, pp. 22–3, though much with the Catholic perspective.

[110] WCC, *The Nature and Purpose of the Church*, pp. 21–2. See Timothy George's evangelical protest against the tendency to a sacramental 'bid for power': Timothy George, in Tamara Grdzelidze (ed.), *One, Holy, Catholic and Apostolic: Ecumenical Reflections on the Church. Faith and Order Paper No. 197* (Geneva, 2005) 27–39, p. 35.

[111] WCC, *The Nature and Purpose of the Church*, p. 22.

[112] See the resignation to evident lack of agreement recorded in WCC, *Nature and Purpose of the Church*, p. 23.

Chapter 9
Twin Problems on Power and Church

This chapter's brief digression into two related key concerns is an acknowledgment that a work on power and church should take account of some persisting, vigorous, debates in other related domains. Two key ones are, first, the apostle Paul's standing with regard to church and power and, second, the continuing problems raised about human power relations in the light of a belief in divine omnipotence. These are huge subjects and we can only hope to take something helpful away from a careful sampling of the issues. This exercise, all the same, should test a possible fruitful comparison between those discussions and other ones in this book.

Paul and Power

Power, Church and the Christian Scriptures

Accounts of early church communities disclose to modern readers a Roman world where stark power towered over the landscape. In contrast to Foucault's description of modern liberal democracies, this really was a world of sovereign power and a zero-sum setting where power was only too clearly in the hands of the very few at the expense of the countless many. Evidence of a world of domination, for instance, speaks through familiar Hebraic themes of liberation and divine readjustments of power which stand out in the Jesus story. Jesus himself, rooted in the Hebraic idea of a covenant of justice, endorsed in his own sense of Messianic calling the Jewish prophetic promise that the prisoner will be set free, the oppressed be liberated (Lk 4.17,18). There are main centres of power, understood as domination and hierarchy, appearing only too clearly at the sites of the socially and religiously privileged. Zero-sum assumptions abound. On the surface it would not be very obvious that anything else existed in the Roman society of Caesar Augustus and his immediate successors. Strict layers of society, privileged patronage and command stood out unmistakably. So, admittedly, a formulation of power as capillary and fluid, as detected in liberal society by the later Foucault, does not occupy the foreground at all. As an ideal, let alone an ideology, it would have carried wildly unrealistic Utopian overtones in first-century times. The zero-sum world was clear and simple. Power was mainly absolute from Emperor down to the humblest slave-owner.

The early accounts of the life of Jesus offer the glints of a revolution amid domination. The centres of power are about to be overturned, and subversive new disparities are to emerge, removing old simplicities. The rich and powerful become the ones who find it hard to enter the kingdom. The religious holders of the high moral ground are doomed unless first humbled. In the new kingdom the first shall be the last and the last shall be first. It is a kingdom that will go not to the strong but to the weak – the poor (Lk 6.20). Everything will be turned upside down (Lk 6.20,21),[1] upsetting a prevailing, and clearly unfair, zero-sum regime.

But in addition, as in the Hebrew Scriptures, it all means that a new fluidity of power-relations is also already on the move! Martha seems to represent a very traditional female domestic role-model but for a moment Jesus wants her to experience his rabbinical circle along with her already enlightened sister Mary, even though this was normally a male preserve. True, in the earliest accounts the apostleship is male, a continuing inner group generated by the resurrection of Jesus. But the prime witnesses to that resurrection in the biblical narrative are not the male apostles but the women (resulting in actions which affect other, male, actions). And a new fluidity of status springs up with the emergence of a mixed-gender inner group of 120 people on the Day of Pentecost, not to mention the Spirit's particular power descending upon 'daughters' as well as 'sons'. Women begin to play key roles with impressive status in the early biblical narrative.

Notably, the 'new covenant' theology still did not turn its back on the clear-cut domination picture of good and evil powers. Recent studies on the book of Revelation, understood now not so as much a crystal ball as a criticism of the Roman Empire, bear this out.[2] But new things happened as the Christian way began not just to turn upside down the old dominations and balances of power but also to shake them out. For 'the Way' loosens the rivets and destabilizes norms of hierarchy.

Paul and Foucault

When we turn to Paul, the main concern is whether he will indeed mediate the distinctive way of Jesus to churches of his own time and ours. Critical to this quest will be the correspondence from his relationship with the church in Corinth. Certainly we can trace without difficulty signs of the elaborately layered society already mentioned and which poke through the letters most widely agreed to be his. However, already in scholarship Foucault and feminism have both made their mark on studies of Paul. Sometimes this is direct and acknowledged.[3] Yet other

---

1 See James Malcolm Arlandson, *Women, Class and Society in Early Christianity: Models from Luke – Acts* (Peabody, 1997). Throughout he takes 'turning upside down' as important for understanding Luke's agenda on status, honour and shame etc., including the meaning of this for women. I am indebted to my colleague, Prof. Christine Trevett for pointing this out.

2 See for instance, Richard Bauckham, *The Climax of Prophecy: Studies on the Book of Revelation* (Edinburgh, 1993).

3 See for instance Elizabeth A. Castelli, 'Foucault and the Church in Late Antiquity', in James Bernauer and Jeremy Carrette (eds), *Foucault and Theology: The Politics of Religious Experience* (London 2004), pp. 19–38, Sandra Polaski, *Paul and the Discourse*

writers seem either to have been indirectly influenced by his ideas concerning the top-down reinforcement of power relations or have come to a similar perspective by another route.[4] More important are the themes of power and discourse taken up by feminist interpretations of power. These often blend quite well with middle and later Foucault, especially when problematizing power and truth, marking the pervasiveness of sovereign power or raising the question of excluded voices in a power-relations setting. However, on other occasions, it seems that the writers have not become aware of ideas of Foucault beyond *Discipline and Punish* and *Power/Knowledge*. There is not so much openness to Foucault's questioning of liberationist convention. Dominant centres of power sometimes seem the only possible scenario for setting out power relations and a principal villain may be considered essential. And that villain sometimes turns out to be the revered apostle Paul. So then, how does Paul measure up in this discussion? The views of those commentators attached to the Foucault revolution vary. Some weigh in with gusto subjecting Paul to withering deconstruction and critique. He cannot open his mouth without getting into trouble, even if he calls himself a servant. It is all power play isn't it?

Paul and the Non-Charismatic

In finding an orientation towards power and church in Christian biblical studies, it is possible only to sample a very small corner of the vast and contentious field of Pauline scholarship. Fortunately, it has recently become well sign-posted. Over the last twenty years Paul has been deconstructed by a series of power analyses with a very critical edge in which Paul has received the Foucauldian treatment. The question this raises is whether Paul's example and teaching is credible and liberating for a community of the *koinonia* today. Or have we only imagined that Paul was one of those early Christians reputed to be 'turning the world upside down'? One of those leading the charge at the beginning of the final decade of the twentieth century was undoubtedly Antoinette Wire.[5] Her work on Paul's relationship to the Corinthian church was one of the first to question the reverence with which Paul has been viewed. Hence according to her book, Paul's only wish was to crush the exuberant variety, spontaneity and freedom (perhaps anarchy) of the newly formed Christian community – all to promote a safe, unthreatening

of Power (Sheffield, 1999), pp. 41–51, Graham Tomlin, *The Power of the Cross: Theology and the Death of Christ in Paul, Luther and Pascal* (Carlisle, 1999), pp. 271–314.

[4] Famously, for instance, in Richard Horsley's treatment of the impact of Roman political rhetoric on Paul's writings to Corinth: 'Rhetoric and Empire – and 1 Corinthians,' in Richard Horsley (ed.), *Paul and Politics*: *Ekkleisa, Israel, Imperium, Interpretation: Essays in Honour of Krister Stendahl* (Harrisburg, 2000), pp. 72–102.

[5] Especially Antoinette Clark Wire, *The Corinthian Women Prophets: A Reconstruction through Paul's Rhetoric* (Minneapolis, 1990).

'sameness' – one which buttressed his own personal power base. But he met more robust resistance than he expected, and had to fall back upon his hierarchical and privileged status to try and enforce his will.

Certain of Foucault's laws are honoured here. Where there is a figure with 'power over' a resistance is implied by the terms of the power relations. Even the underdog pushes back or we are not looking at power. And then again, Foucault would say, whatever the most powerful figure is able and seeking to do, the result may not be exactly that intended. Moreover, power tends to a capillary presence. 'Totalizing' or 'subjectivising' power is apt to invade micro-settings in order to colonize them with its gaze and ensure that ground-up power corresponds to top-down 'power over'. For Wire, Paul's temperament and strategy of power is determined in great measure by his loss of social power through becoming a Christian. On the other hand many of the Corinthian Christians for their part have gained social standing and thus are emboldened to aspire to a fair amount of autonomy. Moreover, on this view Paul shows himself not to be on the right side of liberationist history, seeing he is hell bent on reimposing an unthreatening sameness upon the unsettling diversity that has healthily erupted in early 'charismatic' Christianity. Although not always given the credit, Wire has been immensely influential with this approach and has been appropriately recognized for her impact on their work by such luminaries as Richard Horsley, Rosemary R. Ruether and Cynthia Briggs Kittredge.[6]

Elizabeth Castelli, at around the same time, also questioned the privileging of Paul by traditional scholarship.[7] So, she maintained, either Paul was explained uncritically or when problems arose his grabs for power were somehow rationalized away.[8] For her, Paul is most certainly a mix of both persuasive-speeches and power-speeches. She echoes Wire's concern by seeing Paul as advancing a culture of unity and sameness.[9] She also qualifies Foucault's approach. While power is admittedly everywhere, there is still plenty of room for variety and imbalances in the way it affects relationships.[10] The point here is that Paul still held the upper hand and called upon his 'power over' to bring Corinthian speech to heel.[11] For Paul, apostolic forms of knowledge inscribed certain privileges for the possessor in a debate about Messianic truth and

---

6 See Horsley, 'Rhetoric and Empire', p. 89; Rosemary Ruether, *Introducing Redemption in Christian Feminism* (Sheffield 1998), and *Women and Redemption: A Theological History* (London, 1998); Cynthia Briggs Kittredge, 'Corinthian Women Prophets and Paul's Argumentation in 1 Corinthians', in Richard A. Horsley (ed.), *Paul and Politics*: *Ekkleisa, Israel, Imperium, Interpretation: Essays in Honour of Krister Stendahl* (Harrisburg, 2000), 103–23, especially pp. 103–5.

7 Castelli, pp. 19–38.

8 Castelli, pp. 19–21.

9 Castelli, p. 21.

10 Castelli, p. 24.

11 Castelli, p. 25.

action.[12] Paul was appealing to headship whereas the Corinthians were creating new freedoms.[13]

Paul and Authority

Some of the themes followed here were still alive and well when an important collection on Paul and politics appeared in 2000.[14]

Although driven by a continuing criticism of Paul and power, the volume included some significant voices of dissent. It is therefore a valuable window into contentious issues, especially on which kind of Paul is to be found in Romans, Philippians and the Corinthian correspondence. Ten years on, Wire was still of the same mind about Paul. The wisdom that he spoke of so dismissively was not the speculative wisdom of the Hellenistic intellectual élite, she maintained, but the new found power of prophecy and prayer in the assembly.[15]And as these voices surfaced in the assembly by the power of the Spirit, they constituted a potential threat to the leadership – not excluding Paul.[16] For he, Wire claimed, saw the status of members in the Corinthian *koinonia* as lowly – not many wise or powerful – but they saw themselves as raised up through the charismata to wisdom and power and to a high status of honour.[17] This analysis leads Wire to a counterintuitive conclusion: unlike Richard Horsley, she thinks the new Christians in Corinth, not Paul, were the real threat to the layered, class-ridden culture of Rome and that Paul, by trying to bring a disciplining order to the company of believers, was the opposite: a supporter of the *status quo*.[18] A similar indictment of Paul emerges in the analysis of Cynthia Briggs Kittredge. She lucidly summarizes feminist challenges to conventional Pauline studies posed by such critics as Wire, Castelli and Fiorienza. Her conclusion is clear: they have identified a specific contemporary rhetoric in Paul that unveils the hidden partners in the controversy in the Corinthian correspondence.

By such advances, feminist criticism has not only begun a viable search for dissident voices among Paul's audience. It has done more. Kittredge stresses that

---

[12] Castelli, p. 26.

[13] Castelli, pp. 30–31.

[14] Horsley, *Paul and Politics*. See also a more recent collection of views on what the Corinthian *koinonia* was like: Edward Adams and David G. Horrell (eds), *Christianity at Corinth: The Quest for the Pauline Church* (Louisville, 2004), which also includes Horsley's contribution.

[15] Antoinette Clarke Wire, 'The Politics of the Assembly in Corinth', in Richard A. Horsley (ed.), *Paul and Politics. Ekkleisa, Israel, Imperium, Interpretation: Essays in Honour of Krister Stendahl* (Harrisburg, 2000), 124–9, p. 126.

[16] Wire, p. 126.

[17] Wire, pp. 126–7.

[18] Wire, p. 127.

the correspondence reveals Paul's own authority struggling to get established.[19] She considers Horsley's claim that Paul was an opponent of the Empire more critically on this assumption. Yes, perhaps he did in some measure censure it. And yet, she argues, Paul nevertheless lapsed into bad imperialistic habits himself. Hence she thinks that we need Wire's approach to supplement and correct Horsley's overly generous evaluation,[20] since Wire focuses not upon Paul's message addressed to empire. Her attention is upon his suspect, conservative curbing of what Foucault would call 'transgressive' voices and freedoms in Corinth, particularly where they belong to women.[21] Paul, it is pointed out, remained ever so conventional on the status of women, male domination in family life and the absolute need for ordered relationships (these latter which, she might have added, was partly a legacy of the Augustan reign). Granted, Kittredge agrees that there is a revolutionary note in Paul. But more significant for her is what he does in his letters to those who are even more of a threat to the Imperial rulers than himself.[22] Even Sandra Polaski, who speaks more positively of Paul, feels compelled to admit that even when Paul addressed the equalities in the setting of 'grace', he could not break away from thinking hierarchy – with a pecking order that had him at the top.[23]

We cannot begin to settle the erudite problematics involved in this debate, often rooted in Classical Studies. It seems clear, however, that there is much of which to take stock, whichever viewpoint is held. It looks very much as if feminist critics have greatly enriched and deepened the project of evaluating Paul and the impact of his writing. Much that has superficially been taken for granted as simple and straightforward has given way to a serious consideration of complexity. This new intricacy particularly concerns the aspirations and motives swirling around in the Corinthian setting. Most of all, feminist studies have brought a long overdue highlighting of the triple bind endured by women of the Empire. Even wealthy women whose husbands were still alive endured a status that differed little from slavery. Even rich wives were still the property of their husbands. There also seems fairly wide agreement that the imperial political context was real and significant. For Horsley, the 'rhetoric' of Paul reflected the normalizing function of rhetoric within the Empire,[24] and the apocalyptic strains in Paul set him inevitably against the imperial order.[25] Or perhaps it is not the actual monolithic Empire in itself that Paul opposes but the paganism that animates empire. So perhaps he is using his renunciations of a non-Messianic Judaism in Romans merely as a 'code' to discourage the Christians in Rome from lapsing into loyalty to the

---

19 Kittredge, pp. 103–4.

20 Kittredge, pp. 104–5.

21 Kittredge, pp. 104–5.

22 Kittredge, p. 105.

23 Sandra Hack Polaski, *Paul and the Discourse of Power* (Sheffield, 1999), p. 119.

24 Horsley, 'Rhetoric and Empire', throughout, but especially, pp. 72–87.

25 Horsley, 'Rhetoric and Empire', pp. 93–102.

fast-strengthening cultus of emperor worship.[26] This would be in line with the technique employed by the writer of the book of Revelation.[27]

As a result of feminist scholarship, even more than before, Paul must not be plucked from the context and idealized as transcending mere humanity. He too, throughout the Corinthian correspondence, is a subject in the making just like anyone else, as Foucault also would likely have expressed it. Equally, monochrome descriptions of Corinthian Christians as all poor or ineffectual will not do justice to the complexity of the Corinthian assembly.[28] It is likely that the *koinonia* community there contained many freed slaves, some of whom were fairly well off.[29] And this is, of course, borne out by Paul's protest at the way some people with money in the assembly treated the poor at the 'Lord's Supper'. 'Not many of you noble or powerful', then, could merely be betraying the fact that the highest layers of the local social élite would have nothing to do with this mixed bag that made up the *koinonia* of Corinth.[30] In that case, not all of Paul's audience in Corinth would be so unhappy with the, albeit limited, social layering in Roman society that generated unequal power relations. And maybe, also, few would have been surprised at Paul's emphasis on order.

Hence surely, it is also inadequate to valorize the church assembly as populated entirely by heroic and freshly empowered revolutionaries, suddenly suffering a new onslaught of oppression by Paul. This take on matters can only be maintained by the arbitrary and cynical dismissal of Paul's seemingly passionate concern for justice and mercy in the assembly and for believers' freedom from financial exploitation. It seems strange that someone striving primarily to upgrade his status would be in this way so preoccupied with, even obsessed about, the fate inflicted on those at the bottom of the pile. This kind of priority is not usually the mark of power play. In any case, Paul was many miles away from the Corinthians when he wrote and would only rarely see them again, if at all. Their problems hardly offered him the greatest of power trips. Perhaps from doubts raised by such facts, a solid body of thought has not seen its way to endorse all feminist interpretations of Paul's rhetoric, while still being comfortable with serious changes in the landscape of Pauline studies.

---

[26] N. T. Wright, 'Paul's Gospel and Caesar's Empire', in Richard A. Horsley (ed.), *Paul and Politics: Ekkleisa, Israel, Imperium, Interpretation: Essays in Honour of Krister Stendahl* (Harrisburg, 2000) pp. 160–83.

[27] See Richard Bauckham's approach in *The Climax of Prophecy of Revelation.*

[28] See Sheila Briggs, 'Paul on Bondage and Freedom in Imperial Roman Society', in Richard A. Horsley (ed.), *Paul and Politics: Ekkleisa, Israel, Imperium, Interpretation: Essays in Honour of Krister Stendahl* (Harrisburg, 2000) 110–23, pp. 121–2.

[29] Briggs, pp. 121–2.

[30] Briggs, pp. 122–3.

Counter-voices on Paul

Those expressing caution about the strongest criticisms of Paul are usually far from hostile to the quest for a grounding of liberation, especially concerning women within the early Christian culture. It is more a question of the degree to which Paul led unambiguously from the front. Already even Kittredge does not altogether begrudge Richard Horsley his detection of an anti-Imperial note in Paul's rhetoric.[31] But other women's writing is still more generous to Paul. This is especially true of Sandra Polaski[32] who has also read Wire and, in addition, is positive towards Foucault. Yet she firmly takes a less strident line. The Gospel which Paul preached turned upside down the hierarchies of religious Jew and imperial Gentile alike as well as turning power-relations inside out for Paul too. Even Paul had to negotiate.[33] He repeatedly recognized revelations other than his own, especially among the Corinthians and Galatians. Similarly, forms of grace existed autonomously among Corinthian believers without his presence. They marked a divine power placed alongside the special 'grace' or 'power' to which Paul too had to submit[34] even a divine power over which Paul had no direct control.[35] Whatever happened between Paul and Corinth is also likely to square with his dealings with the equally strong-minded Galatians. Here, it is argued, Paul overturned religious hierarchy as he cashed in the long-held dominance of Judaism and Jerusalem. So far as his apostleship went, he did not see himself as empowered by such things to enforce his views. He could only persuade.[36] He made clear in Romans and 1 Corinthians that he recognized the integrity of revelations received by others,[37] including women. Grace, and its accompanying gifts of 'word' and 'knowledge' were in 1 Corinthians given freely to the whole congregation not just to people like Paul.[38]

Alexandra Brown is well aware of all the arguments touched on above, and takes them into account in her thoughtful assessment of Paul, weakness and power. She challenges Castelli's claim, made along with Wire and others, that Paul undercuts difference and 'inscribes' his own superior power as natural. She sees Paul, rather, at the end of 2 Corinthians as more of an embattled figure than

---

31 Cynthia Briggs Kitttredge, 'Corinthian Women Prophets and Paul's Argumentation in in 1 Corinthians', in Richard A. Horsley (ed.), *Paul and Politics: Ekkleisa, Israel, Imperium, Interpretation: Essays in Honour of Krister Stendahl* (Harrisburg, 2000), 103–8, pp. 106–8.

32 See also more recently Cornelia Cyss Crocker, *Reading 1 Corinthians in the Twenty-First Century* (New York, 2004) (unfortunately not available for me to consult).

33 Polaski, p. 103.

34 Polaski, p. 119.

35 Polaski, p. 129.

36 Polaski, p. 104.

37 Polaski, p. 105.

38 Polaski, p. 115.

one invoking privileges. This happens to him precisely because he is trying to move the Christian community on from hierarchy and sacred centre without cutting them off from their founder.[39] Equally while Paul seemed to be a defender of traditions he actually criticized them.[40] In fact, while his emerging opponents in 2 Corinthians took their stand on a pedigree of authority, status and signs of power, Paul's power emerges in 'apocalyptic' form – that is, in his sufferings and weakness.[41] Hence Paul's apparent bids for power have to be consonant with his clarified conviction that true apostolic power is a power made known through weakness.[42] 2 Corinthians also draws out what it really is that makes Paul so seemingly assertive. He is concerned not with something so trivial as his own status within Corinth. He is thinking globally. He wants Corinth linked in to other church planting endeavours in Asia and Macedonia. He is aiming at a pattern of leadership that will develop local expressions of faith but also be in fellowship with the wider, growing Christian movement. This is all about the burgeoning mission of the Messianic movement and only in the light of this is it possible to properly understand Paul's response.[43]

More especially Paul wants it to be clear that the mainly non-Jewish Corinthian assembly is a full partner in the Christian family.[44] Great care must be taken not to assume that Paul is building on an old, conventional paradigm of power. If he were, as his critics claim, he would not have condemned the divisions based on allegiance to Peter, Apollos and himself, but have urged everyone to get behind Paul.[45] His framework is not 'world power' but a new configuration and conceptuality – one that inverts the use of power to divide and dominate in favour of a power that belongs to lowliness.[46] Paul's apocalyptic power of suffering aims instead, as already suggested, at unifying rather than dividing. This unity for the community drawn from the *koinonia*, we suggest, is Paul's great driving passion rather than any desire for traditional uniformity. As for status, Paul even terms himself and Apollos as inferiors. In Paul's case, he is condemned and made socially inferior by working with his hands – all calculated to undermine any conventional claim to power.[47]

These writers, all sympathetic to the liberating struggle, particularly at the level of gender, take on board the fresh and productive problems presented by talk of Paul's' rhetoric' without diagnosing an uncertain sound in the charismatically

---

39 Alexandra R. Brown, 'The Gospel Takes Place: Paul's Theology of Power-in-weakness in 2 Corinthians', in *Interpretation*, 52/3 (1998): 271–85, p. 281.

40 Brown, p. 271.

41 Brown, p. 271.

42 Brown, p. 271.

43 Brown, p. 272.

44 Brown, p. 272.

45 Graham Tomlin, p. 106, n. 65.

46 Tomlin, p. 279.

47 David Horrel, cited by Tomlin, pp. 94–5.

driven Christian movement. Even if Paul is himself developing his understanding of power in ever-evolving new contexts from the non-Jewish mission, he is mainly of the same mind as his Corinthian readers on the freedom and new hope that comes with the message he has shared with them. So as sympathetic a writer to feminist concerns as Richard Horsley, does not feel driven by Wire's original work on Corinthian prophets to deny goodwill on Paul's part. With a catena of texts, Horsley presents Paul as urging a common interest upon the Corinthians in his first letter and a common cause against division.[48] Horsley might of course be adapting the Imperial rhetoric used for political harmony, but it is at least clear that Paul is not aiming to obliterate difference but to avoid the strife that sometimes comes along with difference. Paul, then, presents a radically alternative 'assembly' to the political one found in Corinth.[49] Moreover, the source of unity is not the typical reinforcement and subjectivization that rhetoric played in the Empire (as Foucault would have spotted). Rather it is built upon a theology of the cross where there are simply no variations in status.[50] In addition, Horsley is probably in the majority in seeing the 'wisdom' that threatens this unity (through élitism and ascetism) as having a Hellenistic, not a charismatic, source and he himself suspects an Apollos caucus.[51] Paul's reproach upon 'wisdom' would then not be an attack on the free use of charismatic gifts of knowledge and revelation. These for him are gifts which he repeatedly commends and reinforces throughout 1 Corinthians (even though love is the highest way of all). Instead he is warning against a hegemony of the intellectual and sophisticated. This is 'wisdom' seen as the term of a Greco-Roman élitism contrasting educated and superiors with mere rustics.[52]

So we are even urged to recognize that it is Paul, not at all the dissonant voices in Corinth, who provides a front line for egalitarianism pitted against the strong and the loudest in the Corinthian assembly.[53] One perspective protests against Castelli, that 'unity' and 'sameness' should not be confused.[54] On this view, to appeal for unity is not to erase difference but to warn against the dangers that

---

48 Horsley, 'Rhetoric and Empire', p. 73.

49 Horsley, 'Rhetoric and Empire', p. 91.

50 Tomlin, pp. 88–9.

51 Horsley, 'Rhetoric and Empire', pp. 88–9.

52 Robert Jewett, 'Exegetical Support from Romans and Other Letters', in Richard A. Horsley (ed.), *Paul and Politics: Ekkleisa, Israel, Imperium, Interpretation: Essays in Honour of Krister Stendahl* (Harrisburg, 2000) 58–71, pp. 63–4. See also Graham Tomlin, pp. 59–61: an ethic of 'love rather than wisdom' is counteracting typically Corinthian Epicurean élitism. See also Timothy Savage on constant Epicureanism and self-importance in Corinth: Timothy B. Savage, *Power Through Weakness: Paul's Understanding of the Christian Ministry in 2 Corinthians* (Cambridge, 1996), throughout but especially pp. 19–53.

53 Jewett, pp. 60–62, with particular reference to 2 Corinthians.

54 Tomlin, p. 106n. The questions raised here could be directed to Wire also.

attend difference. This perfectly parallels the warning of Foucault that differences of status, wealth, position should be distinguished from those power relations to which they nevertheless naturally lead. It echoes Foucault's power theory where difference always brings collision and collusion of varied power streams and behaviours.

Conclusions on Paul and Power

Where then does all this leave us? Certainly, even on the most negative view, Paul undercut some conventional classical culture and posed challenges to traditional pre-Messianic Judaism, as well as to paganism, the imperial cultus and ultimately to the vertical social ordering of the Empire. It then depends on other factors as to whether one finds serious contradictions in Paul's attempt to present things his way. Some see privilege and fear of loss of power in the attempt while others see voluntary powerlessness and a dependence only upon the persuasion of truth without manipulation as Paul sincerely sees it. We are immediately mindful here that for Foucault 'truth' and 'power' are not such separate domains as most people tend to think. Then again, even the entanglement of power and knowledge may not be sinister, for it could be a case of benign 'power to' sending out a knowledge that can broadly be trusted. Willing, costly service tends to fall into this category, though it cannot always be guaranteed as a badge of authenticity and integrity.

In addition, most can accept if in some cases a little warily that Paul's relationship with those in his churches will involve process for him too at some level. He refers to shifting strategies and perceptions himself. Did his pressing on to the full knowledge of Christ (Phil. 3.13,14. Cf. possibly 1 Cor 13.9,10) imply a growing awareness of the fuller and more immense significance of the precious message that he believed himself to carry? If so, development is possible in his understanding of 'power' in political and social relations as it results from the Good News announced in the name of Jesus. This proposal is even adaptable for those holding a very high view of Paul's revelatory powers, so long as it is not held necessary that all the revelation came to him in one initiatory experience.

However, most could agree that Paul, right from the beginning of his itinerant mission, was a messenger to the non-Jews and that he fully welcomed a variety of giftings, especially that of revelatory prophecy for women. If this is so, there seems no reason to rule out that he celebrated the freedom of the Good News just as much as the new, enthusiastic Corinthian Christians did. This still leaves the specific problematic passages that seem to betray a hierarchical approach to gender: in the strange symbolism of head covering, the apparent limitation of women in the congregation and the seemingly pervasive subjection of one human being to another in a way only too familiar to Roman class systems (for example 1 Cor 11.3–16). Straightaway, one must question whether it is appropriate to expect Paul, even on the highest view of him, somehow to wrap the full covering of Enlightenment liberalism around the body of Roman social class tradition feeding off a mass slave culture. Surely no one is disappointed in Jesus for failing to pronounce on the relative values of left and right in modern democracies or on the relationship of religion to modern science. In the case of power, equality and today's Foucauldian analysis it is worth noting that it took many centuries of struggle, exodus and return to recover and affirm the freedom way of Jesus. Paul gets criticized for not having grasped all the implications within a few years and for not completely soaring above his culture, with the flag of modern democratic liberalism fluttering behind him. And he needn't expect any mercy from his critics today either. If he speaks of the need for order to balance freedom, then he is plainly an unconverted, imperialistic Roman. But then if he chooses the way of the servant and relies chiefly on this commendation, well that's obviously bound to be no more than Roman rhetoric isn't it? Even if he had enjoyed miraculous foreknowledge of the liberating privileges that would come upon intellectuals in the comfortable and colonializing European countries of the Enlightment, it would not have earned him any better a press.

It all invites the question of what exactly Paul could have written that would not have been construed by determined critics today in one of these disapproving ways. And the answer to that question is: only what a twenty-first century middle class, enlightened liberal, liberationist would have written enjoying all the privileges of historical hindsight and modern analytical method. To say that he did not manage to achieve this is not to say anything significant or surprising all.

And yet even then, Paul did in fact take some remarkable strides. He had the nerve to insist to Corinthian believers that they had all equally drunk of the Spirit of power without privilege, whether slave or free. He recklessly insisted that the most neglected gift in the *koinonia* community entitled its owner to being affirmed by God whatever other gifts went about. That is to say, he claimed that only love endures to the end and by implication not might, human honour or status. And this also meant that the rich were to give preference to the poor among them. Let the Corinthians go and deal with it. All of these statements were outrageously subversive in a society as status-ridden and gender-biased as that of the Roman world. Some would say that without the challenging message Paul introduced in this way, modern liberals and liberationists themselves may never have come to exist.

If we lose sight of such angles, we might also be plunging into the unjustified denial of an essential primary radicalism in the early Christian mission and its resulting churches, so raising doubts about its validity now. This would mean that we have jettisoned belief in the continuity of the churches of Paul with the radical life and way of Jesus. The historical link between all Christian activists for liberation and the radical Messianic founder of their faith would then consequently have perished. It would be difficult to see exactly what the gains were here for those who wish to engender fundamental Christian discipleship and the struggle to end disempowerment based on race, gender, wealth or class. And it would surely be a strength in the world for such people to be able to say that they genuinely do speak for authentic, Messianic faith and action. This would be the case if they could claim that the reconfiguration of power was already beating away in the heart of its most distinguished exponent and church planter. Dismantling and dispensing that conviction naturally is warranted in the name of truth but only if the evidence absolutely and unambiguously demands it. But in that case, since so much is at stake for so many people, it is not too much to ask that the case be truly watertight and dependent not on tentative speculation but upon actual compelling evidence.

The Problem of Omnipotence

Omnipotence Accused

For many theologians, the real culprit on power in theology is the classical Christian doctrine of divine omnipotence. It is this, not empire nor even Christendom, that explains the alleged obsession of a Christian élite in the past with their privileged positions of power. This one theological tenet, it is felt, especially supports idolatrous attention to power both internally and in external dealings. A theologian as attentive as Jűrgen Moltmann to the long tradition of Christian doctrine, is nevertheless damning in his criticism. A God merely omnipotent is incomplete because unable to experience powerlessness. Omnipotence may be worshipped but not loved. An 'almighty' God in this sense would lack experience, have no destiny and be loved by no creature in the universe. Such a God would be surplus to requirements. [55]

For further critics today, the Christian community is still in some ways a child of its birth-time, and the doctrine of omnipotence is still vulnerable to the evils of that era. In ancient pagan religion the agents of a God such as Zeus, belonged to the ruling group, displaying both the deity's and their own power through association. Connection with the divine realm carried some social and political advantages.[56]

Worse though, the source of this evil, allegedly, is found even in the Christian Scriptures. After all they related Jesus and the apostles to the world as 'cosmic power-brokers'.[57] And according to Douglas Edwards, the early fateful signs surface in primitive Christian attempts to attach deity and spirituality to a cosmic-universal space occupied exclusively by the Christian God.[58] So the question persists: could there still be a hankering today for such a feeling of power just so long as theology clings to divine omnipotence?

At the very least, the allegation arises that the later privileged leaders of Christian churches also came to ascribe to themselves inflated, divinely delegated powers over people's lives, over state and government and over the mass of

---

55 Jürgen Moltmann, *The Crucified God* (London, 2001), p. 230.

56 Douglas R. Edwards, *Religion and Power: Pagans, Jews and Christians in the Greek East* (Oxford, 1996), p. 51.

57 Edwards, pp. 108–18.

58 Edwards, pp. 108–18.

people. And the sheer, audacious breadth and depth of this power-claim sprang from association with a cosmically all-powerful God.

It will be hard to find a more ringing warning of danger than that found in Catherine Keller's evaluation of divine omnipotence. It comes in a tightly argued, probing and defining article which begins with the lament that omnipotence retains its grip over Christian imaginations, holding the faithful captive to a 'bad faith' of self deception.[59] She eventually concludes that this form of theism feeds on images of a power that dominates, and it spells domination for women and children. It brings oppression to exploited workers, 'the darker ones' and eventually all human beings.[60] It is significant that she does not see such a distortion as intrinsic to the biblical narrative, for this dominating power has been projected onto the God of the patriarchs.[61]

For many who share Keller's concern, Christendom has thrown up many heirs clamouring to claim this absolute power. So, it is felt, along with the biblical patriarchs we must also count in not just apostles but also those claiming to assume the apostolic mantle down through the centuries to the present. Even Christian traditions without a special (usually male) 'apostolic' group still display disturbing symptoms. Hence, these other varied church movements can view their preachers, theologians, charismatic leaders and others as especially called and empowered 'of the Spirit' in this world. And the called individuals themselves seem to be quite at home as bearers of a special power and/or authority. These special ones are icons or bearers of an omnipotent God, just like Israel's patriarchs. Keller warns of dualism emerging once again between omnipotence and impotence, between (subtle) power-abuse and helplessness.

The scrutiny of 'power' by such feminists as Keller, claims to spotlight the need to tackle a whole network of dominations springing from the very mother of dominations itself: divine omnipotence. Keller is again characteristically concise and lucid when generalizing on feminist theologies. These theologies, she claims, expose all devotion to power and analyse every relation of dominance, starting with classical deity, focusing on the problems for women, children, the racially oppressed and even animals and the earth itself.[62]

An allied approach is the suggestion that the idea of a God who is 'a unifying, dominating power', was originally constructed by theology to 'explain historical and social reality'.[63] Hence it is desirable today in a much more liberal society to take thought about power and powerlessness away from talk of God's domination

---

[59] Catherine Keller, 'Power Lines', *Theology Today, 55/2* (1995): 188–203, p. 188.

[60] Keller, p. 194.

[61] Keller, p. 194.

[62] Keller, p. 193.

[63] William Schweiker and Michael Welker, 'A New Paradigm of Thelogical and Biblical Enquiry' in Cynthia L. Rigby (ed.), *Power, Powerlessness and the Divine: New Inquiries in Bible and Theology* (Atlanta, 1997), 3–20, p. 13.

and control. It should move instead to considering how to transform distortions in the domains of social reality.[64]

Such writers have a deeper concern than merely exposing all types of power-claims by church leaders who draw moral support from the notion of divine omnipotence. Rather the real problem, we are warned, is not simply a favoured group enjoying an option on the divine power. It is more about foundational issues which reach into the very heart of a discussion of church. For the seed problem is a *framework of domination and dualism*, power and powerlessness in which the reasons of faith (classical teachings of theology) imprison human life.

The significance of this for ecclesiology is that the life of the Christian community is more fully 'dominated' than other groups because of its resting so much on a God of domination. All the relations and relationships between its members fall under the spell of a perverse distortion of reality handed down by the doctrine of divine omnipotence. The fact that members often do not *feel* dominated cannot dispel critical disquiet. For, as Foucault insisted, ideology and control can take their prey quietly. It is an impressive sign of their success that the victims don't even perceive themselves in captivity at all. In other words, suspected to be at work here is something like Foucault's 'disciplinary power'. It is a circulation of hidden normalizing and subjectivizing power, only this time it is governing power directed also from yet higher up, by divine omnipotence itself. This concern about the alleged deep impact of belief in divine omnipotence is so persistent that we shall return to it soon. And one result will certainly be that the issues are indeed serious, and perhaps even more problematical than just posed. But the further question will surface in the rest of the chapter of whether the problems are intractable or not.

Omnipotence as Supreme 'Power Over'

Anything said at this point on divine omnipotence can be no more than a footnote to a long history of debates. The subject is vast, ancient and highly contentious. Hence the main purpose here is quite limited. It is simply to allow some insights from our discussion on power so far to bump against the problem of omnipotence and possibly provoke further discussion. The topic, however, is not insignificant for the question of power in church. After all, church potentates in the darker moments of 'Christendom' have been known to lay claim to God's own authority for many if not all actions. Neither do we see this bid just in a faded Christendom or its remnants today. In our own time quite militarist and triumphalist tones have surfaced in resurgent groups of local churches and networks. It sometimes shows up in the worship and propaganda language of enthusiastic church. No wonder, then, that Anna Case-Winters, like other feminist writers, is concerned at the dangers she perceives beyond political church and which she finds instead in

[64] Keller, p. 19.

the doctrine of omnipotence.[65] She is careful and thoughtful with a subject often enveloped in more heat than light. She recognizes that the mere metaphor of God as 'king' is not necessarily a villain of the piece. For one thing the political context of the pre-modern world offered no other immediate metaphor for a supreme being. Equally, as displaying a more perfect form of kingship, the metaphor can serve to check imperfect forms of human power, so be able to bring about justice, unity and safety.[66] This squares with the Hebrew Scriptures where the desire for a (likely corrupt and wasteful) king in Israel is a betrayal of God as king who upholds justice and shields the poor (1 Sam 8).[67]

However, the history of the metaphor's use in theology is mixed. Consequently, her long-considered view is that the kind of omnipotence so often invested in the metaphor of God as king has not been chiefly benign. It has mainly presented itself as domination and control.[68] It is however another matter to decide whether the alternative she offers instead is persuasive or necessary. What is most striking is that from this point on, despite her opening acknowledgments, she seems to assume that a fullness to divine power must always imply suppression, domination, control and disempowerment. Peter Byrne claims a similar trait in feminist explanations of omnipotence as a projection of male power. He wants this to be shown as a necessary proposition still doing justice to the declared intentions of traditional views.[69]

---

65 See her seminal article: Anna Case-Winters, 'The Question of God in an Age of Science: Constructions of Reality and Ultimate Reality in Theology and Science', *Zygon* 32/3 (1997): 351–75.

66 Case-Winters, 'The Question of God', p. 365.

67 The contentious domain of metaphors and models is too extensive to pursue here. Most famous, if perhaps perceived as problematical is Sally McFague, *Models of God: Theology for an Ecological Nuclear Age* (London,1987). But see also, for example an earlier more technical treatment: Janet Soskice, *Metaphor and Religious Language* (Oxford, 1987). Not consulted for my work here because appearing too late to include is her more directly relevant new book: Janet Martin Soskice, *The Kindness of God: Metaphor, Gender, and Religious Language* (Cambridge, 2008).

68 Case-Winters, 'The Question of God', pp. 36–7. She appeals to her book on the subject: Anna Case-Winters, *God's Power: Traditional Understandings and Contemporary Challenges* (Louisville, 1990). The book and the article both propose an approach through process theology. See also a similar, yet in other ways different, handling in Janet Soskice, 'God of Power and Might', *Theology Today*, 54/1 (1997): 19–28. Like Case-Winters she also introduces process thought. However her subject is really the precise philosophical status of divine intervention in the world, not quite the topic here.

69 Peter Byrne, 'Omnipotence, Feminism and God', *International Journal for Philosophy of Religion*, 37 (1995): 145–65, pp. 146–7. The point is valid regardless of the success or otherwise of his own philosophical approaches to omnipotence. Donald Bloesch indicts individualism and modern liberalism for the fate of divine almightiness in theology today. Donald Bloesch, *God the Almighty: Power, Wisdom, Holiness and Love* (Illinois, 1995) p. 54. There are other culprits as he sees it: pp. 55–6.

The above is fair enough, but it has to be admitted that the wider trenchant critiques of power today have often grown cynical only through disappointing experience of all human power. This must be taken with the utmost seriousness in a world swept along by global capitalism and governmental bureaucracy. Coercive or manipulative forms of 'power over' and domination infest so many human situations that little good is expected from its presence. Not all are as detached as Foucault at the more unappealing strategies of power. Power, as everyone chants, tends to corrupt. So the all-powerful is too horrendous to imagine. Coercion and domination may not necessarily be logically entailed in all 'power over', but they might *seem* an integral part of the package. The fact means that fear of coercion should always be taken seriously. It would indeed be a continuing miracle if power as described here somehow flowed right round churches and never through them. Surely sometimes church people too (especially leaders) have all too easily been trapped into manipulative power-plays which infect group situations (as, of course, Foucault warns us to expect and not deny). Moreover, and the main point here, church theologians have sometimes enlisted divine omnipotence to back up human church power.[70] But it also does not rule out hope of a friendly form of power which belongs also to a positive divine omnipotence itself.

Foucault has already helped us to consider power from a more complex set of vantage points. Power may not always be dangerous. It might also surprise us with its positive results. He leaves open the possibility that even 'power over' might achieve good ends. Despite the bad press, then, benign power can also empower and set free – and sometimes in our human world it does. If it did not, no political lobbyists for just causes would exist. As Foucault wanted us calmly to acknowledge, power is not intrinsically bad. But assumptions about power's necessary badness are widespread in discussions of divine omnipotence, and, we should note, understandably for most of us in today's world. But if the conception of a God very different from the moral frailty and flailing pursuit of power by humans is possible then 'good' power is also possible, just as much as perfect love is possible. Perhaps indeed it is possible only because of perfect love. Therefore, just to be coolly logical for the moment, some form of good 'omnipotence' is possible too. This is especially the case if we take into account all the fruit of this study so far. Suppose power is taken at its highest to mean primarily 'power to'. Or if we to return to Pasewark's preference, it can mean the communicating of a transforming efficacy. Similarly power undergoes yet further transformation by acting sometimes even through weakness and vulnerability rather than natural and obvious strength. Then we have a religiously worthy capacity with which God may work in the world with religiously worthy results for the creatures.

Case-Winters herself provides a further clue when taking divine power through the filter of process thought (and under the model of God as mother) and arriving

[70] Janet Soskice, 'God of Power and Might', p. 25.

at the divine sea of love.[71] Why equally could not a loving omnipotence, primarily a divine 'power to', also be seen as a power that does not diminish another? Actually some might argue that this *must* be the case for just this one kind of power – an infinite one. For such omnipotence, if it exists, by very definition does not fit an artificial zero-sum model of power where power is always clawed in at someone's expense. Scarcity or limitations to this power by definition cannot apply. This really is the situation of infinite power where the miracle of loaves and fishes operates, just we saw in Talcott Parsons's suggestion about economies. This would be infinite divine power supplying abundance of empowerment for others without self-diminishing. Once the intuitive assumption of zero-sum thinking in most minds disappears, there is no need to see omnipotence as automatically disempowering, despite our many understandable low expectations of 'power'. The image of an unevenly cut cake does not apply here. Or to state this positively: divine power particularly works (conceivably) precisely by empowering people – by enabling the life of freedom, as an expression of divine love. In its unlimited freedom it takes pleasure in creating a million other free beings. It has infinite resources to do this without diminishing its own power.

Perhaps most remarkable of all in the assumptions from which divine power suffers is that it must involve coercion. But, again as Foucault has so definitively shown, power can work both negatively and productively without even a moment of coercion. Plainly it would be an uphill task to coerce someone without 'power over' (though the crafty can sometimes get there) but 'powerful' and 'coerce' are not synonyms, nor complements nor necessary partners. So nor is coercion of the essence of either 'power over' or 'power to' despite endemic assumptions that it is. To assume otherwise is to gloss and distort, however unintentionally.[72] If power is assumed to be domination, control or coercion, there is little difficulty in concluding that omnipotence is definitely a bad thing and especially undesirable in a Christian God. But if these are not of the essence of power, at least care and caution is in order when throwing away tradition. But beyond this, further ways have appeared with the offer to reconcile us a little to the possibility of divine power.

Omnipotence as 'Power To'

As it happens, an outstanding contributor to the subject has done formidable groundwork for the above approach.[73] He makes his way briefly through similar

---

71 Case-Winters, pp. 369–70. It looks similar to the process phrase of 'omnipotent love' and accordingly she refers approvingly to Hartshorne's ideas.

72 See how the word turns up unannounced or and with validations in Case-Winters, 'The Question of God', p. 367.

73 Gijsbert van den Brink, *Almighty God: A Study of the Doctrine of Divine Omnipotence* (Kampen, 1996).

territory as our earlier journey through power conceptuality. Hence for him, despite comments about omnipotence above, the real way through is to dispatch 'power over' as the setting for the discussion. More particularly, some distinction is indeed valid between 'power over' and the more preferable theological concept of 'power to'.[74] Gijsbert Van den Brink complains that Steven Lukes's earlier work is too quickly dismissive of 'power to' for failing to take account of the conflictual element in power. Lukes, he claims, falls into the trap of presumptively defining *all* power as governed by conflict before any analysis begins.[75] Restricting the term to personal relations is all right if that is already the context. But it cannot be a principle everywhere. It must not rule out other angles, since one might have power over an environment, over things or even over one's own self without the presence of conflict.[76] Van den Brink admits of course that 'power to' may involve 'power over' but not necessarily in a highly intensive personal way, or even in a well-defined sense. Vagueness often prevails.[77] He prefers 'power to', then, for describing God's power, even though admittedly it can be misconstrued into 'power over' (as in the case of 'Black Power' illustrated by Peter Morriss).[78]

'Power over' is always weighed down by the sometimes problematical zero-sum notion. According to this, we have seen, one party's power always implies an inescapable loss by the other party. Van den Brink, asks: why even in a social setting, should one person's power diminish that of another? On the contrary, the appointment and empowerment of a leader over others by them might instead lead to enhancement of their influence and power. I will leave aside here the likelihood and problem that such leadership probably enhances the said team (whether sales, production, sport, services etc.) in competition over someone else, so a zero-sum aspect is not quite dispatched. The point is that although conflictual or competitive situations likely entail zero-sum somewhere this is not essential to the idea of power.[79] Van den Brink concludes, with some justification, that where the notion of God's omnipotence takes flack today, assumption of power *exclusively* as 'power over' is rarely far away.[80] In fact on this very score he turns his attention to Case-Winters. In fairness, it is noted that she was willing to recognize that conflict was not essential to power conceptions. All the same, she also maintained that tradition had given a conflictual twist to God's power, focusing on domination and power.

Such a view meets a formidable opponent in van den Brink. Much of his book to this point has shown that early Christian writing, even including Augustine, takes the 'almightiness' of God to mean God's capacity to do things rather than

74 van den Brink, p. 120.

75 van den Brink, p. 120.

76 van den Brink, pp. 120–21.

77 van den Brink, p. 122.

78 van den Brink, p. 122.

79 van den Brink, p. 123.

80 van den Brink, p. 123.

dominion over things and even less domination of people.[81] Moreover, if it is claimed that God's power in the tradition really is of a conflictual, competitive, and therefore zero-sum kind of 'power over', then divine omnipotence would render everything else to an absolutely powerless, inactive sponge – a notion not usually associated with the idea. God does not actually *do* everything, as John Lucas notes.[82] Foucault is invoked here too. One of his achievements is to show that power cannot be reduced entirely to top-down action of either repressing or even subjectivizing through knowledge production.[83] On the contrary, the truly theological way to describe divine power is in the language of creating and sustaining infinite abilitie]or in other words 'power to'.[84] Even divine power seen as authority 'over' creation (a key sense to almightiness) is only an example of the higher meaning of 'power to'. At this point van den Brink does not say so, but the implication is that when one shifts into top gear and talks of divine *omni*-potence, the sense of 'power to' as primary and religious should not disappear from view. Hopefully it is not embellishing van den Brink too much to speak of God's 'power to' as nothing other than the 'freedom-of-God-to'. And that 'power to' as often as not has a chiefly positive end. This is the divine 'power to' enable humanity in the direction of freeing the oppressed, protecting the fatherless, feeding the hungry, establishing truth and righteousness. This much can certainly be agreed with Case-Winters and her perceptive work. Divine power, then, leads the way for an understanding of power relations and spiritual power in *koinonia* communities. The stance it commends fits nicely with the direction also of this book.

Conclusion

The approach above, taking in van den Brink's work, leads us to a number of careful statements which if taken together require a very carefully controlled assessment of the religious and logical legitimacy of divine omnipotence for a Christian approach. Van den Brink leads the way.

In the first place he considers it a blind alley to concern ourselves with any defence of, or attack upon, omnipotence which arrives at the concept through detached logic rather than through a Christian understanding of the saving actions of God.[85] This is in line with the view that traditional theology fell too much under the influence of philosophical views that presented God primarily as power.[86] Divine almightiness has a pedigree in Abraham rather than in Anselm, namely with

81 van den Brink, p. 124.

82 van den Brink, p. 124.

83 van den Brink, p. 124.

84 van den Brink, pp. 124–5.

85 van den Brink, pp. 165–6.

86 van den Brink, pp. 103–4.

the promise of Sarah's child, against all human expectation.[87] Secondly, whatever divine almightiness means, it always excludes the notion of God as 'naked power'. It is rather God's capacity to achieve a supremely good end.[88] Thirdly, in the Hebrew Scriptures, where almightiness begins, God's power belongs to promises and actions in the world, not a philosophical project.[89] It is not a way of expanding into theoretical infinity the relations and politics of human interpersonal power with all the blemishes and blotches of 'power over'.[90] Moreover, the setting for thinking about God's extraordinary power is prayer and worship.[91] In addition, all theological concepts are open to abuse[92] and care has to be taken over rejecting caricatures on the one hand or mutants of a belief on the other. So finally, with these qualifications in place the role of a doctrine of divine omnipotence may be seen in a new light. On a biblical understanding it no more permits corrupt power abuse in leaders than the doctrine of God's humility commands snivelling subservience to challengeable forms of injustice. Rather than buttressing human dominations, the divine and salvific almightiness of God's 'power to' relativizes all corrupt human claims to power.[93] By implication it then questions all naked power in our world and all exaggerated authority also, whether in church or out of it. Divine power especially condemns all abuse and tyranny through its benign ascendancy and its religious meaning of love and freedom.

What does this all add up to for a church community living in the presence of power? A number of conclusions confront us. First, a belief in divine power is not there to enhance any kind of human power or authority, as often assumed. That is, belief in divine almightiness as suggested so far does not logically entail the conceivable transfer or leasing of its authority to members of the human race. It does not follow that divine power is distributed to churches in handy packs – especially to its leaders. That would be consonant with applying the zero-sum conception to infinite power. Divine power for the biblical writers does not look the sort of 'power over' that can be franchised from the God (with whom it is benign) to human beings (with whom it would surely be dangerous). Nevertheless, divine power might, from a biblical point of view, be seen to empower, gift and enable people to lead (and then only as serving), and might even enable the *koinonia* community as a whole to a 'reception' of such giftings. Secondly, Foucault's power theory of unpredictable power behaviours springing from power relations, is not threatened by a reality of divine power. In other words almightiness is concerned

87 van den Brink, pp. 166–7.

88 van den Brink, p. 167.

89 van den Brink, p. 178.

90 van den Brink, p. 179.

91 van den Brink, p. 178. However, it should be borne in mind that some feminist theology has raised questions even about that. For example see McFague, discussed above.

92 van den Brink, pp. 179–80.

93 van den Brink, p. 180.

in the mix of power streams precisely with empowering just the weakest and the voiceless to be part of this process. Thirdly, the almightiness of God in Christian thought is not a doctrine implying human passivity, but a call to be empowered and energized in the task of building *koinonia* communities on the Jesus way. It is taken to provoke the members of such a community to be spurred into humble action for the wider world in solidarity with the one who has the 'power to'. Where divine power is seen this way it is good … and even dangerous too, but in a good way.

Chapter 10
Conclusions: Power in the Future of *Koinonia* Community

We began this exploration with a number of questions, to which we turn again. How should power be conceived? Where was it to be found? Was it really 'dangerous' just as Foucault alleged? In particular did it present itself as a critical factor in the life of a church community? What challenges were involved for church as community and leaders in particular? Some answers have at least begun to take shape. And one thing has especially become clear. Church as a living community cannot afford to be casual or complacent about something as formative for its life together as power. It must be alert to power's pervasive presence, the elephant in the room that no-one talks about. And once awakened to the fact that power relations and strategies are indeed dangerous, it has to avoid falling back into any form of denial concerning the sociological reality of power at work within its processes. Especially church should take note of the hidden levers that can in a crisis suddenly clunk into action or defiantly be shifted to a tactical off-position.

But is this really the case where a church is plainly buzzing with life, and is a place of positive relationships and creativity? Put bluntly, vigilance is possibly even more necessary in a healthy church, for the richer the mix the greater the combustible chemistry. But that is not the whole story. We have concluded that power patterns and power moves can be counterbalanced, offset through a continuous culture of transparency, listening and willingness for surprise and respect. For church community these spring from the presence of distinctively Christian values and principles. If a common journey on the way of Jesus is at all important, social and ethical lubrication is desirable in the sometimes dysfunctional mechanisms of power. It is in this way that church might hope to release another more critical kind of strategies and patterns alongside power ones. These further patterns and streams constitute a 'power to' and a 'power with', that is, a positive power, a synergy of service to the world.

So those carrying duties of leadership of various kinds in a church are most responsible and best placed for addressing both kinds of strategies and streams in the community. Their task is fairly simple in aim. Leaders are to be sensitive and vigilant, listening and learning, all the time taking full account of two realities. The first reality is to be the early Christian tradition's understanding of *koinonia* as the fellowship of the way. This community is a company of people convinced of a common and equal share in God's Spirit and journeying together on the way of Jesus as equals, having renounced the vicious layering that has scarred the ancient Roman world and many societies since, including our own, in subtle ways.

The consensus in theology today is beginning to say more emphatically that this *koinonia* character, is of the essence of church in both local or wider contexts. The second reality nevertheless is equally important. It is the basic sociological character of church and its natural vulnerability to whatever power normally finds to do in such micro-groups. Everything that critical and social theory throws at us about power behaviours in human societies, if valid for social groups, also inhabits church however nice church people might be.

The Place of Power Theory

The resources for supporting this approach on power and church have not been insignificant. We can claim a high degree of ecumenical and theological consensus in favour of *koinonia* as the key issue for essential church. It is valid to transpose everything about *koinonia* into either a universal or local key. That enables an intense focus on what power means in particular for local church internally and also for church turned outwards to the world and other forms of church *koinonia*. Within and behind such an approach lies a deep appeal to the Scriptures rather than to any trendy fad. But further help from outside theology helps to ensure some level of analytical sharpness. Group dynamics, systems theory and social psychology each play a part here. But the most incisive contribution comes to our aid from the work of major and influential streams in critical studies, especially for clarification of key distinctions in the analysis of power. These contributions offer more than mere abstract, academic distinctions. They also point straight to what is at stake in the power debate for a church community. Michel Foucault and especially vanguard writers in feminism, raise telling questions about neglected power patterns in groups. Naturally, such contributions from cultural studies should not be received randomly and without critical care. But equally they cannot be completely ignored either.

Foucault does indeed prove his worth, especially in his breaking of the mould in political approaches to power. But yet more important is his exposing of complexity in the anatomy of power. All the same, he is prone to hard overstatement. And on occasion he takes up intellectual causes which are difficult to maintain if not indeed doomed from the beginning. However, it is important that theology works round some of the less convincing ideas of Foucault if his searching analysis is to benefit Christian practices of community. For Christian thought need not let his lapses obscure his insights. True these lapses are often perceived as serious. For instance it is unlikely that he has completely recovered from complaints that he lacks clear normative control for his theory (a criticism, we recall, sometimes termed 'normative deficit'). And he does reject a number of widely shared assumptions such as the value of ideology, a generic defining of humanity and the reality of the human subject. But he therefore often runs his ship without rudder or engine.

It should be remembered that, however inconsistently, unacknowledged ethical principles do swim just below the surface for Foucault. These are perhaps purely instinctive and not integrated with other parts of his work, or maybe simply self-commending. He would not be alone in that. In fact his ethical assumptions must surely be normative legacies from a variety of sources more ethically structured than his own work, ranging through Catholicism, Kant and Marxism to Heidegger. It provides the reverse of a famous punchline: this time we must graciously say of Foucault 'Look! The King's got some clothes on!' Though of course we courteously ignore that they are not his own. This concession at least recognizes some theoretical ethical ballast in Foucault despite his own disclaimers. A good thing too, since he needs this kind of ballast for his varied intellectual campaigns, such as that waged against secretive power. It is such campaigns around power analysis that bring him today within waving distance of church's uneasy relationship with power. Another critical and far-reaching example is the subtle connection of power to truth.

Feminists have shown great resilience in the face of Foucault's gatecrashing of their world (some by adaptability, others by unruffled stability). Concentration of their thought by Foucault's intervention in the struggle for human freedom has enabled many feminists to deconstruct the traditional (male) theoretical obsession with 'power over'. It has also produced clarity on the value of relational foundations for power and ethics. Their responses have provided a focus through which reflection on the patterns and relations in church community may be viewed. This leads to much greater interested in 'power to' and 'power with' as the foundations of effective community. The directing away from preoccupation with 'power over' and its balancing by mutuality, transparency and openness is full of wisdom for church leaders.

The Environment of Power

Granted, it had to be an exaggeration when Foucault denied that one can ever extricate 'truth' from its encasement in power impulses. Can it be that all public 'truth' is suspect by coming somehow from the hands of hidden power? Certainly some differentiation of power from knowledge is needed, or intelligible conversation would be impossible. Without this, no mundane matters of factual knowledge could be generally relied on in daily life, ranging from the information contained in diaries to the efficiency of machines. But all the same, with Foucault's hands at the tiller the matter of truth and power has certainly moved on from simple verbal distinctions between them. What he recounts may be observed routinely in human relations. Claims to truth and bids for power are indeed sometimes hard to disentangle. At least this is so concerning local power relations, and is a major factor in promoting and protecting the vitality of church community.

In a micro-group like church, certainty of local 'truths' about situations and crises can indeed take on the character of dogma. Many church tensions spring from unfounded certainty about the allegedly 'pure truth' of local problems or decisions. We are not speaking here about personal religious beliefs or the doctrines of the faith. Rather these conflicts are about political issues and revolve around perceptions of situations. The differences could especially concern such areas as choice of practices or procedures old or new, local church culture, members' expectations of each other and social post mortems. Perhaps all the contributory voices speak 'truths', but this is far different from saying any of them produce pure truth. A healthy church community learns to accept that sub-groups in church politics express only versions of truth. For behind opinions sometimes lie not only power relations but their concealed fruit: attitudes, impulses and strategies. These traits press buttons and pull levers. Power streams such as fear, distrust, suspicion and anxiety manufacture many different versions of personalized 'truths' backed by the pains and experiences of the past. Power patterns and 'truth' are thus intertwined. But the underlying power stream to these truths can fall away, where there is help from Christian distinctives of truthful attitudes and action, as well as of caring, vulnerability and trustful transparency. In this way, Foucault's challenge would be honoured without deleting 'truth' or even 'knowledge', from the dictionary.

A further, similarly searching analysis from Foucault drives home the message to church about vulnerability and shared power. It comes straight from the corridors of the asylum and the appeal is unadorned: grant a hearing, he says, to the strange voice, the transgressing and the inconvenient questioning. Where possible, Foucault might say, let professionalized 'knowledge' or 'truth' make a way to hear the minority voice. Let pain and perplexity sometimes sound out in the surge of decision-making. Give a place to the transgressive voice in the collision and collusion of power strategies.

All this talk by Foucault about the constructed nature of truth emerges from a definite phase – his middle period. From this period of suspicion about power, there also arose his theory of an encompassing bio-power circulating in society, making up people as it went. Of what interest could this theory be to micro-groups like church? Eventually his later work on local groups provides the answer. The centre and the margins turn out to be connected, the big power with local power relations. But even apart from that, church people too are at least in part the products of circulating culture and norms. Such norms can impact healthily or unhealthily upon church as a community, a shared life. For the community journeys on the culturally unpopular way of Jesus. But not only this. Church too can invent ways of making up people by the power of privileged norms. Some of these are not always relevant to the way of Jesus (manufactured norms of non-worldliness). Some are even against the way of Jesus (favouring the 'respectable' or well off). This process of transformation, or 'normalizing', may be in the image of a fading history, a denomination, a facile niceness, or a taut traditionalism. It may flow from a pious dream of perfection, 'successful' church today, past glories or other causes inferior to the main one of reproducing the way of Jesus in community, and for the world's benefit. It may even be in the image of individual local heroes of past and present church, and include all their idiosyncrasies.

Such seemingly trivial and secondary productive power is not always harmless. It can create power behaviours based on mild idolatry of people or traditions.

The gentle winds of local 'truths' and norms can turn into strong gales blowing through the fabric of power relations, driving divisive power behaviours in a church community. It has become clear that any wise leadership of a shared life in community takes them seriously from the beginning and does not underestimate them.

Local Power Dynamics

Eventually however Foucault turns his sights specifically on power in local institutions and groups. Here he draws out the unpredictability of power streams coursing around a micro-community, and this would include such a social body as church. Church in modern societies will always, like any other group, contain a complexity of inequalities of many kinds, with varied, subtle, maybe unintended, techniques of exclusion. The inequalities may show up in such traits as gestures, silences, exclusive forms of communication and rationed warmth. Most naturally, if unchallenged, each imbalance ('asymmetry') will generate unequal power relations, functions and strategies. And if the different power behaviours are in disagreement there may emerge a stronger party. And in a bad scenario then perhaps leadership styles of surveillance and hierarchy will develop. Norms of exclusion usually accompany them, leading to unseemly division or even splintering. But in the tangling together of different power behaviours, it may not always turn out quite as stronger parties expected. Even the weaker member in a relation has a transgressive voice to offer, and many subtle, effective strategies from the seemingly weak can craftily or unconsciously use collision or collusion to block, delay or hinder.

Consequently the results of varied power behaviours in a group today are unpredictable. Resolutions of conflicting views may indeed happily be reached. Or on the other hand perhaps instead it will be resolved only by one party rising above the rest. Or then yet again division might occur. It is not certain in modern groups that the naturally more powerful will get their way. A question began this chapter, indeed the whole project: Where does power lie? If we mean 'power over', a leadership may be startled to find the answer: not necessarily with the leaders. The famous dictum of Foucault may sometimes be true. Power comes from everywhere. And that means anyone can destroy a community, although it is leaders who are best placed to do it.

So the sociological reality of power behaviours really does affect church and operates just as in any other micro-group. That same social reality, then, underlines the need mentioned above to respect transgressive voices as routinely as possible. It also cautions against overconfidence, since seemingly 'successful' church communities harbour their own special dangers, whether they like to think so or not. For the richer and larger the mix becomes, the greater the complexity of power strategies resulting. It seems that long life and health for a *koinonia* depends greatly on a culture of openness and honesty, along with continuous vigilance, hopefully free of anxiety. The task of leaders, it turns out, includes the regular injection of transparency and teachableness into the mix. In such a culture, deep surveillance of members has no place. For it can only produce externalism and undermine mutual transparency. Healthy church however also hears multiple contributions especially those voices that speak out of pain. It seeks to balance normal social asymmetry by the mystery of the way of Jesus. It was this 'mystery of the Gospel' that sought to level the inequalities of the Roman world. It did so through belief in a shared identity in Jesus himself, not by cherishing any discriminating levels of privilege. This was meant seriously in the Christian Scriptures and so is a solemn quest of church.

Today, in a setting of local and disciplinary power, the traits of equality in Jesus affect life together far beyond a church's own life. As suggested at the beginning, what goes on in the local church community cannot be separated from wider connections. Oppressed and unequal church cannot with confidence confront the world's inequalities (especially in the majority, poor world). It cannot join a struggle against evils not yet tackled within its own life. Now the connections become plainer between power in networks of church and church in networks of power. Indifference within church to injustice, suffering and power abuse steals away from it any voice and action for Jesus in the world at large.

However there has been good news. For it has also been noted that the brute fact of 'power over' is not the only possible major influence at work in a micro-group, as Foucault probably conceded. The power of caring for the other, a 'power to', would also be potent in the mix of strategies. It could balance out the natural laws and strategies of power relations and strategies in the community and negate the negatives. It could also spill over into church's relation to the external networks of power in the world. This, incidentally, all squares with some group dynamics, systems theory and psychology. And it helps us now to consider the seriousness of community to church. Caring, transforming power is essential to the circle of friendship in church community if it is truly to reflect the *koinonia* with all its implications. The stakes here are high and the handling of power streams in church appears imperative because life together in small and great ways is a kind of power-sharing in people's destinies. The commitment to each others' destinies is high and therefore involves high risks wherever power relations are found. The more effective a *koinonia* is, the more precious does the continuation of its shared life become to those who share the journey. And so all the more urgent is the attention required in leadership to power relations and the offsetting of power moves through Christian transparency, openness and caring.

Power and Freedom

In Foucault's final concern with freedom, through 'the care of self', he was still striving to find an answer to the problem of resistance raised by his own power theory. That theory exaggerated the degree that totalizing bio-power shaped us and everything about us, and so subverted our freedom. For it logically implied that any resistance was itself shaped and by definition could not really be resistance. Now late in life he detected a way to qualify that earlier somewhat pessimistic perception. But his solution missed the target so far as a Christian sense of freedom is concerned. It focused on individual self-determination and so diverged from the very value enshrined in the idea of Christian community. According to a Christian definition, freedom is found through investment in others not merely in personal development and autonomy. An approach to freedom springing from the way of Jesus instead lives in service to and respect for the other. It locates authentic freedom in a self's developing ethically and towards freedom only in relation to others.

The apparently restrictive context of life shared together in church may all the same be liberating. But this does not denote a freedom ethic that can be rooted in Foucault's 'care of the self', whether this is aesthetic or ascetic. This freedom lives from quite different energies. The freedoms of *koinonia* are counter-cultural and counterintuive. They consist of such powers as intended by Pasewark's 'communication of efficacy'. We could call it empowerment, a mutual giving way, moral responsibility for other persons. And it extends that responsibility beyond the community to far-flung sections of humanity wherever there is oppression and injustice.

And yet, however much Foucault's struggles with the problem of freedom differed from that of the Jesus way, he still confronted church people with challenges. The forceful enculturing of people in Christian beliefs and practices without giving them time for growth, and space for questioning come under pressure. In Jesus, only the free responses of liberated faith count for anything. Anything else, especially that which results from spiritual docility and passivity belongs to the methods of bio-power not those of authentic Christianity. For the spirit of the *koinonia* is freedom. Similarly, self criticism and re-evaluation, which Foucault commends, have also turned out not to be constraints on freedom but as expressions of it. This is another Foucauldian revolution that brings church up short.

Power and the Spirit

So then, we have some idea what kind of distinctive Christian resources lubricate the frictions of naturally colliding power behaviours in the life together of *koinonia.* The levelling tendency of the Jesus way obviously plays the greatest role in cushioning power's impact in church dynamics. It is with this that power relations meet an extra dimension. But equally important is belief in an invisible bond to the *koinonia* since Christian community is a share in *the Spirit*. It had to be settled that belief in the Spirit did not in principle reintroduce further power behaviours. For did not theology speak of 'the power of the Spirit' and yet also of the Spirit of power? So what did the term mean? It looks suspiciously like something to boost egos in the clashing and competing of power interests. It would have been a strange, inscrutable paradox this – powers from the Spirit of Jesus engendering conflict on the way of Jesus.

However the conundrum proved resolvable. The power of the Spirit could indeed become overly associated with public charisma, powerful signs and wonders or with solemn authorities of church. But we should think more of the Spirit of the *koinonia* as the facilitator of life in the common journey of disciples together. As the Spirit of God this was the breath, the life that vitalized a whole creation. But in the *koinonia* that same Spirit breathed life by means of a mutual life-giving which set free in the Spirit. This occurs in such settings as exchange of abilities which fostered service and friendship.

This Spirit should also be seen as authentically being the Spirit of Jesus himself. This person stood out as the very living expression of the power of caring, and so presented an outrageous transgression against coerciveness and the rule of naked, self-serving power. On a similar note, those on the way of Jesus together can see the Spirit as associated with the deepest forms of vulnerability in Jesus. In the Spirit Jesus showed a special power not represented in Foucault's list of power strategies – the transgressive truth of self-denying love. Early Christian texts expected this self-denial to defuse self-interested, coercive power in the community and its power behaviours. The unity which could grow from this is not a top-down, external imposition. Rather it is a disconcerting unity that welcomes varieties of persons from diverse levels, whatever tensions such a mix carries with it in the form of inescapable power relations. It is this type of unity that would demonstrate the power of the Spirit in the community, rather than great feats or ultra-powerful leadership. Of course, the blunt sociological reality does not at this point disappear in favour of a wonderful ideal. But the Spirit in this theological approach tempers natural power dynamics and adds an extra dimension to the collisions of power strategies. The Spirit that brings synergy thus becomes the hope of *koinonia* in church community.

Here we have yet another connection of church to the world around it so far as power is concerned. The power of the Spirit becomes the power *to be to the world as Jesus living in the Spirit was*, responding to its needs and its cries. Any impressive gifting, leading or speaking then only stands for power if it is of this kind. In other words this is assuredly the power of the Spirit if one can see in it the Jesus-led 'pneumatic calling' expressed in a *koinonia*. That calling is to the mission of the self-giving Jesus to the whole world through the power of the Spirit. Church as community looks to the authentic power of the Spirit of Jesus to set a *koinonia* free to grow towards this goal. So freedom is not primarily freedom *from* but freedom *for* – that is, freedom to become what Jesus was and did for the world. Those opening themselves to such freedom are seemingly not chained and oppressed by it but released and energized.

Hence, the power of the Spirit still implies power for the community through vulnerable venture. It means a willingness in many situations not to resort to forbidden channels of power even if this seems to leave one genuinely in an exposed position of weakness. Hence the power of the Spirit denies to an authentic *koinonia* forms of 'power over' (where this term means benefiting oneself at someone else's expense), even more so those that abuse. Rather, any legitimate 'power over' (that is legitimated authority) is only there for serving 'power to', and its chief functioning will be an enabling and empowering.

To repeat Moltmann's way of viewing it, the Spirit's power is whatever drives out death, welcomes the marginalized and comforts the sad, displaying the true 'powers and energies' of the Spirit of life. Or to put it more simply, the power of the Spirit is ultimately the power of God's life-giving love. Although the social reality is a long way behind the ideal, the doctrine of the Spirit's power is intended to shape a *koinonia* which is living, speaking and embodying the good news of the way of Jesus in human lives.

Power and Vulnerability

Such flights of aspiration however, carry with them a serious difficulty quite apart from the deficit between the ideal and reality in all church communities that gives us the notion of pilgrim church. The problem revolves around the more explicit ideal of power seen to be through weakness or vulnerability. As promised at the beginning, we have indeed accumulated prepositions: 'power over', 'power to', 'power with' (synergy), and 'power from' (the Spirit). To these is added now 'power through' (vulnerability or 'weakness'). It has been clarified that this latter power through weakness is a Christologically-inspired theme. The life-releasing power of his death is the essential Jesus-narrative. His own vulnerability even forms a pattern for relations in the Christian writings (Phil 2.1–19). However this apparent compliment to vulnerability has caused much heart-searching. Have not the poor and disadvantaged experienced enough vulnerability? Feminists especially express concern here. A few sentences now will not of course be enough to reconcile the competing concerns. But one point might be worth making. It is that to be 'weak in Christ' did not mean in Paul's rhetoric to be weak in *character* or even in powerlessness. The idea pointed rather to sharing in the self-renouncing, servant-like, faith centred on God and on drawing down God's power. In fact a costly commitment with integrity is efficacious, powerful and maybe even political, just as the vulnerable works of the Mothers of Plaza de Mayo. For theology, a costly commitment is a dying like Christ's not for its own sake, but so that the perfect power of Christ's could flow right out paradoxically from that same position of disadvantage.

However the principle just explored does not demand yet more from those already downtrodden. Rather for them it puts an unexpected value on what they suffer already in that downtrodden position. Their apparent 'weakness' re-enters as a powerful and honourable player in the list of effective strategies for community and the Spirit's purpose for a suffering world. This is the result whatever the intention: it was meant as evil, but afterwards clothed with surprising value by

God as the one revealing power through weakness. Paul himself came to see his unwanted powerlessness as hidden power so that the divine efficacy ('power to') may also spring from that same site. Those already vulnerable and unable to escape their predicament are not exhorted to go looking for more of the same, but take heart a little from God's revaluing of their lives as honourable and powerful, possibly in hidden ways. Foucault of course also attributes efficacy to positions of apparent helplessness. His system, though not his own personal action, just lacks the balancing biblical passion for justice rolling down like a stream. For in the end, for the Christian narrative, oppression is against the will of God and atrocity an awesome offence. This is a sentiment that squares well with some feminist questioning at Foucault's seeming denial of identifiable villains.

Authority

Just as the power of the Spirit is being rediscovered as the power that empowers and gives life so authority is being developed by some as a communication of the power of divine love through the Trinity. Consequently, specific fields of exercising authority particularly need to be handled with sensitivity and these include preaching, pastoral support and participation in the spiritual formation of another. These need to steer well clear of such traits as the inappropriate searching of another's inner life and the use of 'magic words' and insider jargon resulting in feelings of exclusion. Additionally, new approaches to authority are appearing, careful to put boundaries of voluntary cooperation around authority, to avoid coercion or heavy persuasion. Hence authority works authentically only within a narrow and well legitimated way. However, even this is not a simple matter since the grounds, scope and limits of such legitimation would anyway need to be very watertight indeed and often they are not. Hence the suggestion remains that authority should surely be heavily conditioned by the voluntary notion of faith and life together on the Jesus way and by the equality of voices in the community of the Spirit. Authority also implies not political savvy but total dependence of leaders on the holiness, fruit and gifts of the Spirit, as well as what is these days called 'servant-leadership'. However, with these many conditions and qualifications, there is indeed the possibility that the old wineskins and barrels will simply burst and then there may yet be new conceptions of authority and a recasting of it in theology. These will be rooted in today's rediscovery of a treasury of all the gifts and a wisdom of all the voices. If not so done, then in local church communities tyrants rather than carers will perhaps fill the vacancies.

The Way Ahead

We have quarried, as promised, a highly complex (or we might say 'rich') analysis of power. It has proven to be as demanding as expected. Yet it can be argued as a result that power is indeed interpreted by the varied play of prepositions and that these usages clarify some important distinctions. Power has indeed turned out to be not essentially bad in all its senses, but certainly dangerous and all the more compelling a topic for that. And it is clear that it is indeed possible to hold that church community is an adventure in hope, a sign of the future, without falling into naïve neglect of its character as a sociological reality. There are some territories of thought that deserve deeper attention than could be given here. The disciplines of psychology and group theory will no doubt yield many more insights for handling power relations. The concept of freedom deserves a more thorough critical analysis than could be given here.

But what is most urgently needed is a programme of rigorous survey of power dynamics in local churches, meaning a serious empirical, quality-controlled research based on modern analysis of power. Such a project needs to identify more closely those Foucauldian mechanisms and power behaviours that play upon each other in the setting of church community. But the results need to be allied with ongoing Christian theology that concerns itself with principles about power relations and patterns in line with the way of Jesus. In this way it will foster the best aspirations of every community that is a company of followers on the way of Jesus. Theological resources here especially value desires to empower and enable others as Jesus did under his 'power to' transform for good. With more attention to this, true power could genuinely pervade the community even in its character as sociological. Everyone on the way of the *koinonia* would be empowered to play their part in community decision-making and action, and ready to realize power in the strength of the shared Spirit of power.

Bibliography

Ainley, Stephen C., 'Mennonite Culture Wars. Power, Authority and Domination' in Redekop, B. W. and Calvin, W. (eds), *Power, Authority and the Anabaptist Tradition* (Baltimore: Johns Hopkins University Press, 2001), 136–54.

Allen, Amy, 'Foucault, Feminism and the Self' in Taylor, Dianna and Vintges, Karen (eds), *Feminism and the Final Foucault* (Urbana: University of Illinois Press, 2004), 285–57.

Allen, Barry, 'Foucault and Modern Political Philosophy' in Moss, Jeremy (ed.), *The Later Foucault: Politics and Philosophy* (London: Sage, 1998), 164–98.

Arbuckle, Gerald A., *Refounding the Church: Dissent for Leadership* (London: Chapman, 1993).

Arendt, Hannah, 'Communicative Power' in Lukes, Steven (ed.), *Power* (Oxford: Blackwell, 1986), 59–74.

Arlandson, James Malcolm, *Women, Class and Society in Early Christianity: Models from Luke – Acts* (Massachusetts, 1997).

Armstrong, Aurelia, in 'Foucault and Feminism' in the *Internet Encyclopaedia of Philosophy* p. 1. (http://www.iep. edu/f/foucfem.htm – accessed 1.01.07).

Avis, Paul, *Church Drawing Near: Spirituality and Mission In a Post-Christian Culture* (London: T & T Clark, 2003).

Avis, Paul, *Authority, Leadership and Conflict in the Church* (London: Mowbray, 1992).

Bailey, M. E., 'Foucauldian Feminism. Contesting Bodies Sexuality and Identity' in Ramazanoğlu, Caroline (ed.), *Up against Foucault: Explorations of Some Tensions Between Foucault and Feminism* (London: Routledge, 1993), 99–122.

Bauckham, Richard, *God and the Crisis of Freedom: Biblical and Contemporary Perspectives* (Louisville: John Knox, 2002).

Bauckham, Richard, 'Scripture and Authority', *Transformation* 15/2 (1998): 5–11.

Beasley-Murray, Paul, *Power for God's Sake: Power and Abuse in the Local Church* (Carlisle: Paternoster Press, 1998).

Bernauer, James and Carrette, Jeremy (eds), *Michel Foucault and Theology: The Politics of Religious Experience* (Aldershot: Ashgate, 2004).

Bernauer, James, 'Michel Foucault's Philosophy of Religion: An Introduction to the Non-Fascist Life' in Bernauer, James and Carrette, Jeremy (eds), *Michel Foucault and Theology: The Politics of Religious Experience* (Aldershot: Ashgate, 2004), 77–97.

Bernauer, James, *Michel Foucault's Force of Flight. Toward an Ethics for Thought* (New Jersey: Humanities Press, 1990).

Bloesch, Donald, G., *God the Almighty: Power Wisdom Holiness Love* (Illinois: Inter Varsity, 1995).

Bonnet, Piero Antonio, 'Those with No Mandate in the Church', in Provost, James and Walf, Knut (eds), *Concilium 197: Power in the Church* (Edinburgh: T & T Clark, 1988), 115–22.

Bordo, Susan, 'Feminism, Foucault and the Politics of the Body' in Ramazanoğlu, Caroline (ed.), *Up against Foucault: Explorations of Some Tensions Between Foucault and Feminism* (London: Routledge, 1993), 179–202.

Bousma, W. J., *John Calvin: A Sixteenth-Century Portrait* (Oxford: Oxford University Press, 1988).

Bradley, Ian, *The Power of Sacrifice* (Darton, London: Longman & Todd, 1995).

Briggs, Sheila, 'Paul on Bondage and Freedom in Imperial Roman Society' in Horsley, Richard (ed.), *Paul and Politics: Ekkleisa Israel Imperium Interpretation: Essays in Honour of Krister Stendahl* (Harrisburg: Trinity Press International, 2000), 110–23.

Brink, Gijsbert van den, *Almighty God: A Study of the Doctrine of Divine Omnipotence* (Kampen: Kok Pharos, 1993).

Brock, Rita Nakashima, 'A New Thing in the Land. The Female Surrounds the Warrior' in Rigby, Cynthia L. (ed.), *Power, Powerlessness and the Divine: New Inquiries in Bible and Theology* (Atlanta: Scholars Press, 1997), 137–59.

Brown, Alexandra R., 'The Gospel Takes Place: Paul's Theology of Power-in-Weakness in 2 Corinthians', *Interpretation* 52/3 (1998): 271–86.

Brown, Hedy, 'Themes in experimental research on groups from the 1930s to the 1990s' in Wetherill, Margaret (ed.), *Identities, Groups and Social Issues* (Milton Keynes: Open University/Sage, 1996), 9–63.

Brown, Wendy, 'Genealogical Politics' in Moss, Jeremy (ed.), *The Later Foucault: Politics and Philosophy* (London: Sage, 1998), 33–49.

Burkholder, J. L., 'Power' in Redekop, B. W. and Calvin, W. (eds), *Power, Authority and the Anabaptist Tradition* (Baltimore: Johns Hopkins University Press, 2001), 1–13.

Butler, Judith, 'Bodies and Power Revisited' in Taylor, Dianna, and Vintges, Karen (eds), *Feminism and the Final Foucault* (Urbana: University of Illinois Press, 2004), 183–96.

Butler, Judith, *The Psychic Life of Power: Theories in Subjection* (Stanford: Stanford University Press, 1997).

Byrne, Peter, 'Omnipotence, Feminism and God' in *International Journal for Philosophy of Religion* 37 (1995): 145–65.

Campbell, Charles L., *The Word before the Powers: An Ethic of Preaching* (Louisville: Westminster/John Knox, 2002).

Carr, Anne E., 'Providence Power and the Holy Spirit', *Horizons* 29/1 (2002): 80–93.

Carrette, Jeremy (ed.), *Religion and Culture by Michel Foucault* (Manchester: Manchester University Press, 1999).

Carrette, Jeremy, 'Beyond Theology and Sexuality: Foucault the Self and the Que(e)rying of Monotheistic Truth' in Bernauer, James, and Carrette, Jeremy (eds), *Michel Foucault and Theology: The Politics of Religious Experience* (Aldershot: Ashgate, 2004), 217–32.

Carrette, Jeremy, *Foucault and Religion: Spiritual Corporality and Political Spirituality* (London: Routledge, 2000).

Carrette, Jeremy, 'Prologue to a Confession of the Flesh' in Carrette, Jeremy (ed.), *Religion and Culture by Michel Foucault* (Manchester: Manchester University Press, 1999), 1–47.

Case-Winters, Anna, 'The Question of God in an Age of Science: Constructions of Reality in Theology and Science', *Zygon*, Vol 32/3 (1997): 351–75.

Castelli, Elizabeth A., 'Foucault and the Church in Late Antiquity' in Bernauer, James, and Carrette, Jeremy (eds), *Michel Foucault and Theology: The Politics of Religious Experience* (Aldershot: Ashgate, 2004), 19–38.

Castelli, Elizabeth A., Church Evangelization and the Bonds of Koinonia: A Report of the International Consultation between the Catholic Church and the World Evangelical Alliance (1993 – 2002), found online at www.efg–hohenstaufenstr.de [accessed 22.02.06].

Ciobotea, Daniel, 'Holiness as Content and Purpose of Ecclesial Authority' in Grdzelidze, Tamara (ed.), *One, Holy, Catholic and Apostolic: Ecumenical Reflections on the Church. Faith and Order Paper No. 197* (Geneva: World Council of Churches, 2005), 91–6.

Clapsis, Emmanuel, 'Does the Church Have a Sacramental Nature? An Orthodox Perspective' in Grdzelidze, Tamara (ed.), *One, Holy, Catholic and Apostolic: Ecumenical Reflections on the Church. Faith and Order Paper No. 197* (Geneva: World Council of Churches, 2005), 17–26.

Clark, David B., *Breaking the Mould of Christendom: Kingdom Community Diaconal Church and the Liberation of the Laity* (Peterborough: Epworth, 2005).

Clegg, Stewart, *Frameworks of Power* (London: Sage, 1991).

Cobble, James F., *The Church and the Powers: A Theology of Church Structure* (Massachusetts: Peabody, 1988).

Colle, Ralph Del, 'The Holy Spirit: Presence Power Person', *Theological Studies* 62/2 (2001): 322–34.

Croft, Steven, *Ministry in Three Dimensions: Ordination and Leadership in the Local Church* (London, Darton, Longman & Todd, 1999).

Cronin, Kieran, *Rights and Christian Ethics* (Cambridge: Cambridge University Press, 1992).

Dahl, Robert, 'Power as the Control of Behaviour' in Lukes Steven (ed.), *Power* (Oxford: Blackwell, 1986), 37–58.

Davidson, Arnold I. (ed.), *Foucault and His Interlocuters* (Chicago: University of Chicago, 1998).

Davidson, Arnold I. (ed.), 'Structures and Strategies of Discourse: Remarks Towards a History of Foucault's Theology of Language' in Davidson, Arnold I.

(ed.), *Foucault and His Interlocuters* (Chicago: University of Chicago, 1998), 1–17.

Dawn, Marva J., *Power, Weakness and the Tabernacling of God* (Grand Rapids: Eerdmans, 2001).

Diamond, Irene and Quinby, Lee (eds), *Feminism & Foucault: Reflections on Resistance* (Boston: Northeastern University Press, 1988).

Doyle, Dennis, *Communion Ecclesiology: Visions and Versions* (New York: Maryknoll, 2000).

Dreyfus, Hubert L. and Rabinow, Paul, *Michel Foucault: Beyond Structuralism and Hermeneutics* (Brighton: Harvester Press, 1982).

Driver, Alex, 'Bodies in Space: Foucault's Account of Disciplinary Power' in Jones, Colin and Porter, Roy (eds), *Reassessing Foucault: Power, Medicine and the Body* (London: Routledge, 1994), 113–31.

Droogers, André, 'The Power Dimensions of the Christian Community: an Anthropological Model', *Religion* 33 (2003): 263–80.

Dulles, Avery, *Models of the Church* (Dublin: Gill and MacMillan, 1981).

Edwards, Douglas, *Religion and Power: Pagans, Jews and Christians in the Greek East* (Oxford: Oxford University Press, 1996).

Elliott, Neil, 'Paul and the Politics of Empire: Problems and Prospects' in Horsley, Richard (ed.), *Paul and Politics. Ekkleisa Israel Imperium Interpretation: Essays in Honour of Krister Stendahl* (Harrisburg: Trinity Press International, 2000), 17–39.

Evans, G. R., *Problems of Authority in the Reformation Debates* (Cambridge: Cambridge University Press, 1992).

Falconer, Alan, 'Introduction' in Grdzelidze, (ed.), *One, Holy, Catholic and Apostolic: Ecumenical Reflections on the Church. Faith and Order Paper No. 197* (Geneva: World Council of Churches, 2005), 1–14.

Farrow, Douglas, *Ascension and Ecclesia. On the Significance of the Doctrine of the Ascension for Ecclesiology and Christian Cosmology* (Edinburgh: T & T Clark, 1999).

Faubion, J. D. (ed.), *Michel Foucault: Power* (London: Penguin, 2002).

Fiddes, Paul, *Tracks and Traces: Baptist Identity in Church and Theology* (Carlisle: Paternoster, 2003).

Fiorenza, Elisabeth Schüssler, 'Paul and the Politics of Interpretation' in Horsley, Richard (ed.), *Paul and Politics. Ekkleisa Israel Imperium Interpretation: Essays in Honour of Krister Stendahl* (Harrisburg: Trinity Press International, 2000), 40–59.

Forsyth, Donelson R., *Group Dynamics Second Edition* (Belmont, CA: Pacific Grove, 1990).

Foucault, Michel, 'Truth and Power' (Interview), in Faubion J. D. (ed.), *Michel Foucault: Power* (London: Penguin, 2002), 111–33.

Foucault, Michel, 'The Subject and Power' in Faubion J. D. (ed.), 326–48.

Foucault, Michel, 'Sexuality and Power' in Carrette, Jeremy (ed), *Religion and Culture by Michel Foucault* (Manchester: Manchester University Press, 1999), 115–30.

Foucault, Michel, 'Power, Right, Truth' in Goodin R. E. and Pettit, Philip (eds), *Contemporary Philosophy: An Anthology* (Oxford: Blackwell, 1997), 545–50.

Foucault, Michel, '"Omnes et Singulatem"': Towards a Critique of Political Reason' in Faubion James D. (ed.), *Michel Foucault, Power* (London: Penguin, 1994), 298–325.

Foucault, Michel, 'An Aesthetics of Existence' (Interview), in Krizman, Lawrence D. (ed.), *Michel Foucault: Politics, Philosophy, Culture. Interviews and Other Writings* (New York: Routledge, 1988), 47–56

Foucault, Michel, 'Critical Theory/Intellectual History' (Interview), in Kritzman (ed.), 7–46.

Foucault, Michel, 'On Power' (Interview), in Kritzman (ed.), 96–109.

Foucault, Michel, 'Power and Sex' (Interview), in Kritzman (ed.), 110–124.

Foucault, Michel, 'The Battle for Chastity' in Kritzman (ed.), 224–41.

Foucault, Michel, 'The Concern for Truth' (Interview), in Kritzman (ed.), 255–70.

Foucault, Michel, 'The Minimalist Self' (Interview), in Kritzman (ed.), 3–16.

Foucault, Michel, 'The Return of Morality' (Interview), in Kritzman (ed.), 242–54.

Foucault, Michel, 'Disciplinary Power and Subjection' in Lukes, Steven (ed.), *Power* (Oxford: Blackwell, 1986), 229–42.

Foucault, Michel, *The History of Sexuality Vol 3: The Care of The Self* (London: Pantheon, 1986).

Foucault, Michel, 'Confessions of the Flesh' in Gordon, Colin (ed.), *Power/Knowledge: Selected Interviews and Other Writings 1972–1977: Michel Foucault* (Brighton: Harvester, 1980), 194–228.

Foucault, Michel, 'Body/Power' in Gordon, Colin (ed.), 55–62.

Foucault, Michel, 'Power and Strategies' in Gordon, Colin (ed.), 134–45.

Foucault, Michel, 'Two Lectures' in Gordon, Colin (ed.), 78–108.

Foucault, Michel, *The History of Sexuality Vol 1: An Introduction* (London: Allen Lane, 1979).

Freundlieb, Dieter, 'Foucault's Theory of Discourse and Human Agency' in Jones, Colin and Porter, Roy (eds), *Reassessing Foucault: Power Medicine and the Body* (London: Routledge, 1994), 152–80.

Fuchs, Eric, 'Sex and Power in the Church', in Provost, James and Walf, Knut (eds), *Concilium 197: Power in the Church* (Edinburgh: T & T Clark, 1988), 23–28.

Fuchs, L. F., 'Koinonia: Text and Context for the Church', *Ecumenical Trends* 22/Fall (1993): 1–15.

Gabriel, Karl, 'Power in the Contemporary Church in the Light of Sociological Theories: Max Weber, Michel Foucault and Hannah Arendt', in Provost, James and Walf, Knut (eds), *Concilium 197: Power in the Church* (Edinburgh: T & T Clark, 1988), 29–38.

Galbraith, J. K., 'Power and Organization' in Lukes, Steven (ed.), *Power* (Oxford: Blackwell, 1986), 211–28.

Gascoine, Robert, *The Public Forum and Christian Ethics* (Cambridge: Cambridge University Press, 2001).

Geernaert, Donna, 'Church as Koinonia/Church as Sacrament' in Grdzelidze, Tamara (ed.), *One, Holy, Catholic and Apostolic: Ecumenical Reflections on the Church. Faith and Order Paper No. 197* (Geneva: World Council of Churches, 2005), 62–77.

Gill, Robin, *Churchgoing and Christian Ethics* (Cambridge: Cambridge University Press, 1999).

Goldman, Alvin, I., 'Towards a Theory of Social Power' in Lukes, Steven (ed.), *Power* (Oxford: Blackwell, 1986), 156–202.

Goodin, R. E., and Pettit, Philip (eds), *Contemporary Philosophy: An Anthology* (Oxford: Blackwell, 1997).

Gordon, Colin (ed.), *Power/Knowledge: Selected Interviews and Other Writings 1972–1977: Michel Foucault* (Brighton: Harvester Press, 1980).

Gordon, Colin, 'Afterword' in Gordon, Colin (ed.), *Power/Knowledge: Selected Interviews and Other Writings 1972–1977: Michel Foucault* (Brighton: Harvester Press, 1980), 229–59.

Granfield, Patrick, 'Legitimation and Bureaucratisation of Ecclesial Power', in Provost, James and Walf, Knut (eds), *Concilium 197: Power in the Church* (Edinburgh: T & T Clark, 1988), 86–93.

Grdzelidze, Tamara, *One, Holy, Catholic and Apostolic: Ecumenical Reflections on the Church. Faith and Order Paper No. 197* (Geneva: World Council of Churches, 2005).

Green, Henry A., 'Power and Knowledge: A Study in the Social Development of Early Christianity' in *Studies in Religion* 20/2 (1991): 217–31.

Green, Joel and Baker, Mark D., *Recovering the Scandal of the Cross: Atonement in New Testament and Contemporary Contexts* (Carlisle: Paternoster, 2003).

Grimshaw Jean, 'Practices of Freedom' in Ramazanoğlu, Caroline (ed.), *Up against Foucault: Explorations of Some Tensions Between Foucault and Feminism* (London: Routledge, 1993), 51–72.

Guenther, Haas, 'The Effects of the Fall on Creational Social Structures: A Comparison of Anabapatist and Reformed Perspectives', *Calvin Theological Journal* 30 (1995): 108–29.

Habermas, Jũrgen, 'Hannah Arendt's Communications Concept of Power' in Lukes, Steven (ed.), *Power* (Oxford: Blackwell, 1986), 75–93.

Hacking, Ian, 'The Archaeology of Foucault' in Hoy, David Couzens (ed.), *Foucault: A Critical Reader* (Oxford: Blackwell, 1989), 27–40.

Hamar, Anna Karin, 'Some Understandings of Power in Feminist Liberation Theologies' in *Feminist Theology* 12/May (1996): 10–20.

Hanson, Paul D., 'Divine Power in Powerlessness. The Servant of the Lord in Second Isaiah' in Rigby, Cynthia L. (ed.), *Power, Powerlessness and the Divine: New Inquiries in Bible and Theology* (Atlanta: Scholars Press, 1997), 179–98.

Harder, Lydia, 'Power and Authority in Mennonite Theological Development' in Redekop, B. W. and Calvin, W. (eds), *Power, Authority and the Anabaptist Tradition* (Baltimore: Johns Hopkins University Press, 2001), 73–94.

Haugaard, Mark, *Structures, Restructuration and Social Power* (Aldershot: Avebury, 1992).

Hekman, Susan, 'Feminist Identity Politics: Transforming the Political' in Taylor, Dianna and Vintges, Karen (eds), *Feminism and the Final Foucault* (Urbana, University of Illinois, Press, 2004), 196–213.

Hengel, Martin, *Christ and Power* (Belfast: Christian Journals, 1977).

Henn, William, 'Reflections on Authority and Authoritative Teaching in the Light of ARCIC II' in Grdzelidze, Tamara (ed.), *One, Holy, Catholic and Apostolic: Ecumenical Reflections on the Church. Faith and Order Paper No. 197* (Geneva: World Council of Churches, 2005), 124–32.

Hewitt, Marsha, 'Woman, nature and power: Emancipatory themes in critical theory and feminist theology' in *Science Religieuses* 20/3 (1991): 267–79.

Heywood, Carter, *Saving Jesus From Those Who are Right* (Minneapolis: Fortress Press, 1999).

Horsley, Richard (ed.), *Paul and Politics: Ekkleisa Israel Imperium Interpretation: Essays in Honour of Krister Stendahl* (Harrisburg: Trinity Press International, 2000).

Horsley, Richard, 'Krister Stendahl's Challenge to Pauline Studies' in Horsley, Richard (ed.), pp 1–16.

Horsley, Richard, 'Rhetoric and Empire – and 1 Corinthians' in Horsley, Richard (ed.), 72–102.

Hoy, David Couzens (ed.), *Foucault: A Critical Reader* (Oxford: Blackwell, 1989).

Iveson, Duncan, 'The Disciplinary Moment: Foucault, Law and the Reinscription of Rights' in Moss, Jeremy (ed.), *The Later Foucault: Politics and Philosophy* (London: Sage, 1998), 129–48.

Jansen, Gert, 'An overview of Some Faith and Order Papers on Authority' in Grdzelidze, Tamara (ed.), *One, Holy, Catholic and Apostolic: Ecumenical Reflections on the Church. Faith and Order Paper No. 197* (Geneva: World Council of Churches, 2005), 97–103.

Jewett, Robert, 'Exegetical Support from Romans and Other Letters', Horsley, Richard (ed.), *Paul and Politics: Ekkleisa Israel Imperium Interpretation: Essays in Honour of Krister Stendahl* (Harrisburg: Trinity Press International, 2000), 58–71.

Jobling, David, 'Experiencing the Many: A Response to Camp Meek and Wimbush' in Rigby, Cynthia, L. (ed.), *Power, Powerlessness and the Divine: New Inquiries in Bible and Theology* (Atlanta: Scholars Press, 1997), 281–88.

Johnson, David W. and Johnson, Frank P., *Joining Together: Group Theory and Group Skills (Second Edition)* (New Jersey, Prentice-Hall, 1982).

Jones, Colin and Porter, Roy (eds), *Reassessing Foucault: Power, Medicine and the Body* (London: Routledge, 1994).

Jones, Kathleen B., 'On Authority: Or Why Women Are Not Entitled to Speak' in Diamond, Irene and Quinby, Lee (eds), *Feminism & Foucault: Reflections on Resistance* (Boston: Northeastern University Press, 1988).

Jun, Sung Pyo, 'The Bases of Power: An Analysis from a Resource Dependence Perspective' in *Social Science Journal* 34/2 (2002): 105–30.

Kaplan, Laura Duhan and Bove, Laurence F. (eds), *Philosophical Perspectives on Power and Domination: Theories and Practices* (Amsterdam: Rodopi, 1997).

Kasper, Walter, *Jesus the Christ* (London: Burns & Oates, 1977).

Kasper, Walter , *Theology and the Church* (London: SCM, 1989).

Kearsley, Roy, 'Baptism Then and Now. Does Moltmann Bury Tertullian or Praise Him?', in Porter, S.E. and Cross, A. (eds), *Dimensions of Baptism* (Sheffield, 2002), 236–52.

Kearsley, Roy, *Tertullian's Theology of Divine Power* (Carlisle: Paternoster, 1998).

Kearsley, Roy, 'Calvin and the Power of the Elders: A Case of the Rogue Hermeneutic?' in Lane, A. N. S. (ed.), *Interpreting the Bible* (Leicester: Apollos, 1997), 113–29.

Keller, Catherine, 'Power Lines', *Theology Today 55:2* (July 1995): 188–203.

Keshgegian, Flora A., 'Power and Ambiguity: A Response to Brock Chastain and Hanson' in Rigby, Cynthia L. (ed.), *Power, Powerlessness and the Divine: New Inquiries in Bible and Theology* (Atlanta: Scholars Press, 1997), 199–205.

Kittredge, Cynthia Briggs, 'Corinthian Women Prophets and Paul's Argumentation in 1 Corinthians' Horsley, Richard (ed.), *Paul and Politics: Ekkleisa Israel Imperium Interpretation: Essays in Honour of Krister Stendahl* (Harrisburg: Trinity Press International, 2000), 103–9.

Klemm, David, 'Reconstructing Transcendence: A Response to Welker Keller Rigby and Shweiker' in Rigby, Cynthia L. (ed.), *Power, Powerlessness and the Divine: New Inquiries in Bible and Theology* (Atlanta: Scholars Press, 1997), 125–34.

Kritzman, Lawrence D. (ed.), *Michel Foucault: Politics, Philosophy, Culture: Interviews and Other Writings* (New York: Routledge, 1988).

Kritzman, Lawrence D., 'Introduction: Foucault and the Politics of Experience' in Kritzman, Lawrence D. (ed.), *Michel Foucault: Politics, Philosophy, Culture: Interviews and Other Writings* (New York: Routledge, 1988).

Lenski, Gerhard, in Lukes, Steven (ed.), *Power* (Oxford: Blackwell, 1986), 243–52.

Litke, Robert, in Kaplan, Laura Duhan, and Bove, Laurence F. (eds), *Philosophical Perspectives on Power and Domination: Theories and Practices* (Amsterdam: Rodopi, 1997), 5–12.

Lukes, Steven, 'Power and the Battle for Hearts and Minds', *Millennium: Journal of International Studies* 33/3 (2005): 477–93.

Lukes, Steven (ed.), *Power* (Oxford: Blackwell, 1986).

Lukes, Steven, 'Introduction' in Lukes, Steven (ed.), *Power* (Oxford: Blackwell, 1986), 1–18.

Lukes, Steven, *Power: A Radical View* (London: Macmillan, 1974).

Lynch, John E., 'Power in the Church: An Historico-Critical Survey', in Provost, James and Walf, Knut (eds), in Provost, James and Walf, Knut (eds), *Concilium 197: Power in the Church* (Edinburgh: T & T Clark, 1988), 13–22.

Lynch, Richard A., 'Is Power All there Is? Michel Foucault and the "Omnipresence" of Power Relations', *Philosophy Today* 42/1(1998): 65–80.

McFadyen, Alistair I., *The Call to Personhood: A Christian Theory of the Individual in Social Relationships* (Cambridge: Cambridge University Press, 1990).

McGowen, Randall, 'Power and Humanity: Or Foucault Among the Historians' in Jones, Colin and Porter, Roy (eds), *Reassessing Foucault: Power, Medicine and the Body* (London: Routledge, 1994), 91–112.

McLaren, Margaret A., 'Foucault and Feminism: Power, Resistance, Freedom' in Taylor, Dianna and Vintges, Karen (eds), *Feminism and the Final Foucault* (Urbana, University of Illinois Press, 2004), 214–34.

McSweeney, John, 'Foucault and Theology', *Foucault Studies* 2 (2005): 117–44

Mack, Burton L., 'Power, Purity and Innocence: The Christian Inauguration of the Gospel' in Rigby, Cynthia L. (ed.), *Power, Powerlessness and the Divine: New Inquiries in Bible and Theology* (Atlanta: Scholars Press, 1997), 241–61.

Mackey, James P., *Power and Christian Ethics* (Cambridge: Cambridge University Press, 1994).

Martin, Luther, Gutman, Huck and Hutton, Patrick H. (eds), *Technologies of the Self: Seminars with Michel Foucault* (Massachusetts: University of Massachusetts, 1998).

Martin, Luther, 'Introduction' in Luther, Martin, Huck, Gutman and Hutton, Patrick H. (eds), *Technologies of the Self: Seminars with Michel Foucault* (Massachusetts: University of Massachusetts, 1998), 1–8.

Meehan, Johanna, 'Feminism, Critical Theory and Power', *Philosophy and Social Criticism* 30/3 (1999): 375–82.

Miles, Margaret R., 'Patriarchy as Political Theology: The Establishment of North African Christianity' in Rouner, L. (ed.), *Civil Religion and Political Theology* (Boston: Boston University Press, 1986), 169–86.

Milgram, S., *Obedience to Authority* (London: Tavistock Publications, 1974).

Miller, Patrick D., 'Closing Remarks: An Oral Response Presented to the Plenary Attending the 1994 Conference' in Rigby Cynthia L. (ed.), *Power, Powerlessness and the Divine: New Inquiries in Bible and Theology* (Atlanta: Scholars Press, 1997), 291–301.

Miller, W. and Sparks, Glen, *Refrigerator Rights: Creating Connections and Restoring Relationships* (New York: Perigee Books, 2002).

Mills, Catherine, 'Contesting the Political: Butler and Foucault on Power and Resistance', *Journal of Political Philosophy* 11/3 (2003): 253–72.
Moltmann, Jürgen, *The Church in the Power of the Spirit: A Contribution to Messianic Ecclesiology* (London: SCM, 1998).
Moltmann, Jürgen, *The Source of Life, The Holy Spirit and the Theology of Life* (London: SCM, 1997).
Moltmann, Jürgen, *The Spirit of Life: A Universal Affirmation* (London: SCM, 1993).
Morales, Maria, 'The Corrupting Influence of Power' in Kaplan, Laura Duhan and Bove, Laurence F. (eds), *Philosophical Perspectives on Power and Domination: Theories and Practices* (Amsterdam: Rodopi, 1997), 41–51.
Morris, J. N., 'Can we Over-emphasize God's Immanence in Creation', *Theology in Green* 4/2 (1994): 12–35.
Morriss, Peter, *Power: A Philosophical Analysis* (Manchester: Manchester University Press, 2002).
Moss, Jeremy (ed.), *The Later Foucault: Politics and Philosophy* (London: Sage, 1998).
Mudge, Lewis S., *Rethinking the Beloved Community: Ecclesiology, Hermeneutics, Social Theory* (Maryland: University Press of America, 2001).
Mudge, Lewis S., *The Sense of a People: Toward a Church for the Human Future* (Philadelphia: Trinity Press International, 1992).
Műller-Fahrenholz, Geiko, *The Kingdom and the Power. The Theology of Jűrgen Moltmann* (London: SCM, 2000).
Murray, Stuart, *Church After Christendom* (Carlisle: Paternoster 2004).
Murray, Stuart, *Post-Christendo*m (Carlisle: Paternoster, 2004).
Nyce, Dorothy Yoder and Harder, Lydia, 'Power and Authority in Mennonite Ecclesiology: A Feminist Perspective' in Redekop, B. W. and Calvin, W. (eds), *Power, Authority and the Anabaptist Tradition* (Baltimore: Johns Hopkins University Press, 2001), 155–73.
O'Driscoll, Mary, 'Response to "An overview of Some Faith and Order Papers on Authority' in Grdzelidze, Tamara (ed.), *One, Holy, Catholic and Apostolic: Ecumenical Reflections on the Church. Faith and Order Paper No. 197* (Geneva: World Council of Churches, 2005), 104–8.
O'Farrell, Claire, *Michel Foucault* (London: Sage, 2005).
Ojakangas, Mike, 'Impossible Dialogue on Bio-Power: Agamben and Foucault' in *Foucault Studies* No 2, 5–28 May 2005 (online journal accessed 26.7.06).
Oksala, Johanna, *Foucault on Freedom* (Cambridge: Cambridge University Press, 2005).
Paras, Eric, *Foucualt 2:0: Beyond Power and Knowledge* (New York: Other Press, 2006).
Parsons, Stephen, *Ungodly Fear: Fundamentalist Christianity and the Abuse of Power* (London: Lion, 2000).
Parsons, Talcott, 'Power and the Social System' in Lukes, Steven (ed.), *Power* (Oxford: Blackwell, 1986), 94–143.

Pasewark, Kenneth A., *A Theology of Power: Being Beyond Domination* (Minneapolis: Fortress, 1993).

Patten, Paul, 'Foucault's Subject of Power' in Moss, Jeremy (ed.), *The Later Foucault: Politics and Philosophy* (London: Sage, 1998), 64–77.

Percy, Martyn, *Power and the Church: Ecclesiology in an Age of Transition* (London: Cassell, 1998).

Percy, Martyn, 'Authority in Contemporary Theology' in Grdzelidze, Tamara, *One, Holy, Catholic and Apostolic: Ecumenical Reflections on the Church. Faith and Order Paper No. 197* (Geneva: World Council of Churches, 2005), 141–7.

Pinto, Henrique, 'The More Which Exceeds us: Foucault, Roman Catholicism and Inter-Faith Dialogue' in Bernauer, James and Carrette, Jeremy (eds), *Michel Foucault and Theology: The Politics of Religious Experience* (Aldershot: Ashgate, 2004), 191–213.

Polaski, Sandra Hack, *Paul and the Discourse of Power* (Sheffield: Sheffield Academic Press, 1999).

Presbey, Gail M., 'Hannah Arendt on Power' in Kaplan, Laura Duhan and Bove, Laurence F. (eds), *Philosophical Perspectives on Power and Domination: Theories and Practices* (Amsterdam: Rodopi, 1997), 29–40.

Provost, James and Walf, Knut (eds), *Concilium 197: Power in the Church* (Edinburgh: T & T Clark, 1988).

Ramazanoğlu, Caroline (ed.), *Up against Foucault: Explorations of Some Tensions Between Foucault and Feminism* (London: Routledge, 1993).

Ramazanoğlu, Caroline, 'Introduction' in Ramazanoğlu (ed.), 1–27.

Ramazanoğlu, Caroline, 'Women's Sexuality and Men's Appropriation of Desire' in Ramazanoğlu (ed.), 239–64.

Ransom, Janet, 'Feminism, Difference and Discourse: The Limits of Discursive Analysis for Feminism' in Ramazanoğlu Caroline (ed.), *Up against Foucault: Explorations of Some Tensions Between Foucault and Feminism* (London: Routledge, 1993), 123–46.

Raymond, Aron, '*Macht* Power *Puissance*: Democratic Prose or Demoniacal Poetry?' in Lukes, Steven (ed.), *Power* (Oxford: Blackwell, 1986), 253–77.

Redekop, B. W., 'Power and Religion in the Western Intellectual Tradition' in Redekop B. W. and Calvin W. (eds), *Power, Authority and the Anabaptist Tradition* (Baltimore: Johns Hopkins University Press, 2001), 14–49.

Redekop, B. W. and Calvin W. (eds), *Power, Authority and the Anabaptist Tradition* (Baltimore: Johns Hopkins University Press, 2001).

Redekop, Calvin, Report: 'Authority and Authoritative Teaching in the Church' in Grdzelidze, Tamara (ed.), *One, Holy, Catholic and Apostolic: Ecumenical Reflections on the Church. Faith and Order Paper No. 197* (Geneva: World Council of Churches, 2005), 162–5.

Redekop, Calvin, 'Power in the Anabaptist Community' in Redekop, B. W. and Calvin, W. (eds), *Power, Authority and the Anabaptist Tradition* (Baltimore: Johns Hopkins University Press, 2001), 174–92.

Reynard, Ruth A., *A Discussion of Power as it Relates to a Local Church Context* (no date given), p.1. http://media.premierstudios.com/nazarene/docs/didache_4_1_Reynard.pdf. Accessed 22.08.07.

Richards, Jerald, 'Power Imbalance and Human Worth' in Kaplan, Laura Duhan and Bove, Laurence F. (eds), *Philosophical Perspectives on Power and Domination: Theories and Practices* (Amsterdam: Rodopi, 1997), 93–105.

Rigby, Cynthia L. (ed.), *Power, Powerlessness and the Divine: New Inquiries in Bible and Theology* (Atlanta: Scholars Press, 1997)

Rigby, Cynthia L., 'Someone to Blame, Someone to Trust: Divine Power and the Self-Recovery of the Oppressed' in Rigby, Cynthia L. (ed.), *Power, Powerlessness and the Divine: New Inquiries in Bible and Theology* (Atlanta: Scholars Press, 1997), 79–102.

Rikhof, Hervi, 'The Competence of Priests, Prophets and Kings' (Edinburgh: T & T Clark, 1988), 53–62.

Roberts, Richard H., *Religion, Theology and the Human Sciences* (Cambridge: Cambridge University Press, 2002)

Robinson, Anthony B., 'Power Outage', *Christian Century* (2003): 9–10.

Rose, Nikolas, *Inventing Ourselves: Psychology, Power and Personhood* (Cambridge: Cambridge University Press, 1996).

Russell, Bertrand, 'The Forms of Power' in Lukes, Steven (ed.), *Power* (Oxford: Blackwell, 1986), 19–36.

Saarelma, Antii, 'Church and "Sacrament" in Bilateral Dialogues' in Grdzelidze, Tamara (ed.), *One, Holy, Catholic and Apostolic: Ecumenical Reflections on the Church. Faith and Order Paper No. 197* (Geneva: World Council of Churches, 2005), 51–61.

Savage, Timothy B., *Power Through Weakness: Paul's Understanding of the Christian Ministry in 2 Corinthians* (Cambridge: Cambridge University Press), 1996.

Sawacki, Jana, 'Feminism, Foucault and 'Subjects' of Power and Freedom' in Moss, Jeremy (ed.), *The Later Foucault: Politics and Philosophy* (London: Sage, 1998), 93–101.

Schuld, Joyce, 'Augustine, Foucault and the Politics of Imperfection' in Bernauer, James and Carrette, Jeremy (eds), *Michel Foucault and Theology: The Politics of Religious Experience* (Aldershot: Ashgate, 2004), 57–74.

Schuld, Joyce, *Foucault and Augustine: Reconsidering Power and Love* (Indiana: University of Notre Dame Press, 2003)

Schwahn, Barbara, 'The Sacramentality of the Church: Points of Convergence and Issues to be Addressed' in Grdzelidze, Tamara (ed.), *One, Holy, Catholic and Apostolic: Ecumenical Reflections on the Church. Faith and Order Paper No. 197* (Geneva: World Council of Churches, 2005), 40–50.

Schweiker, William, 'Power and the Agency of God' in Rigby, Cynthia L. (ed.), *Power, Powerlessness and the Divine: New Inquiries in Bible and Theology* (Atlanta: Scholars Press, 1997), 103–24.

Schweiker, William and Welker, Michael, 'A New Paradigm of Thelogical and Biblical Enquiry' in Rigby, Cynthia L. (ed.), *Power, Powerlessness and the Divine: New Inquiries in Bible and Theology* (Atlanta: Scholars Press, 1997), 3–20.

Siebel, Wigand, 'The Exercise of Power in Today's Church', in Provost, James and Walf, Knut (eds), *Concilium 197: Power in the Church* (Edinburgh: T & T Clark, 1988), 39–49.

Simmel, Georg, 'Domination and Freedom' in Lukes, Steven (ed.), *Power* (Oxford: Blackwell, 1986), 203–210.

Simons, Jon, *Foucault and the Political* (London: Routledge, 1996).

Smart, Barry, 'Foucault, Levinas and the Subject of Responsibility' in Moss, Jeremy (ed.), *The Later Foucault: Politics and Philosophy* (London: Sage, 1998), 78–92.

Smith, Austin, *Journeying with God: Paradigms of Power and Powerlessness* (London: Sheed & Ward, 1990).

Smith, Carol, 'Biblical Perspectives on Power', *Journal for the Study of the Old Testament* 93 (2001): 93–110.

Smith, James, K. A., *Who's Afraid of Postmodernism: Taking Derrida, Lyotard and Foucault to Church* (Grand Rapids: Baker, 2006).

Snook, Lewis, E., *What in the World is God Doing? Re-imagining Spirit and Power* (Minneapolis: Fortress, 1999).

Soskice, *The Kindness of God: Metaphor, Gender, and Religious Language* (Cambridge, 2008).

Soskice, Janet Martin, 'God of Power and Might', *Theology Today* 54/1 (1997): 19–28.

Steinke, Peter, *Healthy Congregations: A Systems Approach* (Herndon, VA: Alban Institute, 1996)

Stone, Ronald H., 'Review of A Theology of Power: Being Beyond Domination' (K. A. Pasework), *Interpretation* 49/2 (1995): 222–3.

Strenski, Ivan, 'Religion, Power and Final Foucault', *Journal of the American Academy of Religion* 66/2 (1998): 345–67.

Sykes, Stephen, *Power and Christian Theology* (London: Continuum International, 2006).

Taylor, Charles, 'Foucault on Freedom and Truth' in Hoy, David Couzens (ed.), *Foucault: A Critical Reader* (Oxford: Blackwell, 1989), 69–102.

Taylor, Dianna, 'Foucault's Ethos' in Taylor, Dianna and Vintges, Karen (eds) (Urbana: University of Illinois Press, 2004), 258–74.

Taylor, Dianna and Vintges, Karen (eds), *Feminism and the Final Foucault* (Urbana: University of Illinois Press, 2004).

Theiβen, Gerd, 'The Ambivalence of Power in Early Christianity' in Rigby, Cynthia L. (ed.), *Power, Powerlessness and the Divine: New Inquiries in Bible and Theology* (Atlanta: Scholars Press, 1997), 21–36.

Thurian, Max (ed.), *Churches respond to BEM Vols 1–6 Faith and order papers; 129–144* (Geneva: World Council of Churches, 1986–1988).

Thwaites, James, *Renegotiating the Church Contract* (Carlisle: Paternoster, 2003).

Thwaites, James, *The Church Beyond the Congregation: The Strategic Role of the Church in the Postmodern Era* (Carlisle: Paternoster, 1999).

Tomlin, Graham, *The Power of the Cross: Theology and the Death of Christ in Paul, Luther and Pascal* (Carlisle: Paternoster, 1999).

Torfs, Rik, 'Auctoritas – Potestas – Jurisdictio – Facultas – Officium – Munus: A Conceptual Analysis' (Edinburgh: T & T Clark, 1988), 63–73.

Veyne, Paul, 'Foucault Revolutionizes History' in Davidson, Arnold I. (ed.), *Foucault and His Interlocuters* (Chicago: University of Chicago, 1998, 146–82.

Veyne, Paul, 'The Final Foucault and his Ethics' in Davidson, Arnold I. (ed.), *Foucault and His Interlocuters* (Chicago: University of Chicago, 1998), 225–33.

Volf, M. (ed.), *The Future of Theology: Essays in Honor of Jűrgen Moltmann* (Grand Rapids: Eerdmans, 1996).

Walzer, Michael, 'The Politics of Michel Foucault' in Couzens, David (ed.), *Foucault: A Critical Reader* (Oxford: Blackwell, 1989), 51–68.

Watts, Fraser, Nye, Rebecca and Savage, Sara, *Psychology for Christian Ministry* (London: Routledge, 2002).

Webster, John, 'On Evangelical Ecclesiology', *Ecclesiology* 1/1 (2004): 9–35.

Welker, Michael, 'God's Power and Powerlessness: Biblical Theology and the Search for a World Ethos in a Time of Short-lived Moral Markets' in Rigby, Cynthia L. (ed.), *Power, Powerlessness and the Divine: New Inquiries in Bible and Theology* (Atlanta: Scholars Press, 1997), 39–55.

West, Charles, *Power, Truth and Community in Modern Culture* (Harrisburg: Trinity Press International, 1999).

Wetherill, Margaret, 'Life histories/social histories' in Wetherill, Margaret (ed.), *Identities, Groups and Social Issues* (Milton Keynes, Open University/Sage, 1996), 299–361.

Wink, Walter, *Engaging the Powers: Discernment and Resistance in a World of Domination* (Philadelphia: Fortress, 1992).

Wink, Walter, *Unmasking the Powers: The Invisible Forces that Determine Human Existence* (The Powers. Vol 2) (Philadelphia: Fortress, 1986).

Wink, Walter, *Naming the Powers: The Language of Power in the New Testament* (Philadelphia: Fortress, 1984).

Wire, Antoinette Clark, 'The Politics of the Assembly in Corinth' in Horsley, Richard (ed.), *Paul and Politics. Ekkleisa Israel Imperium Interpretation: Essays in Honour of Krister Stendahl* (Harrisburg: Trinity Press International, 2000), 124– 9.

Wire, Antoinette Clark, *The Corinthian Women Prophets: A Reconstruction through Paul's Rhetoric* (Minneapolis: Fortress, 1990).

Wolin, Richard, 'Foucault the Neohumanist' in *The Chronical Review* (Electronic Version), 53/3 (2006): 1–5.

Woodhead, Linda, *An Introduction to Christianity* (Cambridge: Cambridge University Press, 2004).

World Council of Churches, *The Nature and Mission of the Church: A Stage on the Way to a Common Statement. Faith and Order Paper 198* (Geneva: World Council of Churches, 2005).

World Council of Churches, *The Nature and Purpose of the Church: A Stage on the Way to a Common Statement: Faith and Order Paper No 181* (Geneva: World Council of Churches, 1998).

Wright, Nigel G., *Disavowing Constantine: Mission Church and the Social Order in the Theologies of John Howard Yoder and Jürgen Moltmann* (Carlisle: Paternoster, 2000).

Wright N. T., 'Paul's Gospel and Caesar's Empire' in Horsley, Richard (ed.), *Paul and Politics: Ekkleisa Israel Imperium Interpretation: Essays in Honour of Krister Stendahl* (Harrisburg: Trinity Press International, 2000), 160–84.

Index